Rabbi Saul Zucker
Teaneck, New Jersey

16 *Av* 5771
August 16, 2011

Dear Reader,

The term "Torah" as used by the Sages of Israel has always had an intimate association with the ideals of truth and profound wisdom. These ideals have been transmitted throughout the millennia in the Oral Law, whose origins go back to the Revelation at Sinai. Indeed, the covenant with Israel was made on the basis of the Oral Law. References and allusions to this Oral Law abound in the Written Law, and quite a number of authors have written about the authenticity of the Oral Law as presented by the Sages.

The work that you hold in your hands is a masterpiece of scholarship in that genre. It is, in my opinion, an invaluable contribution to works on the Oral Law. As someone who has been involved in Jewish education on many levels during the past thirty years, as the founding *Rosh Mesivta* of the *Mesivta of North Jersey* and as a *maggid shiur* in various venues, I am well aware of the challenges that face a generation of Jews who are exposed to information from an array of different, competing disciplines. To that generation, my dear friend and erudite scholar Rav Michael S. Bar-Ron has written this excellent book, citing proofs and demonstrations of the authenticity of the Oral Law. His proofs and demonstrations are compelling and profound; they reflect serious scholarship and thorough research. The work is particularly valuable as it presents overwhelming evidence while avoiding the pitfall of loose speculation that is sometimes characteristic of materialistic academia, and while avoiding the pitfall of unsubstantiated dogmatic fiat that is sometimes characteristic of religious zealotry. In short, the book that you hold presents facts and wisdom, designed to speak clearly to the reader's mind.

I have known Rav Michael Shelomo for a number of years. He is a humble servant of *HaShem*, sincere, thoughtful, caring, and very wise. He represents the ideals of Torah wisdom and compassion most excellently. I wholeheartedly commend him for this wonderful book, and I wish him the greatest success, confident that his work will serve its purpose of bringing the truth and wisdom of *HaShem*'s noble Torah to a host of readers seeking knowledge.

I close with blessings of Torah for wisdom, happiness, fulfillment and success.

Sincerely yours,

Rabbi Saul Zucker

אברהם ירחמיאל רבינוביץ
• אוסטרובה ביאלא •
בכ"ק אאמו"ר מביאלא זצללה"ה

פעיה"ק ירושלים תובב"א

בעזרת השם יתברך

יום ה' לסדר 'והוא יהיה לך לאלקים' וגו', כ"ג אלול תשע"א לפ"ק.

בא לפני תלמידי הנכבד והיקר הרה"ח מארי **מיכאל שלמה בר-ריין** שליט"א, אשר כבר פקע שמיה בעולם אודות מסירות נפשו ומאודו בכדי להרבות כבוד שמים בעולם ושלא על מנת לקבל פרס.

ולעת בואו הראה לפני תבריך כתבים יקרים, אשר בהם סובב ומבאר בדרכי השכל, שכלל דברי תורה שבעל פה שנתונים בידינו, כולם מקורם ושורשם מסיני, ובתוכן דבריו ראיתי אשר כל דבריו המה שכל נכון ואמיץ כולם מיוסדים על דרך התורה הקדושה המסורה לנו מדור דור.

ודבר גדול פעל הרב המחבר בפרט לעת עתה שבו נחוץ הדבר מאוד, כאשר שרבים מאחינו בית ישראל נבוכים בהבלי שוא ומדוחים, וניצודים בחבלי האפיקורסות והשקר הסובבים בעולם ר"ל, וע"כ בוודאי שגדלה זכותו מאוד.

ומאחר שאיתמחי גברא ואיתמחי קמיעא, כפי שכבר ראינו ביתר המפעלים המרובים, אשר פועל הרב המחבר ללא לאות למען כבוד תורתנו הקדושה, בוודאי חזקה על חבר שלא תצא תקלה מתחת ידו, וע"כ נכון מאוד לאמץ ולחזק ידיו בכל האפשר בכדי לסייעו במפעלו הכביר להגדיל תורה ולהאדירה.

ויה"ר שזכות הדבר תעמוד לו ולזרעו אחריו, להתברך בשנה טובה ומתוקה בכתיבה וחתימה טובה, לעלות מחיל אל חיל, והשי"ת יזכנו לראות בביאת גואל צדק, במהרה בימינו אכי"ר.

[TRANSLATION]

Avraham Yerachmiel Rabinowits
* [Grand Rabbi] Of Ostrova-Biale *
Son of the Holy Master, the Grand Rebbe of Biale of Blessed Memory
Here in the Holy City of Yerushalayim – May it be rebuilt speedily in our days

With the Aid of HaShem Blessed Be He

5th Day of [the Week of] the Torah Portion *'And He Will Be a God Unto You, etc.'*,

23 Elul 5771 from Creation

Before me has come my honored and dear student, the wise rabbi Mori **Michael Shelomo Bar-Ron** *shlita*, who has already pierced the heavens with his self-sacrifice and efforts for the sake of increasing the honor of Heaven in the world and not for sake of receiving reward.

And at the time of his arrival he showed me a compilation of precious writings in which he encompasses and clarifies by erudite means that the root and source of all matters of Oral Torah in our hands are from Sinai, and I saw in the content of his words, that all his teachings are correct and strong, founded on the path of the holy Torah that has been passed down to us from generation to generation.

And the authoring rabbi has done a great thing, especially at this time when it is so needed, being that many of our brothers of the House of Israel are perplexed in futile vanities, seduced, and trapped in the binds of heresy and lies that circle the world –may the Compassionate One save them– and therefore his merit has surely increased greatly.

And since his expertise has been proven, as we have already seen in his other many works in which the authoring rabbi acts tirelessly for the sake of the honor of our holy Torah, it can be assumed with certainty that no stumbling block will occur on his account. Therefore it is most proper to embolden and strengthen his hand in any possible way, in order to aid him in his mighty effort in magnifying and glorifying Torah.

And may it be G-d's Will that the merit of this thing will stand up for him and his descendents after him, that they be blessed with a good and sweet year, being inscribed and sealed [in the Book of Life], to rise from strength to strength, and may *HaShem* Blessed Be He cause us to merit the arrival of the righteous redeemer, speedily in our days – Amen, may it be His Will.

Avraham Yerachmiel
Son of the Holy Rabbi from Biale Ostrova

Abe M. & Geri Cohen Rabbinical College
The Stephen Isaiah Ades Library
Alsa Azancot Stern Scholarship Fund
Hayden Leah Judeo-Spanish Leadership Training
Max & Shirty Hidary Teacher Training College

ב"ה

Shehebar Sephardic Center

Rabbi Sam Kassin, Dean
Rabbi Elyahou Shamoula, Director

כ"ו אלול תשע"א
September 25, 2011

Board of directors
Alan Dweck
Leo Esses
Avi Esses
Zac Gindi
Joey Habert
Morris A. Sutton
Richard A. Sutton
David R. Ades
Scott Shrem

To Whom It May Concern

It has been fifteen years since the young yeshivah student who would become the intrepid Torah scholar who wrote this book, first entered Shehebar Sephardic Center, the yeshivah and rabbinical academy we founded and directed since 1971. Even from then, the author's good character and commitment to truth, which at times put him at odds with common mainstream thinking, were noted and appreciated at SSC.

It is therefore a distinct pleasure for me to recommend the new work of our former SSC student, "Oral Torah From Sinai". On one hand, we live in an era of unprecedented scientific discovery, with more evidence for Torah truth and more media outlets to spread that wisdom than ever before. Yet never before have religious movements antithetical to Torah been more sophisticated in their attempts to steal hearts away from Torah truth. Through the Internet, truth-seekers are exposed to their attempts to use current scientific findings to "disprove" our Oral Torah tradition through selective, prejudiced presentation of fact and ignorance of our Oral Torah literature.

Rising to meet this challenge, Rabbi Michael Shelomo has enlisted his own broad academic background and command of Torah literature, together with his experience in Torah outreach and writing talent. He has produced an accurate work, well-sourced with current academic research. In it, he addresses key, burning questions and difficulties of lay people and Torah scholars alike. As such, "Oral Torah From Sinai" is not only a source of wisdom and inspiration that can fortify Jewish belief in these trying times, but a significant contribution to Torah thought. We wish the book and the author every success in awakening and fortifying Torah faith the world over.

With Torah Blessings,

Rabbi Sam Kassin, Rosh Yeshivah and Dean of SSC

Oral Torah from Sinai

The Case for the Authenticity

of the Oral Torah Tradition

from *Alef* to *Tau*

Rabbi Michael Shelomo Bar-Ron

Oral Torah from Sinai
The Case for the Authenticity
of the Oral Torah Tradition
from *Alef* to *Tau*

Rabbi Michael Shelomo Bar-Ron

© 2011, all rights reserved

ISBN 13: 978-0-9792618-9-3
ISBN 10: 0-9792618-9-9

Biblical History/Philosophy/Commentary

No part of this book may be reproduced or transmitted in any form or by any means, electronic or mechanical, including photocopying, recording, or by any information storage and retrieval system, without permission in writing from the publisher, except in the case of brief quotations in reviews for inclusion in a magazine, newspaper or broadcast.

Published by Lightcatcher Books, printed in the United States of America and in Israel.

1204 Kissinger Ave.
Springdale, AR 72762
lightcatcherbooks.com

Cover Art: Carol Long

> THIS BOOK CONTAINS
> NAMES OF GOD,
> VERSES OF TORAH, AND
> SACRED TORAH COMMENTARY.
> PLEASE TREAT IT WITH
> THE APPROPRIATE
> SANCTITY IT DESERVES.

DEDICATION

This book is dedicated to all those who broke free
of the lies and vanity of the world, who lost friends
and jeopardized their income and safety to refashion their
lives according to the Torah, and cling to the statutes
of the Almighty.

I particularly salute those who then saw dear friends
who had once begun the same route; friends who then
lost their perspective and inspiration and returned to the
world of lies and vanity, now doing their utmost
to corrupt others. In spite of the pain and confusion caused
by these troubled souls, these loyal servants of God
refuse to be shaken, but continue undaunted to sanctify His
Name openly and in private.

To them I dedicate this work.

I further dedicate this work to my loving parents
Jacob and Ruth Barron and my dear brother Jonathan,
the first person in this world to teach me, as a young child,
about God.

I dedicate this work to the awesome souls that *HaShem*
merited me to bring into this world, my children,
particularly my eldest child,
Gavriel Ya`aqov Bar-Ron,
whose Bar Mitzvah coincides with the
publishing of this work.

Lastly I dedicate this work to those whom He merited me
to bring into the Life of the World to Come:
my worthy students. May the light of faith and
true Torah observance never cease
from all our generations to the end of time.

WORDS OF GRATITUDE

First and foremost, I thank the Master of the Universe for all the blessings in my life; particularly the health, wisdom, ability, time and inspiration required to write this book.

He has provided this by means of many human *mal'akhim* (angels/agents). Among them are the following men, advanced Torah scholars and laymen, Jews and Noahides. I am most grateful to them for their significant contributions to this work, whether or not they were aware.

They are (not in order of the significance of their contribution):

Mori Shelomo ben-Avraham
Rabbi Benjamin Blech
James D. Long
Rabbi David Hanokh Bar-Hayim
Yosef Eliah ben Avraham
Yehudah Barukh Ilan
Andrew Overall
Jacob Scharff and Abigail Sookraj
David Barron (my dear cousin)
Justin Johnson
Yehoyada` `Amos Eisen

My heartfelt gratitude is further extended to other eminent teachers of mine over the years for their example, support and wisdom That remain in my heart always:

The Grand Rebbe *shlit"a* of Biale-Ostrova in Jerusalem
Rabbi Sam Kassin *shlit"a*, Rosh Yeshivah and
Dean of Shehebar Sefardic Center

My deepest thanks is extended to my *esheth hhayil* (woman of valor), for her enduring patience and support.

Without her bearing as much of the yoke of our household as she has, this work would not have been possible.

CONTENTS

(Hebrew translation is decorative and inexact)

TRANSLITERATION AND PRONUNCIATION KEY

INTRODUCTION 1

PART I: TACKLING THE HARD QUESTIONS 29

   1. How Can the Oral Tradition Include Teachings Added Later by the Rabbis? 30

   2. Why Are Novel Rabbinical Laws Not Considered Unlawful "Additions" to the Torah? 34

   3. The Word of God is Perfect, the Word of Man Fallible. Did the Sages Make a Distinction? If So, How? 36

   4. How Can We Trust the Moral Integrity of the Ordained Sages? 38

   5. Does All The Rabbinical Debate in the Talmud Negate an Oral Tradition? 42

   6. What About Post-Talmudic Customs and Rabbinical Enactments that Jews Relate to as Law? 44

   7. Since We Have the Sources of the Oral Law from Sanhedrin-Era Israel, Why Rely on the Babylonian Talmud? 47

   8. What About Post-Talmudic Rulings and Customs Instituted to Meet the Changing Needs of the Times? 59

   9. Is Orthodox Torah Judaism Authentic Oral Torah? 61

PART II: BIBLICAL PROOF
– Revealing the Oral Tradition in the Written Word 69

1. היחוד המופשט המוחלט של **א**לוהי ישראל
   The Oral Tradition of the Incomparable Oneness of Hashem 73

2. תורה ש**ב**על פה מ**ב**ראשית
   The Oral Torah Wisdom Known to the Generations Before
   Sinai 79

3. בית דין ה**ג**דול דן את ירמיהו הנביא
   The Sanhedrin in Action in Jeremiah 80

4. מניין **ד**יני המלוכה של ישראל בתורה?
   The Oral Details of the Powers of an Israelite King 85

5. **ה**וסיפו את פורים וימי צום בנוכחותם של נביאי ישראל
   Where Were the Prophets When Purim Was Added? 86

6. איסור טלטול בשבת ברשות הרבים ו**ב**רשות היחיד
   Oral Details of Sabbath Laws Enforced by the Prophets 90

7. "ושחטתם ב**ז**ה ואכלתם"
   Oral Torah Details Of Ritual Slaughter 94

8. בזמן שמד, דניאל איש **ח**מודות מוכן למות על דיני כשרות מדבריהם
   Daniel Risks Death to Keep Rabbinical Dietary Restrictions 97

9. "והיו ל**ט**וטפות בין עיניך": תפילין בתנ"ך
   Oth (Sign) and *Totafoth* (Ornament) : *Tefillin* in
   The Bible 99

10. זהות **י**שראל דרך האם בלבד
    Jewish Identity Passes Through the Mother Only 106

11. **כ**ניסת רות המואביה ל**כ**נסת ישראל
    How Could Ruth the Moabitess Enter the People of Israel? 114

12. **לֹא** עין תחת עין ממש
   The Oral Tradition of "An Eye for an Eye" 116

13. בזמן שמד, דניאל **מִ**סכן את חיי נפשו על שמירת דיני תפילה **כְ**דבריהם
   Daniel Risks Execution to Pray According to Oral Tradition............ 118

PART III: SCIENTIFIC PROOF
– Hard Science Reveals the Antiquity of the Oral Tradition and Hints of its Divine Origin 127

14. זכויות שבט **נ**פתלי בים כנרת עדיין בתוקף
   Naftali's Fishing Rights: Still in Force 130

15. **ס**ודות עתיקות-יומין במדרשי חז"ל מנבאות על עידן הנוכחי
   Obscure Talmudic Tradition Reveals Prophecy of Modern Times 132

16. תפילין ב**ע**תיקות קומרן ומצריים
   What Scientific Evidence is there that *Tefillin* are from Sinai? 144

17. מסורת שנשתמרה על **פ**ה 1,500 שנה עד כתיבת המשנה
   Proof at *Tel Shilo* of Tradition Maintained Orally 1500 Years.......... 151

18. האם חז"ל היו **צ**וללים בעמוקי ים תהום רבה?
   Were the Talmudic Sages Deep-Sea Biologists?..................... 156

19. האם חז"ל **ק**בעו מראות על הירח?
   Did the Sages Make Use of Mirrors on the Moon? 160

20. האם חז"ל **ר**או שינויים מיקרוסקופיים בתוך גוף עובר אנוש?
   Were the Ancient Sages Embryologists? 167

21. מסורות בעל פה מימות **ש**עיבוד ישראל במצריים
   Oral Tradition Preserved Since Our Slavery in Egypt............ 172

22. הזכר בידי כומרי חבש לקבלה וזריקת דם זבחים על פי **ת**ורת הכוהנים במשנה
How Did Priestly Rites in the Mishnah Enter Ethiopian Tradition?... 178

CONCLUSION 193

APPENDIX I: Why were Jews of Israel Pressured to Abandon Their Tradition? 199

APPENDIX II: The Sixth Day Continues to Unfold *(Original Torah Commentary by the Author)*.................. 205

APPENDIX III: A Brief Guide for Those Perplexed by "Alien Astronaut" Theory 213

APPENDIX IV: The Shared Tradition of the Ancient Ark-Cults of Africa and Its Significance until Today 221

Transliteration and Pronunciation Key

Besides places where it might confuse the reader (such as names of books and individuals from the Bible), an effort was made to transliterate Hebrew words as authentically as possible, according to the faithfully maintained traditions by Jewish communities throughout the Middle East – most notably Yemen, Iraq, Syria and Tunisia. The following scheme is used:

Alef (א), a letter for vowels beginning or ending with a glottal stop, especially when found in the middle of a word, is marked by ' as in *mal'akhim* (angels).

Heh (ה) with a possessive *mappiq*-point at the end of a word, pronounced as a breathy "h," is written "ḥ" as in *roshaḥ* (her head).

Waw (ו) is written and pronounced as "w" as in *wa-hayu* (and they shall be) and *hhuqaw* (his statutes).

Hheth (ח), pronounced as an aspirated "h," is written "hh" as in *milhhamoth* (wars).

Khaf (כ/ך), pronounced like "ch" in the name of the classical composer Bach, is written "kh" as in *halakhah* (practical Torah law).

*`Ayin* (ע), a voiced consonant produced deep in the throat, is marked by ` as in *`eruv* (an enclosure within which Jews may carry on the Sabbath day.

Sadi (צ), an "s" sound produced deeper in the mouth instead of next to the teeth, is written as *S* as in *Sadduqim* (*S*adducees).

Resh (ר) without a *daggesh*-point, pronounced as a lightly rolled "r" on the tip of the tongue like the Spanish letter *ere* (not the hard *erre*), is written simply as "r."

Thau (ת) without a *daggesh*-point is written and pronounced "th" as in *totafoth* (head phylactery).

Transliterating other distinct sounds of the Holy Tongue — such as the letter *Teth* (ט) and authentic vowel pronunciation— was found impractical, as it would have detracted from the comprehension of the lay reader. These sounds were simplified.

INTRODUCTION

וּבְחָנוּנִי נָא בָּזֹאת, אָמַר יְהֹוָה צְבָאוֹת,
אִם לֹא אֶפְתַּח לָכֶם אֵת אֲרֻבּוֹת הַשָּׁמַיִם,
וַהֲרִיקֹתִי לָכֶם בְּרָכָה עַד בְּלִי דָי.(מלאכי ג:י)

...and test Me now in this, says *HaShem*[1] of Hosts,
if I will not open for you the windows of heaven,
and pour you out a blessing
that there shall be more than sufficiency. (Malachi 3:10)

Oral Torah from Sinai

DISPELLING ILLUSIONS ABOUT TORAH PROOFS

It is the simple, ignorant person who believes that if only he were presented with incontrovertible proof, or would experience a great miracle on a biblical scale, that then he would certainly believe. The Bible itself is full of examples of generations who were given the most awesome proofs possible of God's Existence and the Divine backing of the Torah of Moses – only to return to serving idols. The very generation that crossed the Red Sea and experienced the Giving of the Torah at Sinai —after "seeing the sounds" of God's thundering voice speaking to Moses (Ex. 20:14)— fell quickly from that lofty state, worshiping the Golden Calf only forty days later. The very generation that witnessed fire from heaven consume the offerings of Elijah the Prophet on Mt. Carmel —immediately falling on their faces, crying, "*HaShem*[1] is the God! *HaShem* is the God!"— slid right back in to Ba`al-worship afterward.

Fittingly, Elijah was brought to Mt. Sinai itself to be taught a fundamental lesson by the Almighty: *HaShem* is not "to be found" —one does not arrive at true faith— simply by witnessing dramatic, fearsome miracles. Rather, He is found (true faith in Him is only born and nurtured) by means of a "still, small voice." This could be the voice of a patient Torah teacher. I understand it to be the still small voice of one's inner conscience zone — the conscious, inner decision to open one's eyes even to the mundane miracles of our lives, recognize *HaShem*, and live a life of *faithfulness*.

The choice to accept Torah is the choice to leave one's comfort zone —the easy, self-serving way of life one is accustomed to— and begin a long, challenging road to molding his life to a high standard of goodness, and remain accountable to it always.

Yet in spite of this truth, we all know that proofs do help.

If not to convince those in denial, at least to solidify and strengthen the faith of those who have made the right choice, to help sincere fence-straddlers to choose the correct side, and even to rattle non-believers into reconsidering their position. But at the end of the day, the question is: *Who has the maturity and self-mastery to translate proof into action?* It becomes far easier for many to explain away the proof, or find ways to discredit the source – anything in order not to feel obligated.

NOTE: *This is why any Torah-based society, no less than one that is non-Torah-based, must have a strong justice system. There is a limit to how much human society can tolerate of those who wreak havoc because they cannot bring themselves to do what is right simply because it is right.*

THE CHALLENGE OF FREE CHOICE

If it is such a challenge for human beings to change their lives, and society must be partly coerced into behaving properly, why did *HaShem* give man free choice?

According to Torah tradition, it is the very purpose of Creation for an intelligent creature to freely choose to recognize *HaShem* and follow His ways, and build a good world accordingly. Without that freedom, mankind would be reduced to a robotic race, enslaved against our will. Only by being fully free to give in to one's evil inclination can a human being be meritorious for his choosing good, and receive his just reward (most of which we enjoy in the eternal life of the soul). To make such free choice possible, *HaShem* gave man the ability to harden his heart like the Pharaoh of the Exodus, no matter what miracles and proofs he encounters.

Introduction

A sign of God's unfathomable benevolence is how —no matter how great one's denial of God, no matter how bitter his hate for those who bear His truth in the world— *HaShem* remains fair to all. Until it is for the best that his soul leave the world, God continues to give him air to breathe, sustenance to remain alive, and enables his body to continue living through biological processes so miraculously complex, they will forever defy even the cutting edge of human science.

WHY PROOFS BECAME IMPORTANT

For thousands of years, the faithful remnant of the Jewish People through the ages required few if any such proofs. As "believers, descendants of believers" we trusted our tradition and held fast to it. Truth be told, the other options were not very appealing. Even the more advanced non-Jewish cultures, such as the Greeks and Romans, were savage and morally corrupt, with religious cults that insulted not only the intelligence of learned Jews, but truth-seeking non-Jews as well (many of whom converted to Judaism or joined the large Noahide movement of the time). Among the Jews it was mainly the spoiled, wealthy class that fell prey to the worldly temptations of joining the gentile world[2].

However, as history progressed and knowledge advanced to the Enlightenment era, secular society and its ways of thinking became very attractive even to the poor and middle-classes of Jewry. Without a clue as to how advanced the Torah's wisdom is — containing secrets that the scientific world is only beginning to discover— they dropped out of Torah observance *in droves*. It was no help that, in response to the challenge of the Enlightenment in Europe, the ultra-Orthodox world turned inwards, adopting an anti-scientific stance.

Thank God, that has changed. Scholars such as Rabbi Dr. Weissmandl of blessed memory, Dr. Gerald Schroeder, Prof. Natan Aviezer and Rabbi Natan Slifkin (notwithstanding those who have banned him) —being highly proficient in Torah as well as science and mathematics— as well as others behind outreach programs such as Aish HaTorah's *Discovery* program, are responsible not only for preventing the assimilation of those within the fold, but for attracting quality truth-seekers from the outside. They follow in the tradition of RaMBaM (Moses Maimonides, 1135-1204), who wrote the *Guide For the Perplexed* for those who struggled to maintain their faith in light of general scientific knowledge in their own day.

Unfortunately, a few of the new proofs based on scientific and yeshiva logic that have become widely disseminated online are weak. More than one has been disproved. Thanks to loud-mouths who broadcast such mistakes on the Internet, defeated proofs can actually become a "turn-off" for educated souls. In fact, the very use of the word "proof" instead of "point of evidence" is asking for trouble. Is any proof great enough that it cannot be called into question by writers with their own agenda?

In this book, while I only tackle the issue of the authenticity of the Oral Tradition (not the Written Bible, nor the Existence of *HaShem*), I will attempt to present more sophisticated and resilient points of evidence, including arguments that have never been published before. (For scientific proof, see Part III, Points 14-22).

SPEAKING TO THE UNDERLYING ISSUE OF THOSE *WITH* BASIC BELIEF

While it must be searched for, resilient Torah proof does exist in print and on the internet. However, there is a more basic problem. Too often, the whole multi-pronged scientific approach employed by those doing Torah outreach does *not* speak to the mindset of many people who neither trust, nor are moved by scientific proof, no matter how sound it may be.

They are already believers in the Bible (who may also be exploring the Qur`an) who have much more fundamental issues that are not treated in any book I've come across. Due to this lack of attention, Karaism, Islam and Messianic Judaism —which have become very sophisticated in their approaches— have made considerable inroads among those seeking religious truth. *Without treating the underlying issues that bother such truth-seekers, scientific proofs have little potency.*

Torah teachers must come to grips with the reality that there is a very real, underlying reason why so many intellectually-minded, college-educated youth have difficulty accepting the legitimacy of Torah Judaism over other scripture-based faith communities. *Many laws and principles are not clearly spelled out in the Bible; certainly not in any useful detail. In the absence of an authoritative interpretation from Sinai (to their awareness), the Bible's verses are open to anyone's interpretation.*

The rest of this Introduction, Part I and Part II will speak to those of this mindset – honest, thinking Jews and non-Jews who have general belief in God and a basic reverence for the Bible, yet have trouble resisting the arguments of competing religious movements.

* * *

To begin with, the very vagueness of the Bible on the details of its laws screams out the existence of an authoritative interpretation from the outset. Otherwise, how could the ancient Hebrews, to whom the laws of the Bible alone were their sole Constitution, be governed? For example, when the Written Word commands that meat be slaughtered "as I have commanded you" with no further detail (Deut. 12:21), how could Israel's elders achieve consensus as to what the laws of slaughter actually were? Even if this were clear in the first few generations after Sinai, how could the Rabbis quoted in the Talmud —who split hairs over so many issues, great and small— largely relate to those laws plainly as a received tradition? (See Part I Point 6) *The very vagueness of the Written Torah cries out the existence of an accompanying Oral Tradition.*

NOTE: In this book, the ancient Sages/Rabbis quoted in the primary literature of the Oral Tradition are capitalized to distinguish them from post-Talmudic rabbinical leaders who neither have mosaic ordination, nor sit on a rabbinical court that represents the Jewish nation as a whole as the Babylonia Sages.

UNIVERSALLY-KNOWN AND RECOGNIZED ORAL TRADITIONS OF ISRAEL

Without realizing it, critics of what they call "Rabbinism" (or "Pharisaic Judaism") take for granted and overlook certain Oral Torah traditions maintained by the people of Israel; traditions that are uncontested and respected the world over.

Take, for example, the commandment of circumcision. God commanded that a Hebrew baby boy be circumcised on its eighth day of life. On one hand, it is generally accepted that rabbinical Judaism retained an unbroken Oral tradition since Abraham as to precisely where on the body circumcision should take place, and exactly how much flesh is to be removed. I have never seen an argument anywhere arguing against this.

However, for some strange reason, for those who have no difficulty with rabbinical Judaism having preserved such an oral tradition, the notion that the Rabbis preserved the authentic meaning and practical details of *other* Commandments that are just as much a part of everyday life and less technical than circumcision (i.e. the Oneness of God, dietary laws, the parent through which Jewish identity passes on to offspring, etc.) is a *very big deal*.

Similarly, I have never seen an argument anywhere claiming that Rabbinic Jews have forgotten which day is the 7th day. All know that the Church chose the following day as their day of rest, while the followers of Mohammad chose the sixth day. Note that the opportunity to practice and remember the Sabbath laws (every week) occurs in a Jewish community with much greater frequency than circumcision ceremonies (only when a baby boy is born). However, for the same people who fully accept that we have preserved the Oral Tradition as to which day is the 7th day; to recognize that we also preserved the meaning of God's Commandment *"to cease from labor"* on that day suddenly becomes a *very big deal*.

Few realize that an authoritative Oral Tradition was required even to have a readable written Bible in the first place. The original Torah was written without vowels or spaces between the words.[3] It is only according to an Oral Tradition from Moses that the ancient Hebrews could know where one word ends and the next word begins, how much more so the punctuation (i.e. the mid-sentence breaks and pauses), enabling us to identify the beginning and ending of sentences and phrases. *Without an Oral Tradition, even the individual words of the Written Torah could not be known, much less their vowels and the meaning of the text.*[4]

Moreover, the Written Torah itself plainly shows the Oral Tradition to far predate the written Word. The careful Bible reader will note that the scroll of the Torah as we have it today was only written towards the very end of Moses' life. Only in the last year of Moses' life, in the Plains of Moab, did he write the Torah down on a scroll as we have it to this day (Deut. 31:24-26). Considering all of Moses' instruction to the early nation of Israel after leaving Egypt, it is clear that Oral Torah instruction *preceded* the Written Word – not the opposite. In fact, the Torah makes it clear that ancient Oral Torah wisdom was known to the progenitors of mankind long before Sinai. (See Part II Point 2)

THE HYPOCRISY OF CHRISTIAN & ISLAMIC REJECTION OF THE ORAL TORAH

Ironically, Christianity and Islam —whose members have historically been classic rejecters of the Oral Law— revere texts that, unbeknownst to the simple masses, require solid faith in the Oral Tradition of the *Perushim* (*'Pharisees'*). This is how the Rabbis, the bearers and teachers of the *Perush* ("Interpretation"; the system of official Torah interpretation and tradition with roots going back all the way back to Sinai), were referred to in Israel 2,000 years ago. *The purpose of this book is to provide proofs and strong hints that the true 'Perush' is far older than that.*

Christian Hypocrisy

NOTE: There is no intention here to offend anyone, much less the growing number of righteous Christians who do not believe in the divinity of Jesus, but recognize the authority of the Hebrew Bible, respect Israel's obligation to fulfill the Torah in its entirety and her rights to the Land of Israel, and worship the true God according to His utter, abstract Oneness.

Let us consider honestly what is clearly taught in Matthew 23:2-3 in the name of Jesus himself:

Introduction

> The teachers of the law [translated as "the scribes" in other versions] and the Pharisees sit in Moses' seat. So ["Therefore" in other versions] you must obey them and do everything they tell you. But do not do what they do, for they do not practice what they preach.[5]
> —New International Version ©1995

Lest anyone make the ignorant claim that "the seat of Moses" here refers to some special "seat" that was supposedly featured in synagogues of the time, and that there was no intention here to put the Sages on a pedestal as fulfilling the leadership role of Moses, see the full context of Jethro's words to Moses in Exodus 18:13-26, and the implementation of God's Command in Numbers 11:16-17. The court ordained by Moses literally took over a major part of his daily role of judgment. Furthermore, in the above text, Jesus is using the fact the Rabbis sit "in the seat of Moses" as the reason why one must "do and observe" "all that they tell you" *even if they are corrupt* (God-forbid). Why would they be entitled to such obedience simply by virtue of their sitting in a fancy seat in the synagogue?[6]

Most versions of the New Testament (henceforth referred to as "NT") —such as the King James Bible, Webster's Bible Translation New International Version, etc. — are honest about the meaning of Matthew 23:2-3. Because the authority of the Rabbis is of Mosaic origin, what they say is authoritative and must be obeyed – even when it contradicts their actions. Accordingly, the New Living Translation (©2007) translates 23:2 refreshingly as:

> The teachers of religious law and the Pharisees **are the official interpreters of the law of Moses**. So practice and obey whatever they tell you, but

don't follow their example. For they don't practice what they teach.

However, other Christian translators were too bothered by the ramifications of this and other verses which expose the NT's internal contradictions to follow suit. They translated to the tune of "The scribes and the Pharisees *have seated themselves* in the chair of Moses" (New American Standard Bible (©1995) – as if the Rabbis had arrogantly assumed that power. But if that were so, why does Jesus then use that fact as the very reasoning why his followers must obey everything that they tell? Do his alleged words here not echo the very words of the Torah, as discussed above: "And you shall observe to do according to all that they will teach you?" *In other words, if they had co-opted the authority of Moses, why must people obey it?*

If they should then respond that it was merely Jesus' begrudging appeal that his followers obey the law of the land as good citizens —despite the Rabbis having unjustly assumed their power— that would reveal rabbinical law to be full of unlawful additions and unauthorized interpretations. Would a true prophet enjoin Israel to obey teachings that included additions or unauthorized interpretations of the Torah? It makes no Torah sense.

Moreover, how could the Rabbis' words carry such weight in spite of their own actions? Jesus is clearly holding their teachings on a pedestal in spite of their alleged bad behavior. This makes no sense from the standpoint of a religion that denies the authority of the Oral Tradition.

In fact, this may be a key that unlocks a great historical truth:

Through all the smoke of anachronisms and internal inconsistency within the Gospels, there is one profound method for deriving from the Gospels what may, indeed, have been teachings of a true, historical Jesus. If a verse attributed to Jesus appears to have escaped the Church censors' eyes —since it appears to teach *the opposite* of what the Church founders preached (an embarrassment to Christianity)— there is a chance it is historically accurate. *Can there be anything more embarrassing to the future Church than Jesus promoting the Pharisee Rabbis as "sitting in the seat of Moses," exhorting his followers to fulfill "all that they will tell you"?*

Believers in the NT are forced between accepting the Pauline antinomianism (the belief that the Torah's laws are no longer applicable) of most of the NT, or accepting the authority of bearers of the Oral Law per Jesus' own command; as it is written in their own NT: "And why do you call me 'Lord, Lord' and do not the things which I say?" (Luke 6:46) Rejection of the Oral Tradition by the Christian world is but a smokescreen hiding the fact that, by their actions, classical Christianity does not show any real subordination even to the Written Torah.

Even beyond Christian rejection of Matthew 23:2-3 (Jesus' alleged sweeping commandment that his followers "do and observe" all the Rabbis would teach), major observances in classical Christianity are not rooted even in their NT, much less the Hebrew Bible.

For example: While the holiday of Christmas is supposed to celebrate the birth of their god-man, where is a source for this observance in their own sacred writ? The religion's founders clearly created this holiday and ordained it to coincide with, and thereby replace other pagan celebrations such as the Roman holiday of Saturnalia and the holiday of Yule (December 25). But again, where is there a commandment —even according to NT— that devotees celebrate his birth?

Although there is textual support in NT that devotees mark Jesus' death at the time of Passover, how did this turn into a pagan rite, referred to in Greek as "*kiriakon [deipnon]*"? This term is so explicitly connected to pagan rites involving wine, bread, blood and other elements which were current at the time; that the early Patristic sources (Early Christian writings) opt for the rite being called *efchariston* ("Eucharist") instead. *It is not only a rite of human invention, but pagan to the core.*

This is not to mention the replacement of the Sabbath day (Saturday) with Sunday as the Christian sacred day of rest. Again, this begs the question: Where, even according to their sacred writings, are non-Jews expected to ritually observe any day of rest? If the Church regards itself as an extension or replacement of Israel (God forbid) by what right did the religion's founders obviate themselves of the Torah's Commandments concerning idolatry, circumcision, *tefillin*, and the prohibitions of consuming swine and shellfish? *By what authority do clergy who claim to guide their flocks in the service of the God of the Bible declare his eternal statutes to be defunct?* [7]

Did the Creator not state unequivocally (in text considered as sacred to Christianity as it is to Judaism) that the Commandments of the Torah were Given to Israel *for all time*:

> "an eternal law for all your generations"
> (Lev. 3:17 and another 7 places)

> "and the things that have been revealed belong to us and our children for eternity, that we may execute all the teachings of this Torah."
> (Deut. 29:28)

Introduction

These are the words of the Living God from the same Torah that includes stunningly-accurate prophecies of future times when Israel would sin and be thrown into exile, only to be restored to our Land (Deut. 30:1-5).

No one can say that *HaShem* "changed His mind" at any point to choose another people, or to change or replace his Commandments with others – unless the deity he refers to is not the God who said, "I, *HaShem*, do not change." *(Malachi 3:6)* He could not be referring to the God of David who confirmed in his prayer, "And You established for Yourself Your people Israel to be Your people ["a people unto You"] *forever*, and You, *HaShem*, became their God." (II Samuel 7:24)

Neither can anyone honestly entertain the notion (as many Christians do) that *HaShem* commanded what He did with the hidden intention of proving that His Word could never be kept... not unless the deity he refers is not the God Who said through Moses, "God is not a man that He should deceive." (Num. 23:19)

One of the 613 immutable Commandments of His Torah and the foundation of the Noahide Covenant as well, again, is to observe **"all that they will teach you."** This can only refer to the Oral Torah taught by the ordained sages of the Great Court (Sanhedrin), which were preserved and clarified by the Talmudic sages, and codified succinctly in RaMBaM's *Mishneh Torah* until the day when the Great Court is re-established according to Law.

NOTE: RaMBaM is an acronym for Rav Moshe ben Maimon, also known as Moses Maimonides (1135-1204). The author is a scholar in the unbroken tradition of RaMBaM, and this work is written strictly upon the legal foundation of Mishneh Torah. Cited abundantly in the text, it is usually referred to henceforth as M.T.

Islamic Hypocrisy and Hate

NOTE: there is no intention here to offend anyone much less the growing number of righteous Muslims and Druze who respect Israel's obligation to fulfill the Torah in its entirety and her rights to the Land of Israel, and worship the true God alongside Israel with one consent.

In traditional Islam, Jesus is considered to be one of the true prophets of Allah. Vicariously, the reverent Muslim must either accept the above teaching of Jesus, or contradict his religion, which regards Jesus as a true bearer of Allah's word in his time. Therefore, even according to Islam, if one is to heed the teachings of *Nebi `Issa* ("prophet Jesus") —which he must— then every Torah instruction of the "scribes and Pharisees" must be obeyed. Again, since Matthew 23:2-3 undermines the Christian religion, they can be certain that this verse is no later addition to, or corruption of the historical words of their *Nebi `Issa*.

Moreover, the *teachings of the Rabbis* are explicitly referred to in the Qur'an as having been given to the Jews by Allah:

> We [Allah] have revealed the [Written and Oral] Torah, in which there is guidance and light. By the prophets who surrendered themselves judged the Jews, and so did the rabbis and the Torah scholars, according to God's Book which had been committed to their keeping and to which they themselves were witnesses.
> (Qur'an, The Table, *Sura* 5:44)

According to *Nebi Musa* ("prophet Moses") those laws are eternal, never to be replaced, as it is written, "an eternal law for all your generations." (Lev. 3:17 and another 7 places)

Introduction

At this point Muslims should be reminded that, according to Israel's eternal Torah from Allah, *Allah Commanded that Israel bring all of mankind to the Seven Laws of Noah.* There should be *nothing* in the Seven Laws that any intelligent, sincere Moslem should find offensive, if he would only approach the subject honestly and objectively, *with no hate in his heart.* But that brings us to the far more nefarious hypocrisy from the Moslem world in our time– their hateful lies.

Specifically, too many Muslims have a religious attachment to hateful lies that the nation of Israel stole another people's land, that they are guilty of mass-murdering the Palestinians as the Germans did to the Jews, along with other blood libels.

The supposed usurping of Arab land contradicts their sacred writ as well. None but their own prophet allegedly taught that the Land of Israel was given to the People of Moses by Allah, as it is written:

> Bear in mind the words of Moses to his People [Children of Israel]. He said: "Remember, my People, the favor which God has bestowed upon you. He has raised up prophets among you, made you kings [Kingdom of David and Solomon and the Davidic Dynasty], and has given you that which He has given to no other nation [i.e. the Written and Oral Torah – see above Qur'an citation]. *Enter, my People, the holy land* [Land of Israel] *which God has assigned for you. Do not turn back, and thus lose all.*
> (Qur'an, The Table, *Sura* 5:20)

This is according to Allah's special favor for the Jews, as it is written:

> Children of Israel, remember the favor I [Allah]
> have bestowed upon you, and that I exalted you
> above the nations.
>
> (Qur'an, The Cow, *Sura* 2:47)

The miraculous ingathering of her exiles, rebirth of the Jewish homeland, and Israel's repeated victories over so many Muslim foes (irreverent to their own sacred text, I must add) should be a clear sign to any rational Muslim with eyes to see– *The People of Moses have retained Allah's favor*; Israel is Allah-blessed. Moreover, Israel's long exile, Allah's enduring favor, and Israel's eventual return to their Allah-given land were clearly prophesied by Moses – a true prophet in their eyes (Deut. 30:1-5). Therefore, even Muslims cannot claim the Rabbis "changed" these verses, since they were truly fulfilled.

Therefore, the defensive wars Israel fought to defend Israel's right to her Allah-given land cannot constitute murder. If Israel wanted to do to the Palestinians as the Germans did to the Jews, they would have easily massacred them systematically long ago. On the contrary —even against the laws of war in the Torah— Israel's liberal defense establishment puts Jewish soldiers at risk, fighting surgical wars that fail even to eradicate the rogues at the helm of terrorist organizations (the most impious Muslims of all). Meanwhile, Israel supplies those wicked regimes with water, electricity, and all the needs of modern society, and allows the flow of cash into their banks. Again, this is not for lack of the power to crush such criminals, but out of misplaced compassion for those who not only lust for the blood of Jews and Christians, but brutally murder and oppress their own.

Allah's enduring love for the Jews is according to another principle that Allah does not change His mind precariously, as prophet Malachi (another true prophet in Muslim eyes) wrote, "I, *HaShem*, do not change" (Malachi 3:6). Prophet "Daoud" (King David) confirmed Allah's eternal love for Israel in his prayer, "And You established for Yourself Your people Israel to be Your people ["a people unto You"] *forever*, and You, *HaShem*, became their God" (II Samuel 7:24).

When will more Muslims open their eyes and recognize Allah's enduring love and Providence for Israel? When will they note how —while the Jews indeed fell from the proper observance of Allah's laws for Israel (Torah), bringing upon them much suffering and degradation— the nation has been steadily returning to strict Torah observance?

Most pertinent to the subject of this book, when will they realize the importance of the Oral Law of Israel to their own lives, and open their minds and hearts to the Seven Laws of Noah?

WHOM THIS BOOK CAN HELP, AND WHOM IT CANNOT

Sadly, over the centuries, competing religious movements have learned to conveniently ignore or wiggle away from the wealth of textual evidence in the Bible and other ancient literature that prove the deep antiquity of the Oral Torah tradition. In their resentment for the teachings of the *Perushim* (Pharisees, Torah Sages of the late-Second Temple era characterized as the "founders" of rabbinical Judaism) and to further their own agenda, they have painted a twisted picture of the *Perushim* as corrupt legalists who came to *replace* God's earlier system (which they suppose to have been closer to the simple understanding of the Bible) with their own ideas. This includes "adding to the Law" against *HaShem's* decree not to do so (Deut. 4:2).

With considerable monetary resources, those organizations disseminate their own literature, winning over many who are ignorant of history, ignorant of the Bible even as it is translated in their own tongue (how much more so in Hebrew), and lack training in logic, and objective, critical thinking. As a result of all the controversy generated and the general cynicism that characterizes today's young people (particularly those with higher education), the youth —not wanting to take any side— tend to come to see all religion as a single monolith and reject it as a whole.

Despite this trend, many young people, Jews and non-Jews, are serious about finding the truth, which can be found by those who are open, patient, wise, and honest enough to make a thorough search. However, considering the pitfalls along the way, people with the following issues are likely not to be convinced, regardless of the evidence presented here or anywhere:

(1) *Primary religious issues,* such as those who have no belief in God or the Written Torah to begin with. Despite the scientific proofs in this book (14-22) that pose a challenge to the atheist and Bible critic, those who lack these basic beliefs will have the most inner resistance to its content. This book can only help those who have a basic belief in the Creator and, besides Part III, a basic reverence for the Bible.

(2) *Emotional issues,* such as those with deep-seated prejudice, and those who cannot see past the powerful, warm feelings for their birth religion. Included are those who, due to all the controversy, have a basic mistrust in their own ability make sense of it all —much less take a stand— no matter how great the evidence may be. This book can only help those who can rise above their prejudices, can approach the subject objectively with an

open-mind, *and are ready —if they become convinced— to act on that conviction.*

(3) *Social issues,* such as family and peer pressure. This book can only help strong-minded individuals who are willing to free themselves of those binds, to stand up to those challenges in pursuit of the truth

(4) *Business and political issues,* such as belonging to, or depending on a group that has a vested interest in the de-legitimization of authentic Torah tradition. This book can only help strong-willed individuals who are ready to sacrifice such associations out of good conscience, if needed.

(5) *Authority-related issues,* namely those whose natural rejection and distrust for religious authority will not allow them to consider the truth in an organized religion. Included here are those who insist on looking down on the ancient Sages as primitive and thereby ignorant. *This book can only help those individuals who are ready to let go of their ego and pain based on past experiences with false religions.*

For those sincere questioners whose main obstacle is their struggle with the issue of the authenticity of the Oral Tradition and God-given authority of its torch bearers, the Talmudic Sages, this book will be of great benefit. It will show how, between Orthodox Jewry —heirs to the teachings of the *Perushim* (Pharisees) and the prophets— and their critics, it is simple and uncomplicated for an objective person to identify whose historical and religious perspective is rooted in fact, and whose is not.

THE AUTHOR'S COMMITMENT

With *HaShem*'s Help, I will do my utmost to help critical truth-seekers to realize the truth of Oral Torah from Sinai. I will not rest until I have answered the hard, intelligent questions that gnaw at their heart, namely: *How can we safely assume the rabbinical understanding of the laws to be legitimate? Do the rabbis truly speak for God? Which rabbis? How can one know for certain?*

Introduction

NOTES

(1) Meaning simply "the Name," this is the common, respectful reference to God's most sacred Name. Written as YHWH in Hebrew, it is forbidden to be pronounced in the absence of the Holy Temple in Jerusalem. May the Holy Temple be built again speedily in our days, and God's sacred Name will be heard once again. We use the terms *"HaShem"* and "God" interchangeably.

(2) Based on the exhaustive historical portrayal of the life and times of Rabbi Akiva: Lehmann, Meir (translated by Zucker, Pearly). *Akiva: The Story of Rabbi Akiva and His Times.* Feldheim Publishers, Jersualem 2003. 292 pp.

(3) Introduction to the RaMBaN's (Rav Moshe Ben Nahhman) commentary to Genesis cf. Talmud Tr. Sukkah 49a.

(4) The nature of Hebrew (a terse language made of simple word-roots) is such that, without spaces, neighboring words strung together can be broken up differently, generating alternate wording and different meaning. Only by Oral Tradition from Moses could it be known where one word in God's Torah ends and the next word begins. Even so, the meaning of many words would be unclear without the Oral Tradition of the voweling, as Hebrew writing has no vowels. Even if we knew the basic meaning of the words, without the Oral Tradition of the Torah's punctuation (i.e. the mid-sentence breaks and pauses), we could not know with certainty the beginning and ending of sentences and phrases. In short, people take for granted that the written Bibles of the world incorporate a great deal of Oral Torah and Tradition. *Without the Oral Tradition from Sinai, the Written Torah would be a largely sealed book.*

(5) All quotes from translations from the New Testament and information about parallel translations are from the Online Parallel Bible at *Biblos.com.bible.cc*

(6) Christian and Karaite thinkers try their best to derail the plain meaning of these alleged words of Jesus (Matthew 23:2-3), lest one imagine that they actually imply that the judicial authority of Israel's ordained rabbis is Mosaic in origin. It has caused people to see actual, physical "seats of Moses" everywhere and in all things

(i.e. Nehemiah Gordon's *Hebrew Yeshua vs. Greek Jesus*.)

Consider the scholarly piece on this alleged ancient synagogue phenomenon by Kenneth Newport (Newport, Kenneth. *A Note on the "Seat of Moses" (Matthew 23:2)*. Andrews University Seminary Studies, Spring 1990, Vol. 28, No. 1, 53-58. Copyright 1990 by Andrews University Press.

He first reports a "seat" carved from a single block of limestone found at Hammath-by-Tiberias, complete with its "back towards Jerusalem," as one would expect for an important rabbi who faces his congregation. Sounds impressive. Then he tells us of a *better preserved* "seat of Moses" found in 1962 at Chorazin. We learn that this relic *originally had* armrests and a back. Translation: these features are not evident in the artifact today. Thanks to the author's thoroughness, we then learn of an ancient inscription on the front of the chair, translated, "Remembered be for good Judah b. Ishmael who made this *stoa* [Greek for a column-like structure] and its staircase. As his reward may he share with the righteous."

What precisely is it about a small, badly broken stone with no base (much less feet), no back or arm rests of sufficient size to speak of, removed from its archaeological context, labeled as a 'stoa', makes it a chair? (If this "seat of Moses" is the better preserved one, what about the former artifact from Hammath-by-Tiberas?) Apparently for that reason, the small, broken stone needed to be propped high up on wooden beams and placed against the wall, so all can see what a venerable "seat of Moses" it is. (See photographs at:
darkwing.uoregon.edu/~dfalk/courses/ejud/synagogues.htm and *www.biblewalks.com/Sites/Korazim.html*)

The author then nobly admits that his third and final example, unearthed at Delos, was found in a building whose identity as a synagogue is strongly contested.

Even if such prominent seats were indeed found in 1st century synagogues, what would make them "seats of Moses" according to a forced interpretation of Matthew 23:2? Why not the customary "seat of Elijah" (a customary feature in synagogues for time immemorial, upon which the circumcision of males is traditionally performed) or simply a seat for the one given the honor to hold the

Introduction

Torah scroll while the *haftarah* (the accompanying portion from the Prophets read on the Sabbath) is read, per ancient Jewish custom?

In truth, such forced interpretation by Christian thinkers undermines their own agenda. The more mundane the meaning of "the seat of Moses," the more ridiculous Jesus' alleged words are made out to be – that simply by virtue of their sitting in such a "seat," the rabbis must be obeyed. Even Mr. Newport admits later in his piece that the words in the verse "therefore do all that they tell you" implies that the rabbis were "teachers who were in some way considered authoritative expounders of Torah."

As for the Karaites, it is bad evidence for an even worse historical theory which it is supposed to support.

(7) Some might argue that Jesus indeed bestowed such authority upon Simon Bariona (subsequently known as "Peter") per Matthew 16:13-19. Here Jesus allegedly declares that Peter is the rock upon which the new congregation of Jesus will be built, bestowing him with authority which "binds" and "looses" in heaven and earth. However, to argue that Jesus' official adjudicator was above the word of God, and could undermine the Sinaitic Covenant (or even the Seven Laws of Noah binding upon the nations) renders the Torah —which declares repeatedly that the Torah's laws are eternally binding, even in the far future— meaningless.

Other Christian scholars invoke the verse, "For where two or three are gathered in my name, there am I among them." (Matt. 18:20) This verse is traditionally used by the church to "prove" by what authority Peter, "the first pope," could introduce anti-Torah changes in their religion. However, besides the heresy of this thinking (as explained above), none other than Adam Clarke, a classical Christian commentator, admits that the concept of this verse was clearly taken from the Jewish teaching that even if two or three Jews learn Torah together, *the Divine Presence is among them* (Clarke's Commentary on the Bible: *www.godrules.net/library/clarke /clarke.htm*).

Indeed, it is the famous teaching of Rabbi Hhalafta from the Mishnah (Tr. *Avoth* 3:7[6]), teaching the sanctity and importance of Torah learning in groups of any size. It has nothing whatsoever to do religious authority. (Distinct from the idolatrous concept of "Holy Spirit," the nature of the Divine Presence spoken of by the Rabbis is explained in Part II Point 1.)

Another classical Christian commentary slams the traditional interpretation as anathema to the teachings of their deity.

(Halakhic Note: "Christ" is simply the English term for the Greek Χριστός (Khristós) meaning "the anointed one." It is a translation of the "mashiahh" or "messiah" in English. [Wikipedia article on "Christ"]. While Christianity chose to deify the man they erroneously believe to be the messiah, and they call their deity by the title "christ," my understanding is that this term is not the "name of an idol," and is therefore permitted to be pronounced by Jews.)

We have abundant reason to think, that if Christ ever intended that Peter and his successors at Rome should be heads of the church, and his chief vicars on earth, having so fair an occasion given him, he would now have let his disciples know it; but so far is he from this, that his answer disallows and condemns the thing and itself. Christ will not lodge such an authority or supremacy anywhere in his church; whoever pretend to it are usurpers.
(*Matthew Henry's Whole Bible Commentary*, public domain)

Indeed, ancient Jewish sources (most notably the *Toledoth Yeshu* traditions and the *Aggadeta D'Shim`on Kepha*, which can be dated as early as the 3<sup>rd</sup> Century CE), record that "Shim`on Kepha" (Simon Bariona, "Peter") was, in fact, a prominent rabbi who was chosen to infiltrate the Nazarene sect in order to get them to follow other [non-Jewish] religious rites so that they could be

Introduction

distinguished from other Jews. It is recorded that this Shim`on HaKepha originally instituted the changes in the calendar, etc.

We see that antinomianism (the belief that the Torah's laws are no longer binding) was not even a natural tendency among the earliest Christians. It needed to be introduced from the outside in order to save the Jewish People from the madness of a messianic cult, that —in the name of a dead, false messiah— threatened the Torah observance of Israel.

Even non-Jews should escape this heresy-laced confusion and cling to pure, unadulterated Torah – the Seven Laws of Noah.

(A special thank you to Mr. Yehudah Barukh Ilan for the contribution of his knowledge and wisdom to footnotes 6 and 7.)

Oral Torah from Sinai

PART I:

TACKLING THE HARD QUESTIONS

וּבָאתָ אֶל־הַכֹּהֲנִים הַלְוִיִּם
וְאֶל הַשֹּׁפֵט אֲשֶׁר יִהְיֶה בַּיָּמִים הָהֵם,
וְדָרַשְׁתָּ וְהִגִּידוּ לְךָ אֵת דְּבַר הַמִּשְׁפָּט.
וְעָשִׂיתָ עַל פִּי הַדָּבָר אֲשֶׁר יַגִּידוּ לְךָ
מִן הַמָּקוֹם הַהוּא אֲשֶׁר יִבְחַר יְהוָה;
וְשָׁמַרְתָּ לַעֲשׂוֹת כְּכֹל אֲשֶׁר יוֹרוּךָ.
עַל פִּי הַתּוֹרָה אֲשֶׁר יוֹרוּךָ
וְעַל הַמִּשְׁפָּט אֲשֶׁר יֹאמְרוּ לְךָ תַּעֲשֶׂה;
לֹא תָסוּר מִן הַדָּבָר אֲשֶׁר יַגִּידוּ לְךָ יָמִין וּשְׂמֹאל.

(דברים יז:ט־יא)

And you shall come to the priests the Levites
and to the judge **that will be in those days**; and you shall inquire;
and they will declare to you the sentence of judgment.
And you shall do according to the word that they will tell
you
from the place that *HaShem* will choose;
and you shall observe to do according to all that they will teach you.
According to the law that they will teach you, and according
to the judgment which they will tell you, you shall do;
you shall not turn aside from the sentence that they will
declare unto you to the right nor to the left.
(Deuteronomy 17:9-11)

1.
HOW CAN THE ORAL TRADITION INCLUDE TEACHINGS ADDED LATER BY THE RABBIS?

Rabbinical tradition —the Oral Law— not only includes the original interpretations of God's Own Commandments given to Moses at Sinai, but novel ordinances by the rabbis of the "Great Court" (Sanhedrin) in every generation until the court was dissolved in the 5th century C.E. This body of knowledge was committed to writing by the Sages of Israel after the destruction of the Holy Temple in Jerusalem. It is critical to realize that this is the very judicial system God gave Israel from the beginning.

The Written Torah makes it clear that the Law given at Sinai was *a complete, closed system* that would not require any future revelations from Heaven to add or take away from what was Commanded to Moses at Sinai:

> All this Word that I command you, that shall you observe to do; you shall not add to it, nor take away from it. (Deut. 13:1)

> The secret things belong to *HaShem* our God; but the things that have been revealed belong to us and to our children for eternity, that we may execute all the words of this Torah. (Deut. 29:28)

> For this Commandment that I command you this day, it is not too hard for you, neither is it far off: It is not in heaven, that you should say: 'Who will go up for us to heaven, and bring it to us and cause us to hear it, so that we may do it?' Neither is it beyond the sea, that you should say: 'Who will go across the sea for us and bring it unto us, and cause us to hear it, that we may do it?' But the

> Word is very close to you, in your mouth, and in
> your heart, so that you may fulfill it.
>
> (Deut. 30:11-14)

NOTE: In Part II Points 6, 7 and 13, examples are given of Torah Commandments that are stated in the most brief and vague wording. They cannot be understood, much less fulfilled, without an accompanying tradition of practical instruction. Yet the above source in Deut. 30 clearly teaches that Israel has all the instruction it needs to obey the entire Torah. "The Word," the closed Torah system being spoken of that is "very close to us, in our mouth and in our heart", clearly includes such a tradition.

In fact, no future prophets were ever permitted, much less charged with adding or changing the law or its official oral body of interpretation. All future revelations henceforth were strictly for the purpose of instructing prophets and kings in how to lead, teach, and rebuke the people in the ways of the Torah, and guiding those leaders on their holy missions. Consider the final words of Malachi, the very last prophet to the nation until full prophecy returns to Israel:

> Remember the Torah of Moses My servant, which
> I commanded him at Horeb for all Israel, statutes
> and ordinances. (Malachi 3:22)

The Torah's vision is from the beginning of time to the end of history as we know it, including Israel's long exiles to the ends of the earth (Deut. 30:1-5) – such as the current Diaspora that is gradually coming to an end, as Israel returns to their native Land. From the beginning, it has taken into account all the cultural and technological revolutions that would ever come about.

What mechanism did the original system contain by which the original intent of the Commandments could be preserved over thousands of years, while allowing the nation's practical laws to adapt and remain relevant across vastly changing times? *There had to have been an official body to whom the interpretation of the 613 Commandments would be entrusted; a select, ordained body of righteous men who would preserve and teach the laws in the authoritative, correct manner from generation to generation.* It would need to be a source of teaching whose authority would be absolute in the face of any dispute in any future generation. Moreover, it would need to be empowered with the authority to adjudicate *new practical law* to preserve Israelite society in the face of challenging circumstances in the future.

According to the Written Word, that is precisely what *HaShem* did:

> And you shall come to the priests the Levites and to the judge that will be in those days; And you shall inquire; and they will declare to you the sentence of judgment. And you shall observe to do according to all that they will teach you from the place that *HaShem* will choose, *and you shall observe to do according to all that they will teach you.* According to the law that they will teach you, and according to the judgment which they will tell you, you shall do; you shall not turn aside from the sentence that they will declare unto you, to the right, nor to the left. (Deut. 17:9-11)

By those words, *HaShem* established an authoritative judiciary and legislature. It was the "Great Court" or "Sanhedrin" of 70 elders, 71 including Moses. (71 is the official number of seats on the Great Court for all generations.) Their original ordination by Moses is described in Numbers 11:24-25. *Thus began a chain of "semikhah" –Mosaic ordination of Torah judges– and a flow of divinely-ordained teaching in the careful hands of a judiciary appointed by HaShem Himself.* This chain of sacred Torah teaching and ordination of qualified students by their masters continued uninterrupted for over 1700 years.[1] This is why, even though the Court was forced to disband at a few junctures during that time, the integral traditions were maintained and the Great Court could always be re-established. Not until the Sanhedrin dissolved in the early 5th century C.E. (Ibid.) did *semikhah* cease completely. Despite a few attempts to renew Mosaic ordination, none have been successful.

Although the Torah's term for "judge," *shofet*, was replaced in late Second Temple times with the title "Rabbi" (pronounced *"rabbee"* in Hebrew, meaning "my master"), they mean the exact same thing: a judge ordained with authentic Mosaic ordination *semikhah*). Among the ordained Levites and *kohen*-priests, their word must be obeyed in all matters of Torah practice. Therefore, when we use the terms "Rabbis," "Sages," or "Talmudic Sages," we are referring to *those judges* —the ordained Torah masters *(Tannaim* in Hebrew*)* who sat on the Great Court— and even their un-ordained master students *(Amoraim)*, mainly in Babylonia, who acted as the bearers of unbroken Torah tradition until the Talmud was completed in 475 C.E. (Ibid.).

NOTE: The Torah explicitly qualifies that the ordained teachers whose word carries Divine sanction are those ruling "from the place that HaShem will choose" – meaning the national court which convenes at the Tabernacle and later the Holy Temple [when it is standing]. Although it is customary to refer to modern Torah teachers with a degree of certification as "rabbi", in fact there have been no truly ordained rabbis for 1500 years. There are only Torah scholars who do their best to teach, counsel, judge, and lead according to their wisdom and training, in the absence of Mosaic ordination. Fittingly, there is no obligation whatsoever for any Jew or non-Jew to accept Torah teaching from a Torah personality simply because he is regarded as a famous rabbi, but only by virtue of that scholar's faithfulness to the authentic 'halakhah' [practical Torah law] as it was preserved and codified by the Sages.

If, perhaps, the Second Temple Sages had used the biblical term *shofet*, or had the Torah used the latter-day term *Rabbi*, it would have been more difficult for detractors for the last 2,000 years to portray the Sages as the founders of a new religious movement ("Pharisaic Judaism" or "Rabbinism"), as if the Sages of that generation replaced the original Torah system with a new, artificial one.

2.
WHY ARE NOVEL RABBINICAL LAWS NOT CONSIDERED UNLAWFUL "ADDITIONS" TO THE TORAH?

We quoted the verse above, *"you shall not add to it, nor take away from it."* (Deut. 13:1) While the Torah passage quoted above (Deut. 17:9-11) establishes the authority of Israel's ordained *kohen*-priests, Levites and Sages as the bastion of the Oral Tradition and seat of judgment, how can we know that it was lawful for them to add new, original laws that *add* to Torah observance both for Jews and non-Jews according to their respective Covenants?

Let us revisit the verses discussed above:

> (9) And you shall come to the priests the Levites and to the judge that will be in those days; And you shall inquire; and they will declare to you the sentence of judgment. (10) And you shall observe to do according to all that they will teach you from that place which *HaShem* shall choose, *and you shall observe to do according to all that they will teach you.* (11) According to the law that they will teach you, and according to the judgment which they will tell you, you shall do; you shall not turn aside from the sentence that they will declare unto you, to the right, nor to the left.   (Deut. 17:9-11)

The first time the Torah commands in verse 10 "And you shall observe to do according to all that they will teach you," it appears that this is only in the context of judging case law; and determining the solution to legal dilemmas. However, the Torah goes even further, restating the idea in the same verse, giving the court even broader powers:

> ...and you shall observe to do according to ALL that they will teach you.

However limited the context of the previous statements were, this exhortation gives the Court the authority to institute novel legislation of their own *in order to safeguard Torah observance, to guard and guide society according to the needs of the times, and repair the world* (M.T. Laws of Rebels 1:3-4).

According to Oral Tradition, Leviticus 18:30 is actually an explicit command to the Sages to enact rabbinical fence-laws to distance the public from breaking *HaShem*'s Commandments in the Torah. It comes after a list of severe Torah prohibitions on account of which the nation could be destroyed, and the souls of unrepentant sinners utterly cut off from the eternal life of the soul *(kareth)*. *HaShem* then gives the following command to the nation's judiciary:

> *So you shall safeguard My Charge, so that you will not [come to] do any of these abominable practices* which were done before you, and so that you will become defiled through them: I am *HaShem* your God.   (Lev. 18:30)

How can one safeguard God's Charge, words of instruction? The simplest understanding is that Israel is to erect legal safeguards to prevent the infraction of God's Charge. *It is the nation's judges and lawmakers who are directly responsible for how the Law is defined and enforced.* Even without the voice of tradition, it is common sense that this Commandment seems to be aimed at the nation's judiciary.

Beyond such legal safeguards (fence-laws), the Bible itself is replete with indirect references to entirely new laws enacted by their predecessors in the days of Ezra, such as the reading of the Scroll of Esther on Purim and the four rabbinical fasts. As discussed below in Part II Point 5, these novel legal additions to Torah practice were enacted by a court of Sages staffed by prophets such as Haggai and Zechariah. *If such rabbinical additions contradict Torah law, would the prophets of the Bible have remained silent?*

It is simple. Rather than infringing God's law, they were acting according to the authority vested in them in Deut. 17:10.[2]

Clearly, *HaShem*'s Command not to add to the Law (Deut. 4:2, 13:1) means something else. *It means not adding laws in God's Name —as if HaShem Himself had commanded thus— or to add content to HaShem's Torah Commandments* (see M.T. Preface 3-5). An example would be adding more words to the priestly blessing as it was commanded in the Torah (M.T. Laws of Prayer 14:12 cf. Num. 6:22-27), or adding an 8th day to the Passover festival in the name of God, as though it were commanded thus in the Torah.

3.
THE WORD OF GOD IS PERFECT, THE WORD OF MAN FALLIBLE. DID THE SAGES MAKE A DISTINCTION? IF SO, HOW?

Despite the Torah commandment to hearken to the Sages of the Great Court, the ordained Rabbis made a clear, healthy distinction between Torah Law (the 613 Commandments in the Written Torah) and their own decrees, *and they legislated that distinction into law*. They decreed that in a case of doubt involving a Torah law, one must be strict, while in a case of doubt involving a rabbinical law, one is to be lenient. (M.T. Laws of Rebels 1:9[5])

The following example shows to what extent the Court went to ensure that the simple meaning of the Torah's verses, the Word of God, would be protected even against faulty interpretation by a Sanhedrin, God forbid.

Consider the Torah law regarding a case in which the Court should ever err by *unwittingly* ruling against Torah law. In times when the Holy Temple stands in Jerusalem, such a sin can only be atoned before death by giving the appropriate sin offering, since it is an *unwitting* transgression of the Court (Lev. 4:13).[3] The sages defined this as a situation when the interpretation of the law was a matter of controversy with the Sadducees. (*Sadduqim* were apostates who rejected the Oral Tradition, ruling according to their understanding of the plain meaning of Scripture.) However, if the meaning of the Torah wording is *so* simple that *"[even] the Sadducees agree with it" and a child understands it from his repetitions of Scripture in school,* the transgression cannot be considered "unwitting." Consequently it cannot be atoned for with such a sin offering. (Tractate *Horayoth* 4a [henceforth cited as 'Tr.' It is a source in the Babylonian Talmud unless otherwise stated.]) Despite the general Torah obligation to obey the decrees of the court, such a ruling is not to be followed.

This is according to the principle that *"a verse* [in Scripture] *does not leave its plain meaning"*. (Tr. *Shabboth* 63a, cf. RaMBaM in *The Book of Mitzvoth*, Principle 2)

4.
HOW CAN WE TRUST THE MORAL INTEGRITY OF THE ORDAINED SAGES?

From the above section, we come to sense the high caliber of the men the Sanhedrin, their fear of *HaShem* and undying loyalty to upholding His true Word. These are two of the required traits of Torah judges in the Written Word:

> Moreover you shall seek out of all the <u>people men of valor who fear God, men of truth – hating unjust gain;</u> and place such over them, to be rulers of thousands, rulers of hundreds, rulers of fifties, and rulers of tens.
> (Jethro's words to Moses in Ex. 18:19-22. Note where *HaShem* actually Commands Moses to do thus in Num. 11:16-17)

After summarizing the full meaning of these verses, RaMBaM describes the selection process the Sages employed to find such men:

> The Sages said that from the Great Court, they would send agents throughout the Land of Israel and check: Whomever they would find to be <u>wise, God-fearing, humble, discerning, mature, and amicable,</u> they would make him a judge in his town. And from there they would advance him to [the court at] the entrance of the Temple Mount, and from there they would advance him up to [the court at] the entrance to the Temple Courtyard, and from there they would advance him up to the Great Court.
> (M.T. Laws of the Sanhedrin and the Penalties Under Their Jurisdiction 2:11[8])

In addition to the above requirements, a judge had to possess an all-encompassing grasp of Torah and secular knowledge, as well as Torah mysticism. He even had to meet physical criteria, in that the judge was to have a robust healthy appearance (Ibid. 2:5[6]).

Clearly the Sanhedrin was not like most governments throughout history, who have been run by entrenched, corrupt political families. Israel's Supreme Court justices were carefully selected from all of Israel based not only on wisdom, but moral virtue. This is how men of lowly birth such as Hillel, a woodcutter from Babylonia; Eli`ezer ben Hurqanos, a simple farmer or Aqivah ben Joseph (Rabbi Akiva), a poor ignorant shepherd, could rise through diligent growth in Torah to become the greatest Sages of their respective generations.

The legendary humility and fear of Heaven of the Sanhedrin Sages shines through in stories recorded in the Talmud, how even the greatest among them would cast their personal opinions aside (no matter how right they thought they were) to uphold the ruling of the majority, when they had been overruled.

One of the greatest astronomical minds of history was Rabbi Yehoshua` ben Hhananiah. Rabbi Rappaport (1790-1867), former Chief Rabbi of Prague, a scholar with broad secular wisdom in his own right. He proved that the comet which appears every 70 years, a discovery attributed to Sir Edmund Halley, had already been mentioned by Rabbi Yehoshua` (Tr. *Horayoth* 10a).[4]

This astronomical genius had an opinion as to when the month began that differed from that of the Rabban Gamliel, *Nassi* (President) of the Sanhedrin and his Court. The *Nassi* understood that the Rabbi was intending to observe the coming holidays according to his own calculations, which could cause great turmoil and confusion among the nation. Although he was a lesser authority, the *Nassi* overruled Rabbi Yehoshua`. The *Nassi* then commanded that he appear before him with his money-belt and staff on the very day that, according to Rabbi Yehoshua`'s calculation, was *Yom Kippur*, thus constituting a desecration of the holiest day of the year–an act that would carry the penalty of spiritual excision from the eternal life of the Soul! Despite his great frustration, preferring to remain ill and bedridden for an entire year than to comply, the great rabbi acquiesced. When he stood before the Rabban Gamliel on the appropriate day, carrying his purse and staff, the *Nass*i rose to his feet, embraced and kissed him, calling him both his teacher (due to Rabbi Yehoshua`'s greater wisdom) and his student (since he had accepted the judgment of the *Nassi*) (Tr. *Rosh HaShanah* 24b-25a).

Another example is Rabbi Shim`on ben Yohhai, arguably the greatest of the Sages of his generation. In the Jerusalem Talmud (Tr. *Berakhoth* 6b), we learn how Rabbi Shim`on staunchly stood up for the law as it was instituted by his colleagues, despite the fact it contradicted his personal opinion. During the *Shemitah* year (the last of a 7-year cycle), it is well known that Jews are forbidden to work the land of Israel; they must let the land lay fallow. While Rabbi Shim`on had once ruled it should be permitted to reap produce that grows of its own (called *sefihhin*) during the *Shemitah* year, his colleagues on the Sanhedrin had overruled him, forbidding it. The Talmud records:

> Rabbi Shim`on ben Yohhai proved a point about Shemitah. One came to pick *sefihhin*.
>
> He [the sage] said, "Isn't it forbidden [what you are doing]? Aren't those *sefihhin*?"
>
> "Yes, but aren't you [the one] who permits them?"

"Yes, [the Rabbi answered] but didn't my colleagues disagree with me [and overrule my opinion]?" And he recited over him [the verse from Ecclesiastes 10], 'he who breaks a fence [a legal safeguard instituted by the Rabbis], a snake will bite him.' And so it happened. [*HaShem* fulfilled the word of the righteous Sage, and a snake bit the man]."

This source is so precious because it demonstrates how a Rabbi of such high stature would subjugate himself to the majority opinion of the Sanhedrin, even when it contradicted his own.

It also proves that even if the Sage indeed wrote the Zohar [the classical work of esoteric mysticism] as it exists today, he would never have agreed to future generations relying on its teachings against the *halakhah* as it was ultimately codified after his time. If he were alive today to see the current state of the Torah world, I am convinced he would have us follow the *Mishneh Torah* of RaMBaM (the Code of Jewish Law) as practical *halakhah*, until a new Sanhedrin is established.

When we consider the awesome integrity of these men, we can understand God's Wisdom in entrusting the teaching and development of the Oral Law into their hands. Rather than a group of men who assumed the right to impose "their ideas" on the Torah (God forbid), the Great Court was a Divinely-ordained institution (Ex. 18:19-22 cf. Num. 11:16-17) staffed by men of outstanding virtue and wisdom. Together they acted as the pillar of the Oral Law (M.T. Laws of Rebels 1:1) *to preserve and guard the true meaning of the Written Law* over the ravages of time, and *to ensure its proper execution according to God's Will* in each generation, even by means of innovative legislation.

5.
DOES ALL THE RABBINICAL DEBATE IN THE TALMUD NEGATE AN ORAL TRADITION?

Absolutely not. The argumentation in the Talmud is not about matters of Oral Tradition from Sinai. It is about how Oral Torah principles —recognized by all— should be applied in terms of practical *halakhah*, in light of various traditions as to how those principles were applied in the past by earlier authorities. In Part II Point 3 the reader will see that the same type of argument, debating the proper application of the law based on legal precedent, characterized the discussions of the Great Court in the First Temple era.

Moreover, just as every effective government contains more conservative and more liberal voices, so would the Sages argue as to whether or not an extra rabbinical safeguard should be instituted or not. Or they might argue whether, according to the principles agreed upon by all, whether a person or article should be declared pure or impure. In fact, *if there were no known Oral principles to the Law recognized by all —no sacred traditions as to how the law could be interpreted— there would have been no possibility for agreement by the ancient Sages, and a common 'halakhah' could never have been established for the Jewish People.*

The arguments and solutions of the Talmudic Sages prove the opposite to have been true. For example, there are continual references throughout the Talmud to a watershed event in the history of the Great Court known as "that day." It is a reference the historical day when the young Sage, Rabbi El`azar ben `Azaryah, ascended to the presidency of the Sanhedrin. On that day, every unclear point of the law was clarified; every last pending legal dispute settled (Tr. *Berakhoth* 28a). Again, such incredible progress could only have been made in so short a time if the Sages were operating according to sacred, traditional legal principles agreed upon by all.

The many disagreements found in Talmud arose later in the intervening centuries before the Talmud was written down in Babylonia. As explained below in the next section, during this time the nation of Israel suffered cruel conquest, persecution, exile, and a considerable decline in scholarship. The Talmud and later the *Mishneh Torah* of RaMBaM were later efforts to restore the law to the form it had reached before the last Sanhedrin dissolved. The debates came about as a necessity in order to restore and codify the Law accurately. The reason they are recorded for posterity is for a simple reason many fail to realize. *The Talmudic Sages desired that the old debates over rejected opinions be included so that future generations of scholars —ideally ordained judges on future Sanhedria— would know that these opinions had been considered and dealt with.*

Even so, the Sages teach that *the very mark of an ancient oral tradition from Sinai is that there never was an argument about it.* There may be discussion to clarify such received traditions, but no argument. RaMBaM explains:

> *Matters of oral tradition – there is no argument about them ever.* And any matter in which you find an argument [among the original Talmudic sages], it is certain that it is not a received tradition from Moses our teacher. And matters that are derived from the law: If the entire Great Court agrees about them, behold they agreed. And if they are divided [in opinion], they are to rule according to the majority and they produce one law for the masses.   (M.T. Book of Rebels 1:5[3])

It should be noted that each and every one of the 22 points of evidence for the Oral Tradition in Parts II and III are based on received Oral Tradition about which there is no argument among the Talmudic Sages, to my knowledge.

6.
WHAT ABOUT POST-TALMUDIC CUSTOMS AND RABBINICAL ENACTMENTS THAT JEWS RELATE TO AS LAW?

Even in various Torah-observant circles, many Jews do not understand where the ancient sages drew the line, and where modern rabbis must as well.

It cannot be stated loudly enough that the greatest *halakhic* decisors of post-Talmudic history —such as RaMBaM— made a clear and critical distinction between post-Talmudic additions to Jewish practice (which are non-obligatory and often legally problematic) and ordained Rabbinical Law as it was preserved and clarified in the Talmudic literature. According to the pure, critical scholarship of RaMBaM, only the Sanhedrin of 71 ordained Sages has the Divinely-sanctioned authority to interpret the Torah. It is also the only court with the authority to legislate decrees and institute customs (rabbinical law) that are legally-binding on the entire Jewish People and the rest of the world. It is they who composed and ratified the first written code of the Oral Law, the Mishnah, in about 200 C.E., and the Jerusalem Talmud about 175 years after that.[5]

The only judicial authority understood by the classical *halakhic* decisors to be an exception to this rule was one unique post-Sanhedrin court whose legislative authority was universally recognized – that of Rav Ashe and Ravina in Babylonia, who compiled and sealed the Babylonian Talmud in 475 C.E. Some fifty years earlier, due to the intense Roman persecution, the last Great Court of 71 dissolved in 425 C.E. When Mosaic ordination in the Holy Land ceased, authoritative scholarship deteriorated and precious legal wisdom was lost. Disputes arose regarding legal traditions and their applications, which had become unclear. *The law required a final re-codification even though no Sanhedrin existed.*

Meanwhile, first-class Torah scholarship flourished in Babylon. Some Babylonian scholars of the age, called *Amoraim*, were actually born and educated in Israel. In fact, the mighty Torah centers of Babylonia —Sura and Pumbeditha— were *founded* respectively by Rav and Shemuel, by the Israeli students of Rabbi *Yehudah HaNassi* Judah the President (commonly mistranslated as "the Prince", head of the Sanhedrin and compiler of the Mishnah). These schools retained the purity and strength of their traditions from the Great Sanhedria of old, giving them the unique ability to determine and officially codify what the original law was. As explained in the above section, this is the single reason for the compilation of the Babylonian Talmud – *that the original law could be restored and preserved in its entirety.*

While questions remain regarding novel Babylonian legislation (it is largely impossible to distinguish with certainty between their decrees and the authentic Israelite law), certainly no post-Sanhedrin court or individual after Rav Ashe has the authority to add to, nor give an alternative ruling to rabbinical law as it was codified up to the time the *Talmud Bavli* was formally sealed circa 475 C.E. *Since then, only authentic Talmudic Law (based purely on the written word from the original Talmudic literature) is halakhah.*

Whoever doubts this truth should consider the RaMBaM's responsum to Rabbi Yosef ben Gabir of Baghdad.[6] The RaMBaM wrote him a sharp response regarding the

Baghdadi custom to be extra strict, beyond the actual legal safeguards enacted by the ancient ordained Sages – the basic laws that distance a man from the biblical prohibition of intimacy with one's wife during her monthly period of separateness (Lev. 20:18). The rabbinical safeguards require that during this time, the couple may neither touch one another nor eat from the same dish, and that the wife may neither wash her husband's hands or feet, nor make his bed in front of him, nor pour wine for him. *Beyond* these rabbinical safeguards, the pious Baghdadi Jews would keep laws of ritual purity that are only in effect at the times of a Holy Temple in Jerusalem (and that, only for one who wanted to visit the Temple or eat from sanctified offerings) – not eating of the food prepared by one's wife at that time, and not sitting on the same couch on which she sits (see Lev. ch.15).

While RaMBaM stops short of forbidding this extra strictness altogether (so long as the individual regards his extra measures as acts of piety, not as legal requirements), he looks down on it, saying, "This is nothing but obligating [others] in that which is not obligatory." However, to prevent unlawful adding to the Torah, he gives a severe warning to those who dare relate to such customs as having the force of law:

> *It is fitting... to compel people to keep the law of the Talmud and no more,* like we [the rabbinical leaders] have done in the land of Egypt [where RaMBaM lived, where the same custom was commonly upheld]. We told [our congregations] that touching garments and foods [of a woman during her period of separateness] is permissible. However, keep your custom, but whoever wishes to permit [the leniency of the Talmud], may do so. And whoever is revolted [by touching her food and clothing] because of un-cleanliness or in order

to distance oneself from [intimacy with] the woman in her impure state, he may do so [to uphold the custom]. But should one understand there to be an actual halakhic prohibition in touching the food and drink that she touched, and distances himself from her because of this "prohibition," *he is no longer considered a rabbi* [or "rabbinical Jew," like a Karaite]**,** *and has become an apostate in regards to the Oral Torah.*

(Ibid.)

Despite the harshness of RaMBaM's wording, it did not prevent a few customs of extra piety from spreading throughout the Jewish world, and being treated with the force of law. More problematic are the few, pernicious, widespread customs that literally contradict *halakhah*.

Despite these trends, the truth remains. While there is nothing wrong with sensible stringencies for those who want to follow them voluntarily, *the further legal development of the Oral Torah is not a creative endeavor in the hands of un-ordained Torah leaders.* For post-Talmudic rabbis (no matter how wise, pious, or charismatic), to add or detract from our sacred legal structure —which was defined by the one human institution into whose hands God entrusted the adjudication of law— is tantamount to apostasy… *even when it is done for the noble goal of enacting a new safeguard to prevent sinning against a severe Torah crime.*

7.
SINCE WE HAVE THE SOURCES OF THE ORAL LAW FROM SANHEDRIN-ERA ISRAEL, WHY RELY ON THE BABYLONIAN TALMUD?

Why did the *Amoraim* (Babylonian Sages) and the great *halakhic* decisors and codifiers of the last 1500 years not simply rely on the older codes of law —those actually ratified by the ordained Sages of Israel— namely the Mishnah, *Sifre, Sifra, Tosefta, Mekhiltoth* and *Jerusalem Talmud*? Being that the Sanhedrin had disbanded by the time the Babylonian Talmud was compiled in exile, should we not defer to the earlier works created under the reign of the Great Sanhedrin in the Holy Land? This is an excellent question that requires a full, detailed response.

Needed: The Most-Updated Court Record from the Last Sanhedrin

While the legal codes from the land of Israel were an excellent legal record in their day, some of their rulings were considered outdated, since the Great Court had persisted for some 50 years after the Jerusalem Talmud was completed. It is of great significance that when Christianity became the official religion of the Roman empire, *the actual written archives of the Sanhedrin —including that last period of legislative activity— were moved to Babylonia.*[7] This coincides with the time of the Sanhedrin's dissolution circa 425 C.E. When the court of Rav Ashe and Ravina compiled the Babylonian Talmud (circa 475 C.E.), they had direct access to the most complete, accurate and up-to-date legislation from the last Sanhedria.

During the waning years of the Great Court, it appears that the last ordained judges of Israel, who viewed their Babylonian counterparts as their superiors, indeed continued to enact new legislation. The most famous of these is the Hebrew Calendar. It can be assumed that among these were rulings that had been enacted by their non-ordained counterpart (the Babylonian court) in an effort to bring greater unity to the Jewish People. One good example of this is the observance of two days of Rosh HaShanah in the land of Israel.

Tackling the Hard Questions

Here is a short historical background:

Only one century before the Great Court's dissolution, the Jerusalem Talmud still taught that Rosh HaShanah is only one day in the land of Israel. It is a clear from a note by the RaMBaN (Nachmanides, 1194-1270 C.E.) that this remained the practice of Jews in the land of Israel until the community was pressured into accepting the practice of the greater Jewish world.[8] It is tempting to say that 12th century Jews in Israel were keeping an unbroken tradition.

However, when a student of Rav Haye Gaon (939-1038 C.E.) asked the leading Torah giant regarding the Rosh HaShanah practice of the Jews in Israel, Rav Haye's response was that the Jews of Israel were unlearned (Ibid. [8]). RaMBaM would later explain in *Mishneh Torah*, despite the fact that Rosh HaShanah indeed could now be held for one day in the land of Israel (according to the Torah obligation in Num. 29:1), *there had been an actual late "taqqanah"* (official ordinance) *from one of the final Sanhedria before the Court was dissolved, that Rosh HaShanah be two days in Israel as well, so that the practice of the Jews in the land and abroad should be in uniform* (M.T. Laws of Sanctification of Months 5:8).

(For a fuller discussion of this subject, see Appendix I: "Why were Jews of Israel Pressured to Abandon Their Tradition?")

In fact, we learn from the epistle of HaRav Sherira Gaon to the Jewish community of Kairouan that the deference of the ordained Israeli sages to their Babylonian peers went back generations.[9] As far back as the generation that saw compilation of the Mishnah (the time of the first generation of *Amoraim*), ordained Sages in Israel saw their Babylonian counterparts as their superiors in rank, if not in wisdom. *Despite his role as Nassi (President) of the Sanhedrin,*

Rabbi Judah the President saw Rav Hunah —an early head of Babylonian Jewry— as his superior. Similarly, Rabbi Yohhanan (head of the Sanhedrin, compiler of the Jerusalem Talmud) was so impressed by the wisdom of Shemuel —founder of the Torah academy in Pumbeditha— he became his student.

> He [Rabbi Yohhanan] sent him thirteen camel-loads of [questions and answers regarding] *treifah* [non-kosher meat]. He said, "It is clear that I have a teacher in Babylonia; I will go and meet him," as we learn in Tr. *Hhullin*. (Ibid. [8])

While Shemuel was himself from the land of Israel, no one can argue that the school he founded was built on a legal foundation cut off from the pure Oral Torah of the early Israeli Sages. On the contrary, while Torah study weakened due to persecution in the land, it became strengthened in Babylonia, continually refreshed with scholars from the Land of Israel seeking safe haven.

Babylonian Torah, Planted By Israeli Sages, Revived Torah in Israel When it Nearly Dried Up

One of the reasons for the great respect commanded by the Babylonian Sages, is (as mentioned above) that their Diaspora schools, the mighty Torah centers of Sura and Pumbeditha, were founded respectively by Rav and Shemuel, students of Rabbi Judah the President (head of the Sanhedrin and compiler of the Mishnah) from the land of Israel. It is unlikely that such men would have founded schools that would rebel against the rulings of the Great Sanhedrin in the Land of Israel.

On the contrary – The Babylonian schools retained their own traditions from the Great Sanhedria of old, giving them the unique ability to determine and officially codify what the original law was. As we will see in the next section, they may have occasionally had genuine grounds for disagreement with later Great Courts in Israel after the generation of Rabbi Judah the President, judged to be weaker; namely the Court of Rabbi Yohhanan, which produced the Jerusalem Talmud.

As demonstrated in the above section, the exit of Rav and Shemuel from the land of Israel was no break-off point between the two communities by any means. Babylonian scholars, notably Rabbi Hhiyya, Rabbi Ammi and Rabbi Assi (3rd century C.E.), are examples of scholars who moved between Babylonia and the land of Israel. They moved to Israel in order to improve the weak state of Jewish education in the Land. They came bearing Torah from the wellsprings of Babylonia, and awe for its teachers. When quoting a doctrine of Rav or Shemuel, Rabbi Ammi and Rabbi Assi would begin with the expression, "Our masters in Babylonia say." (Tr. *Shevu`oth* 47a) In turn, they received training and Mosaic ordination from the most distinguished Israeli scholars, coming to be known by their Babylonian contemporaries as "the distinguished priests of the Land of Israel". (Ibid. Tr. *Gittin* 59b, Tr. *Sanhedrin* 17b) All the while, Rabbis who were born and raised in the land of Israel were fleeing Roman persecution to become teachers in Babylonia. *The Torah world of that age was clearly more unified than one might assume purely based on the written literature they left behind (as it exists in our hands today).*

The Need for More Detailed Teaching in the Diaspora

As great as the Babylonian sages eventually became through the seeds planted and nurtured by the ordained Sages from Israel, there remained issues of *halakhah* that were common knowledge among Jews in the Land of Israel, but not as widely known among the exiled communities in Babylonia. These issues, considered too obvious for the Rabbis to write into the Israeli literature, were not so obvious in Babylonia and therefore needed to be formally written into the Oral Law's final layer of codification.

The perfect example of this is precisely how one kindles the Hanukkah lights. The Mishnah only makes a passing reference to Hanukkah lights in the context of laws of injuries without any explanation (Mishnah Tr. *Bava Qama* 6:8[6]). It is on the assumption that all, even children, are familiar with their simple details. Accordingly, the later Israeli Talmudic literature is silent on the subject. According to the greater needs of the Jewish People in their day, the Babylonian Talmud would include those details (Tr. *Shabboth* 23a-b).

Genuine Reasons for Permitted Disagreement with the Great Court

The power of the Sanhedrin is not unlimited. While the Great Court is permitted to contradict a *judgment* of a previous Great Court in a given case, such is not the case regarding an earlier ordinance or decree (rabbinical law). Aside from their right to suspend even a Torah law on a temporary basis [10], a present Sanhedrin may only uproot a previous Sanhedrin ordinance or decree under two conditions: It must be (a) "greater in wisdom," its rabbis being more knowledgeable or better skilled in Torah judgment, and (b) "larger in number," meaning that the number of Rabbis and scholars of the generation who accept its legislation must be larger than those who accepted the legislation of the earlier Court. (M.T. Laws of Rebels 2:1-5[3])

Not only does a Sanhedrin not have free reign to uproot earlier ordained legislation, its own rulings must be accepted by the majority of the nation before becoming legally binding (Ibid. ch.2:10-12[5-8]). After the Great Court issues a ruling, there is a waiting period during which it is observed whether or not it is accepted by the majority of the Jewish people. If, after this time period, the majority has still not accepted it, the unpopular new law is repealed.

Consider now the demographics of the Hebrew nation after the Sanhedrin of Rabbi Judah the President in about 200 C.E. (which enjoyed the loyalty the entire Jewish People, both in Israel and abroad). As noted above, Israeli Rabbis were fleeing Roman persecution to Babylonia, leading to a decline in scholarship in the land of Israel. After the centers of Sura and Pumbeditha were founded, it took little time for the number of Torah scholars in Babylonia —with ordained Sages among them— to eclipse the number of scholars in the land of Israel. There arose a situation that had never existed before.

For novel Sanhedrin legislation to take effect, the Sages evidently understood that it needed to be accepted by Babylonian Jewry, the majority of the nation. If the Babylonian Sages considered the new Sanhedrin rulings to contradict previous ordinances (according to the ancient ordained traditions they preserved), their refusal to accept new Israeli legislation on the matter would render the present court as "smaller in number" of adherent scholars.[11] In other words, although there were no ordained courts in Babylonia, their scholars held considerable power over what legislation was considered to take effect halakhically, and which did not.

Consider, for example, the seemingly aloof way in which the Babylonian Sages mention (as a side note only in the context of a legal proof), how the Jews of the land of Israel make a blessing upon removing their *tefillin* (phylacteries), separating their own schools from the picture:

> But according to the Westerners [Jews of the land of Israel] who after removing their *tefillin* say the blessing of "...who sanctified us by His Commandments, and commanded us to keep his statutes [*lishmor hhuqaw*]," what does this include? It includes [the blessing on] fragrant odors. (Talmud Tr. *Niddah* 51b)

Indeed, the Jerusalem Talmud mentions this as an obligatory blessing (Jerusalem Talmud Tr. *Berakhoth* 14a).

Inexplicably, in one responsum I found, Rav Haye Gaon (whose court in the 11th century C.E. stood in an unbroken line of tradition from the *Amoraim)* stated bluntly, "We are not accustomed to blessing 'to keep his statutes'" (the above blessing after removing the *tefillin*). Notably, RaMBaM follows Babylonian Jewish custom here, mentioning no such blessing. *How could the greatest post-Talmudic rabbis of be so careless regarding a required blessing from the mouth of the ordained Sages of Israel?* The only explanation is that, since the practice of this blessing never spread to Babylonia (where the majority of Jewry dwelt), it was understood in hindsight to have never attained true *halakhic* status, and hence repealed.

The lesson is that not everything written in the old literature of the land of Israel represents legally-binding legislation, having been accepted by the majority of the Jewish nation.

Only Babylonian Talmud was Intended to Complete the Writing Down of the Oral Law

This last point is strengthened by the fact that, unlike the Israeli Talmudic literature, only the Babylonian Talmud was intended to serve as the "finishing act" of the transmission of the Oral Tradition. Its compilers, Rav Ashe and Ravina, were known as "the final great Sages of Israel to write down the Oral Tradition." (M.T. Introduction 29)

While the verb *g'mar* in Aramaic means "learned," it is also related to the Hebrew form of the verb G-M-R, *gemirah*, meaning "completion." This may be a key reason why the Babylonian Talmud came to be known as *Gemara*. It alludes to the Talmud being "the finished work"; the work that was *nighmar* – written as an act of completion.

Teachers of Loyalty to the Sanhedrin are Unlikely Rebels

Naturally, there was a low-lying friction between the two communities of scholars. Nonetheless, the Babylonian Sages were fully aware of the severe Biblical judgment of the "rebellious elder," which is any Torah teacher who dares teach contrary to the decrees of the Sanhedrin in the Land of Israel. The Babylonian Talmud spares no detail in his punishment – death by strangulation (Tr. *Sanhedrin* 84b-88a). As explained above in Point 4, this Talmud even includes instructive stories of Sages who let go of their honor to follow the majority opinion of the Sanhedrin – even when it contradicted their personal opinion.

Therefore, despite the occasional differences, all evidence points to the loyalty of the Babylonian Sages to the authentic Oral Torah of Israel.

Early, Ordained Israeli Rulings in Disguise

That loyalty may not be apparent to the student of the Babylonian Talmud. That is because opinions that appear to contradict rulings from earlier Israelite works, are cited in the name of the Babylonian Sages, while in fact they may well have been the opinion of their ordained counterparts in Israel. An opinion cited in the name of Rabbah Bar Bar Hhannah in Babylonia would have had more appeal among Babylonian Jewry (the majority of the Jewish nation at the time) than one cited in the name of a Rabbi Yohhanan or Resh Laqish – Israelite sages from a century earlier. This is very much like the modern rabbinical opinions, which are commonly ascribed to recent rabbis, rather than in the name of their earlier classical sources.

It is yet another reason why the Babylonian Talmud is regarded, for the most part, as more accurately reflecting the rulings of the final Great Courts. In the majority of cases, it is recognized as the final and most authoritative written source from which the Law is determined.

Where We Do Stand By the Rulings of the Sages of the Holy Land

Nonetheless, even the Babylonian Sages lacked the authority to overrule the authoritative laws and traditions established in the Land of Israel. Therefore, in places where it seems the Babylonian Sages erred by ruling contrary to the older, ordained sources from the Land of Israel, the greatest *halakhic* decisors of post-Talmudic history (namely the RaMBaM and Vilna Gaon) were known to rule according to the more accurate opinions from the earlier works, over the conclusions of the Babylonian court. According to Rabbi David Bar-Hayim of Machon Shilo, who specializes in the legal traditions of the Land of Israel, there are many as twenty places in *Mishneh Torah* where RaMBaM "entirely ignores" Babylonian legislation for the older, more accurate legal tradition of the Land of Israel (from private conversation).

RaMBaM became uniquely fluent in these traditions during his personal sojourn in the Land, before threats to his life forced him to flee to Egypt. One notable example of this is the true *Shemitah* year – the "seventh year" during which the land of Israel must lie fallow (Ex. 23:10-11). There are two conflicting Talmudic traditions as to how to calculate the seventh year, and what year it was in the cycle. In his codification of these laws, RaMBaM first explains the logical calculation of the first tradition. From the depth and convincing detail of this first explanation, it seems that this was the tradition whose logic he might have personally preferred, if not the very tradition of his own scholarly line. According to it, the current Hebrew year of 4936 A.C. ("<u>A</u>fter <u>C</u>reation," corresponding to 1175-1176 C.E.) was a *Shemitah* year.

He then turns right around, however, to briefly present the second tradition which, as he explains, carries more weight simply by virtue of its being the tradition maintained by the men and *Geonim* of the Land of Israel. According to it, the current year was actually an eighth year in the cycle – the year following a *Shemitah* year. Despite the perfect rationale of the first tradition, *RaMBaM rules unequivocally that we are to uphold, in this case, the tradition of the residents of the Land of Israel, since they are 'qabbalah' (established Oral Tradition) and 'ma`aseh' (living, unbroken practice of the community)*. (M.T. Laws of the Sabbatical Year and the Jubilee 10:8[1-6])

This is a precious example of the highest regard the authentic traditions of the Sages of the Land of Israel are afforded in *halakhah*. Due to the chief priority given such traditions in RaMBaM's *Mishneh Torah*, the work remains to this day the chief guidebook for Jews and Noahides interested in practicing Torah according to those authentic, ancient traditions of the Land of Israel that are still legally binding.

What is the Babylonian Torah that Rabbi Zera Fasted In Order to Forget?

Another attempt by scholars to de-legitimize Babylonian Talmudic tradition is the following teaching about Rabbi Zera (or "Zeira"):

> When R. Zera emigrated to the land of Israel, he fasted a hundred fasts to forget the Babylonian Gemara, that it should not trouble him.
> (Tr. *Bava MeSi'ah* 85a)

In light of all the above evidence, there is no reason to assume this referred to the actual *halakhah* (law) being taught in the Babylonia. On the contrary, it seems much more likely that Rav Zera wished to forget the method of study of the rabbis in Babylonia. Indeed, this is the conclusion found in the explanatory footnote in the Soncino edition of the Talmud: [12]

> The Palestinian [Israeli] method of study was far simpler than the Babylonian, and R. Zera was anxious that his keen dialectic method acquired in Babylon should not interfere with the clearer course adopted in [the Land of Israel]. Cf. Sanh. (Sonc. ed.) p. 138, n. 11. [On the term *Gemara* v. supra p. 206, n. 6. Kaplan, op. cit., pp. 258ff., on the basis of his definition, explains that Gemara texts as recorded by different schools frequently presented variations in substance, style and phraseology to the confusion of the student, and it was for freedom from this handicap that R. Zera prayed when he decided to join the school in Palestine Land of Israel].

Equally suspect, are the strange superstitions and mystical beliefs found in the Babylonian Talmud (such belief in demons and reliance on astrology), which hardly exist in the literature from the Land of Israel.

This is why RaMBaM only used the Babylonian Talmud for its role in reconstructing the final Sanhedrin law and knowing its most authoritative interpretation, but related to the law in a different spirit – *that of the Sages of the Land of Israel*. While the schools in Babylonia related to *halakhah* as the result of complex logical proof, RaMBaM related to *halakhah* as a settled tradition that can and should be mastered in one's youth. Once it has been mastered, the young scholar is free to delve into the *Pardes* —the mystical secrets of the Torah— and aspire to prophecy. It should be clear to any Bible scholar which approach is more authentic.[13]

8.
WHAT ABOUT POST-TALMUDIC RULINGS AND CUSTOMS INSTITUTED TO MEET THE CHANGING NEEDS OF THE TIMES?

For 1500 years, the scattered communities of Israel have been stumbling in a darkness prophesied by the prophet Jeremiah when he lamented, *"ein Torah"* – there is no ordained Torah judgment (Lamentations 2:9)! He foresaw this long era without any single, nationally recognized, compulsory legal authority over the nation.

There can be no doubt: The Jewish people —nay, the world— needs the Torah to be "taken out of deep-freeze," so to speak. As times change, there has been considerable pressure on Torah leaders to consider the reasoning behind the law as the Sanhedrin is to do, and reinterpret the written sources contrary to the *halakhah* as it was codified. At times, new rabbinical decrees seemed in order according to the needs of the times. However, since post-Talmudic legislation was made without the proper authority, it does not have the status of *halakhah*.

The truth remains – *In the absence of a Sanhedrin, new rabbinical legislation and customs cannot obligate the Jewish People* (except in a specific area of law which the *halakhah* explicitly left to follow the local custom, such as monetary law). In other words, our failure as a people to restore the Sanhedrin until now does not grant legitimacy to novel Torah legislation enacted by un-ordained scholars in its absence. It is still the prophesied time of *"ein Torah."*

Un-ordained sages are expected to lead by example. Their principal task is to instruct their flock in the law, teaching how the law applies to their lives, in their environment. Beyond that, they may rally their communities to act according to the needs of the times – to refrain from what is permitted, and even to introduce new voluntary customs that do not contradict the law. *However, they have no authority to legislate.*

In short, there is no way out for Torah Judaism. Israel was given a Torah Commandment —a mandate from Heaven binding upon every generation— to establish *HaShem*'s judicial system in the Land with a Sanhedrin of 71 at its head, as it is written:

> Judges and officers you shall appoint for yourselves in all your gates, which *HaShem* your God is giving you for your tribes; and they shall judge the people with righteous judgment.
> (Deut. 16:18)

Only when the nation's greatest rabbinical leaders unite for this purpose, will the *halakhah* be "taken out of the freezer" so to speak. Only then can it be adapted to our changed world according to God's very own system of reform. *May the Great Sanhedrin be restored speedily in our days!*

In the meantime, let us strengthen ourselves with clear proofs that the Oral Torah, which will soon be restored to its pristine glory, has roots that far predate the ordained Sages of the Mishnah who began to commit the Oral Torah to writing. The Oral Torah is far more ancient, going back to Moses at Mt. Sinai.

9.
IS ORTHODOX TORAH JUDAISM AUTHENTIC ORAL TORAH?

However common Orthodox practice and philosophy may occasionally differ from authentic Talmudic *halakhah*, Orthodoxy should be synonymous with authentic Oral Torah. However, when I speak of the "Oral Law" and authentic, Orthodox Torah Judaism, *I do not refer to all the different modern ways the ancient religion is practiced today.* Authentic Talmudic Torah practice has clearly eroded during the long, tortuous exile. This is one reason why some non-Jews feel that reading the Bible conjures up an image of how a pious Hebrew should speak, dress and practice Torah-living that stands in contrast to what they see among Orthodox Jews.

However, while there is some truth to this, such feelings by non-Jews (and non-traditional Jews) are too often exacerbated by the beliefs and prejudices they bring into Bible study, their inability to understand the original Hebrew, and their failure to read the entire text. It is therefore little wonder that they may fail to see the authenticity in normative Orthodox Jewish practice.

For example, one may be trained in a Christian outlook, so that he imagines that sin can only be atoned for through blood sacrifice. But if he were only to study Hosea 14:3, he would find the prophet counseling the people that "the offering of our lips" can take the place of bulls on the altar:

> *Take with you words*, and return in repentance to *HaShem*; say to Him: 'Forgive all iniquity, and accept that which is good; *so we will render bull-offerings with our lips.*'

In Micah 6:6-8, he would discover that carrying out righteous judgment, pursuing mercy and humility are worth far more to *HaShem* than sacrifice. He would find that to be an echo of a much earlier source – King David's words in Psalm 40:7:

> Sacrifice and meal-offering Thou hast no delight in; mine ears hast Thou opened; burnt-offering and sin-offering hast Thou not required.

On the other hand, fueled by such sources, one might be swayed to the claims of "animal rights" crusaders and their New Age rabbinical proponents who portray sacrifice as a crude, primitive, outdated form of worship. They might claim that Judaism is now "prayer oriented," since Western religions have made most of the world thus. But again, careful, exhaustive Torah study reveals the holes in those who read such reformist fantasies into God's Word. The same King David who understood that burnt offerings do not please *HaShem* in and of themselves, gave offerings on the altar, to which God responded approvingly with fire from Heaven (I Chr. 21:26). Moreover, if sacrifice would no longer be the Will of *HaShem* in the End of Days — once mankind achieves its highest state and full potential— why is it included in the prophet Ezekiel's vision of the future Temple service? (Ez. 43:27)

The prophet Isaiah foresaw the End of Days as follows:

> And I will I bring them to My holy mountain, and make them joyful in My house of prayer; *their burnt-offerings and their sacrifices shall be acceptable upon My altar,* for My house shall be called a house of prayer for all peoples.
>
> (Isaiah 56:7)

Tackling the Hard Questions

Although serious Torah study reveals certain places where Jewish practice has gone awry and erroneous beliefs have crept in, it also reveals many precious details of our timeless laws that have been well maintained – *Commandments of God that the People of Israel have never forgotten.* My approach involves examining rabbinical tradition (according to the primary sources of the Oral Law and RaMBaM's *Mishneh Torah*) through the lens of the Bible itself (*Tanakh*), hard science, and straight, scholarly analysis of outside literary sources. With as unprejudiced an eye as we can muster, we will see how ancient, authentic and accurate the Oral Tradition in the hands of the nation of Israel truly is.

NOTES

(1) *Seder `Olam Rabbah*, the 2nd century C.E. work by Yose ben Hhalafta, is the authoritative voice on the sequence and dating of events in Jewish history according to Torah tradition. With the exception of dates in Part III Point 22, this is the source for all dates for ancient events in this book. This information as well as dates of later events in Jewish history over the last 1800 years, are found in Kantor, Rabbi Mattis, *Timeline of Jewish History*. Copyright 2010 (online source at *www.askmoses.com*, Copyright 2010).

The rough figure of 1700+ years between the Giving of the Torah and the dissolution of the Sanhedrin is derived as follows: According to tradition, the Revelation at Sinai occurred in 2448 A.C. (After Creation), or 1313 B.C.E. According to the Jewish Encyclopedia *(jewishencyclopedia.com)*, the Sanhedrin dissolved in 425 C.E., an event that RaMBaM teaches occurred *kamah shanim* – "some years" or "a few years" before the Talmud was compiled (M.T. Preface 32). With the Talmud's completion at 4235 A.C. (475 C.E.) according to *Seder `Olam Rabbah,* this fits the academic opinion cited in the Jewish Encyclopedia.

See also: Ben-Sasson, Haim, *A History of the Jewish People*. Harvard University Press (October 15, 1985). Cited in entry for "Sanhedrin" in Wikipedia, The Free Encyclopedia. *en.wikipedia.org/wiki/Sanhedrin*

(2) It is for this reason that the Sages of the Great Court instituted blessings to be recited before the performance of rabbinical commands, such as kindling the Sabbath lamp on Friday evening before sundown. Such commands are nowhere to be found in the Written Torah. Yet one is to recite, *"Blessed are You HaShem our God, King of the Universe, who sanctified us with His Commandments and Commanded us to kindle the Sabbath lamp."* Nearly all of these blessings were authored and instituted by the Great Court of Ezra the scribe (which included biblical prophets in its ranks), called the "Men of the Great Assembly" (M.T. Laws of Blessings 1:5 cf. Preface 7). The prophets and Sages wanted to infuse us with the awareness that fulfilling *their* authentic commands properly is no less than the fulfillment of God's own

Commandment, *"and you shall observe to do according to ALL that they will teach you."* (Deut. 17:10)

(3) Even in the times when the Temple stands, burnt offerings are no magical ritual. Without sincere repentance (confession of one's sin and taking upon oneself never to repeat the sin again), sacrifice is impotent and meaningless (M.T. Laws of Repentance 1:3[1]). However, at a time when there is no Temple, sincere repentance alone brings about God's full forgiveness. (See Point 9 above) Even if one must suffer in this world for what one has done, nothing stands in the way of true repentance (Ibid. 1:8[3]). Ultimately, even if one did not repent properly in this world; so long as one dies truly repentant in his heart, death atones for what was left undone in life (Ibid. 2:2 cf. Laws of Marriage 8:9[5]).

(4) Lehmann, Meir (translated by Zucker, Pearly), *Akiva: The Story of Rabbi Akiva and His Times*. Feldheim Publishers, Jerusalem (2003). 292 pp.

(5) The Jerusalem Talmud was completed 300 years after the destruction of the Temple, a century before the Babylonian Talmud was sealed (M.T. Preface 18, 23).

(6) Responsum #320 in *Teshuvoth haRaMBaM* (Responsa of Maimonides), compiled by Blau, Rabbi Yehoshua`. Reuven Mass Publishing, Jerusalem (5746/1986).

(7) *Teshuvoth HaGeonim* (Responsa of the Geonim), Sha`are Teshuvah in Pirush Iyye Hayyam, of Rav Yisra'el Moshe Hazzan, No. 187.

(8) Rav Moshe ben Nahhman (RaMBaN/Nachmanides), *Milhhamoth HaShem* in Tractate *BeSah* of the Talmud Bavli (Babylonian Talmud), Friedman Edition. `Oz ve-Hadar Publishing, Jerusalem (5766/2006). (See *Ba`al ha-Ma'or, ha-Ra'avad, we-ha-RaMBaN `al Masekheth BeSah*, p.6.)

(9) Rav Sherira Gaon, *The Iggeres of Rav Sherira Gaon* (translated and annotated by Rabbi Nosson Dovid Rabinowich). Moznaim, Rabbi Jacob Joseph School Press – Ahavath Torah Institute, Jerusalem

(1988). pp.90-96. Our translation of the quote is original; it does not perfectly follow that of Rabbi Rabinowich.

(10) This is similar to the authority of a true prophet of Israel. A clear biblical example is the sacrifice of Elijah the prophet on Mt. Carmel, despite the severe Torah prohibition of sacrificing anywhere but the altar at the site of the Tabernacle or Temple (Deut. 12:13). RaMBaM explains:

> And if they had asked Elijah, telling him, "shall we uproot what is written in the Torah, 'lest you offer up your burnt offerings in any place that you see...'?" [Deut. 12:13] – he would have said: "No, on the contrary, one who sacrifices away [from the Temple altar] will always be liable to spiritual excision [kareth], just as Moses commanded. However, today I will sacrifice away [from the Temple altar] by the Word of God, in order to disprove the prophets of Ba`al.
>
> Accordingly, if any of the prophets commanded to transgress for a limited time [according to the need of the hour], it was a Commandment to hearken to him. But if they said that the law is uprooted forever, they would be liable to the death penalty... as the Torah says, "for us and for our descendants forever" (Deut. 29:28). (M.T. 9:6-7[3])

Similarly, a Sanhedrin may suspend Torah law (besides the prohibition of idolatry) for a limited time, due to the great need of the hour, such as concern for public safety. For example, it is extremely difficult for an individual to be put to death according to the Torah's merciful justice system. In the wake of a formidable wave of violent thuggery or lawless public fornication, the Sanhedrin might need to create a powerful enough deterrent to stop the menace. They could do this by suspending the Torah's long due process of law for criminals for a short period of time.

(11) This despite the rule taught in the context of unintentional sins, that only the inhabitants of the Land of Israel are considered a *qahal* – a congregation whose acceptance of the Court's legislation need be considered (M.T. Laws of Unintentional Sins 13:9[2]).

Tackling the Hard Questions

---

(12) Babylonian Talmud, translated and annotated by Epstein, Rabbi Dr. Isidore. Soncino Press. Published online at *www.halakhah.com*

(13) This is one aspect of RaMBaM's *Mishneh Torah* that makes it so attractive to the truth-seeker who desires to know and live by this most effective, authentic, and complete codification of God's Law. There are more reasons that a growing number of Jews and Noahides are coming to recognize *Mishneh Torah* as the most authoritative Torah foundation for their lives. As I wrote in *The 14 Fundamental Principles of our Torah Tradition (*a web-article at *www.torathmoshe.com)*:

> Mishneh Torah is the only code of Jewish Law that relates to the entire Torah as a whole, and practical for every generation. It was written in order to put the entire breadth of Halakhah in the hands of laymen, women, and children, besides Torah scholars. *The best way to learn, practice and teach halakhah in our times is straight from the Mishneh Torah.* It is also the only comprehensive summary of the entire Talmudic literature.

> Theoretically, the entire *halakhah* can be completely learned, successfully practiced and taught straight from the written sources: Bible and the sum total of Talmudic literature (Mishnah, *Tosephta, Mekhilta, Sifre, Sifra, Talmud Yerushalmi, and Talmud Bavli*). Practically, however, this is very complicated. Many years of intense learning are required to master this vast literature. The most authoritative work, the *Talmud Bavli (Gemara)*, is written in a difficult dialect of Aramaic mixed with other languages. Furthermore, in our times, we no longer have texts of the *Gemara* that are uncensored and totally accurate. We no longer have the tradition required to identify non-authoritative conclusions added into the *Gemara* by post-Talmudic sages. We no longer have the ability to accurately distinguish between the authentic traditions received by the *Geonim* —which were not included in the *Gemara*— and their non-authoritative conclusions.

> RaMBaM, one of the greatest masters of Talmud ever, was a highly critical researcher, who possessed all of the above. *Mishneh Torah* preserves the most authentic understanding of that literature

from 800 years ago. Written in relatively simple, clear Hebrew, it requires far less time to master.

Normal, serious individuals with the proper guidance and discipline have the ability to master the entire halakhah using the *Tanakh* (Bible) and the RaMBaM's *Mishneh Torah*. This is, in fact, the very purpose for which the book was written.

[M.T. Preface 40-42 cf. RaMBaM's Epistle to his foremost student, Rav Yoseph ben haRav Yehudah, points 24,25 in *Iggerot – Letters by Moshe ben Maimon (Maimonides)*. Arabic Original With New Translation And Commentary by Rabbi Joseph Qafihh. Mossad haRav Kook, Jerusalem (5754 / 1994). 172 pp.]

While a purist RaMBaM approach to halakhah may seem revolutionary to some, there is in fact a fresh wave of honest Torah scholarship that is restoring the work of RaMBaM to its proper place as the source par excellence of practical Torah law. An example of this blessed trend in the traditional Orthodox Torah world is the refreshing work of Rabbi Asher Benzion Buchman, *Tradition! Tradition? Rambam and the Mesorah* (Published in *Hakirah: The Flatbush Journal of Jewish Law and Thought*, Vol 8, Summer 2009).
http://www.hakirah.org/Vol%208%20Buchman.pdf

PART II: BIBLICAL PROOF

Revealing the Oral Tradition in the Written Word

תּוֹרַת יְהוָה תְּמִימָה, מְשִׁיבַת נָפֶשׁ
עֵדוּת יְהוָה נֶאֱמָנָה, מַחְכִּימַת פֶּתִי.
(תהילים יט:ח)

The Torah of *HaShem* is perfect, restoring the soul; the testimony of *HaShem* is trustworthy, making wise the simple. (Psalms 19:8)

Oral Torah from Sinai

INTRODUCTION TO PART II

The following section is only *a selection of 13 points of evidence* among many more throughout the Bible, which give testimony to the authenticity —the Divine legitimacy— of the Oral Tradition, as it was ultimately preserved in the Talmudic literature. I chose the following proofs because they concern pillars of Torah faith and observance, and are easier for the layman to follow and verify. They will show most plainly what should be made known throughout the world – The Written Torah and Oral Torah tradition are a harmonious, indivisible whole. *The Commandments of the Written Torah can only be properly understood and practiced according to the Oral Tradition.*

Note that people's perspectives vary widely in what impresses them as convincing evidence or proof. Every point cannot possibly impress every type of reader. However, all that is ultimately required to demonstrate the deep antiquity and accuracy of the Oral Tradition is a single strong line of evidence or proof. *My hope is that every intelligent reader will find at least one point that convinces him of the rational basis for believing in the authenticity of Israel's Oral Tradition.*

A KEY NOTE TO READING AND UNDERSTANDING THE BIBLE:

Like other ancient Semitic literature written before the time Greco-Roman culture left its permanent mark on how books are written and organized, the Torah reads differently than the way to which the Western mind is accustomed. One difference, for example, is in the flow of information. Rather than collections of Torah teachings organized neatly into categories according to subject, the books of the Bible were written in an organic flow of concepts. Based on subtle moral principles, the order is meant to generate deeper thinking.

In another departure from Western thinking, from the Torah's viewpoint, not everyone is considered ready for or worthy of deeper knowledge. Beyond the simple meaning, there are deeper layers of meaning that require fluent knowledge of the entire text in Hebrew for the diligent, God-fearing student to discover and enjoy. While the actual Commandments are worded clearly and emphatically, only multiple readings —ideally in Hebrew— will reveal the more subtle, profound concepts. *In short, the Torah is worded the way it is in order to throw off the impatient, careless reader, while reserving its pearls of wisdom for the deserving, diligent student as his just reward.*

Unlike Western literature, the Torah is incomprehensibly brief on some of its most important topics. In fact, the Torah's brevity is one proof that it was given with an accompanying Oral teaching. The Torah does not teach how to circumcise; only to do so. Neither does it teach how to properly slaughter animals; only to slaughter "as *HaShem* Commanded" (See Point 7). The Torah expects that, as a Jew, one has access to the Oral traditions as to how *HaShem* expects His Commandments be fulfilled. In the presence of Oral instruction, there is no need for wordy explanations; only simple statements to anchor the living traditions.

In short, *HaShem* clearly has His Own reasons as to why the Torah was written as it was. The result, however, is that it is not always simple for the outsider to appreciate the wisdom it contains. In contrast, the Talmudic Sages — besides the traditions they had received from earlier generations— knew the Hebrew text forwards and backwards. A sage of the caliber of the Vilna Gaon even knew the number of times a letter appears in a given section.[1] Fittingly, when the novice ponders the Biblical sources for certain traditions — "anchors" of the Oral Law in the Written Word— they may be "under-whelmed," not being sensitized to the subtleties in the Hebrew text.

Nevertheless, I will proceed to present points of evidence that I believe any honest, rational mind can appreciate. I dearly hope that my explanations will help even the untrained student to appreciate how clearly the Biblical text itself proves the existence of the Oral Tradition from the time the Torah was given at Sinai.

1.
היחוד המופשט המוחלט של אלוהי ישראל
THE ORAL TRADITION OF THE INCOMPARABLE ONENESS OF HASHEM

The sublime statement of faith recited by Jews morning and night is, "Hear O' Israel, *HaShem* is our God, *HaShem* is ***One***" (Deut. 6:4). Without having given Israel an Oral Tradition as to what that Oneness truly means, however, neither His nation nor the world would be able to fulfill the Creator's Command that we recognize that Oneness. We shall soon see that *HaShem*'s Oneness is not as simple as it may seem to those who have not given it much thought. RaMBaM wrote:

> This God is One. He is not merely 'not two or more', but One such that there is none like His Oneness among the unities in the universe. Not "one" such as a single category that includes other single entities, and not "one" such as a body that is divisible into different parts and extremities; but rather a oneness such as there is none like it in the universe.
> (M.T. Laws of Foundations of Torah 1:5[7])

It is no coincidence that the opposite doctrine, the notion of God as a composite unity (a trinity in this case) is well-known to be the doctrine of the Catholic Church – an idolatrous movement that arguably did more to extinguish the light of Oral Torah than any in history. It is no less than a miracle that —in spite of their putting the Talmud "on trial" in medieval Europe in public debates between rabbis and priests, publicly burning the Talmud and *Mishneh Torah*, and massacring those accused of practicing Judaism in the Inquisition— the tradition of God's abstract Oneness continues to thrive among Jews of European descent.

Indeed, the classical Christian concept of God is true of *a live human being*. RaMBaM teaches that a living person is actually three entities in one: (1) the physical person himself, (2) his soul or life force, and (3) his *"da`ath"* (his consciousness, awareness, or knowledge). While these are unified during one's life, they separate when they person loses consciousness, and when he dies. But if *HaShem's* Oneness were such a composite unity, we would worship three united entities: *HaShem*, His Life, and His Awareness or Knowledge. *Yet HaShem is perfectly one in every aspect -- something that our finite minds cannot grasp* (M.T. Laws of Foundations of Torah 2:13[10]).

His Incomparable Oneness

The above sources will do little to convince die-hards who cling to a mystical belief that "the One is Three, and the Three are One." After all, so they muse, there are verses in which God speaks of Himself in the plural, as in Gen. 1:26, "Let us make Man…" However, the Oral Tradition claims the opposite: *HaShem's Oneness is utterly indivisible.* How can we know which doctrine is true for certain?

In Hebrew, as in many other languages, the plural form is used to denote respect. Even in modern Israel, rabbis are sometimes referred to in the plural. Known as *Pluralis Majestatis*, it is found in many languages. The Qur`an, for example, uses it extensively and its author certainly intended no allusions to a trinity. Regarding Gen. 1:26, Rav Sa`adiah Gaon wrote:

> Those who say that this verse implies a plurality of creators are ignorant. They do not know that the Hebrew language gives an important person license to say, "let us make" or "let us do" even though he is but a single individual. As Daniel said, "This is the dream and *we* will tell its interpretation to the king." (Dan. 2:36) There are many other examples in Scripture. *(Sefer Emunoth we-De`oth* [Book of Beliefs & Opinions])

A profound source for *HaShem*'s incomparable unity is Isaiah 40:25: *"To whom will you liken Me, that I can be compared?"* As shown above, if *HaShem* were a trinity, he could be compared to a person. If He descended to earth, adopting a physical form, he could be compared to an angel such as the one who appeared to the parents of Samson: It appeared in a physical form, only to leap into fire and ascend to Heaven, back to the non-physical realm (Judges 13:19-20). Similarly, in their song after the parting of the Red Sea, the Israelites sang, "Who is like you among the mighty powers, *HaShem*" (Ex. 15:11)? *HaShem* is beyond comparison even to angels, to stars, or to mighty forces of nature like rain, which descends to earth from heaven.

Moreover, if *HaShem* were to descend to earth in a physical form and live a human life, then that aspect of Him would undergo change. What, then, do we do with the principle taught in Malachi 3:6: "I, *HaShem*, do not change…?" If He did so in order that He would fully know our suffering, as some Christians claim, can any believing person rightly imagine that anything exists outside of *HaShem*'s full understanding? Could "the Judge of all the earth" (Gen. 18:25) not fully understand those whom He Judges? Could it be that the "Wise King" (Proverbs 20:26), the One who "searches out the compartments of the heart" (Proverbs 20:27), the God who "sees the heart" while man can only see the outward appearance (I Samuel 16:7) – does not understand His subjects well enough?

With the principle in mind that *HaShem* does not change and therefore does not physically descend to earth, note the places in the Bible where He is mentioned as "dwelling" in different places. He is mentioned in no uncertain terms as "sitting" or "dwelling" on earth – upon the *keruvim* (the angelic figures that adorned the cover of the Ark) (I Samuel 4:4, II Samuel 6:2, II Kings 19:15). He is referred in Psalms 2:4 as "sitting" or "dwelling" in Heaven. *It should be clear by now that He "dwells" not by means of a body.* Rather this refers to *HaShem* who causes His Presence to be perceived in the Heavens and earth. *HaShem —who does not change— neither has nor needs a physical form to do this* (see M.T. Laws of Foundations of Torah ch.1).

This also negates the widespread, false notion that "God is everywhere, and in all things." Consider how clearly the Bible negates this concept in the narrative of the prophet Elijah's experience on Mt. Sinai:

> And He said: 'Go forth, and stand upon the mount before *HaShem*.' And, behold, *HaShem* passed by, and a great and strong wind rent the mountains, and broke apart the rocks before *HaShem*; *but HaShem was not in the wind*; and after the wind an earthquake; *but HaShem was not in the earthquake*; and after the earthquake a fire; *but HaShem was not in the fire*; and after the fire a still small voice. (I Kings 19:11-12)

Although He can cause His Presence to be felt and manifested through nature, *HaShem* Himself is clearly separate from it. What fills all creation is His limitless power and might. (See the blessing recited upon hearing thunder in M.T. Laws of Blessings 10:16[14])

'Elohim': A Sacred Name with Singular Meaning When Referring to God

The Biblical "source" most touted for God being a plurality is the very first verse of the Torah: "In the beginning, *Elohim* created the heavens and the earth." The sacred Name of God used in that sentence and many that follow, has the ending *-im*, which is the well-known plural masculine noun-ending in Hebrew. What the Catholic priests and followers of UFO-cults (see Appendix III) seldom consider is how the Oral Tradition, regarding that Name (that it is a singular form), is firmly rooted in the Written Torah itself.

The simple, unlearned masses have always accepted the teachings of their clergy on faith. However, the Catholic priests of the Middle Ages, who studied the Bible in Hebrew, had little excuse. How did they handle the names of individual men in the Torah whose names have that "plural" ending? Consider Ephra*im*, son of Jacob. He was a singular individual. Ephraim is no isolated example -- Consider his cousins Mupp*im* and Hupp*im*, two of the ten sons of Benjamin (Gen. 46:21). We know they were individuals and not twins because of how they are counted: They are mentioned as part of the Torah's tally of 70 souls who made up Jacob's household, which descended into Egypt (Gen. 46:8-27). In short, the singular meaning of the end form *-im* is not unique to that sacred Name of God; it is found among names of individuals in the Bible.

The following verse is another example that illustrates the singular meaning of the Name:

> And *HaShem* said to Moses: 'See, *I have set you to be **elohim** to Pharaoh* [meaning "in God's stead"]; and Aaron your brother shall be your prophet.' (Ex. 7:1)

The Bible uses *elohim* to refer to false deities in the plural. However, if its meaning as "lord" was inherently plural, how could Moses be that to Pharaoh? The Name of God is being used as *a title for a single individual*, so that Moses could fully understand the role he was to fulfill. As a title and as God's Name, it is clearly a singular noun.

One need not look further than that very first Torah verse: "In the beginning, Elohim created…." The Hebrew word for "created," *bara,* is in the singular form. The past plural form of the verb "created" is *bare'u*. The singular verb form in the verse declares the Oneness of the subject, *Elohim*.

The nature of God's Oneness and the truth of the Name *Elohim* are but one example of a number of apparent contradictions in Scripture that can only be fully resolved by an outside explanation of an accompanying tradition.

I hope the reader can begin to see the relationship between the Written Law and the Oral Tradition. While the Written Law treats this deep subject with terse, subtle statements scattered across the Bible —and that, amidst dozens of anthropomorphisms (verses that speak of *HaShem* in human terms by way of metaphor)— *the Oral Tradition is a natural voice of explanation for the Written Word, so that the truth of its content would never be lost.*

2.
תורה שבעל פה מבראשית
THE ORAL TORAH WISDOM KNOWN TO THE GENERATIONS BEFORE SINAI

Ahead of the coming Flood, Noah was commanded to take seven pairs of "clean species" of beast and fowl, and only one pair of the "unclean species" – all the other animal species he was to bring aboard to the Ark (Gen. 7:2-3). 1600 years would pass before Moses would actually enumerate in the Written Torah, by *HaShem*'s Command, which species are "clean" and which are "unclean." (Lev. ch.11) Since the Written Word did not exist in the pre-Flood world, how could the righteous be privy to this knowledge? *There must have been an Oral Tradition of Torah wisdom that hailed back to the earliest generations of man.*

This body of teaching is referred to by *HaShem* when He relates to the patriarch Isaac the reason for Abraham's great merit. It is through this merit that Isaac, his son, would merit the blessings of His Covenant with Abraham:

> …because Abraham hearkened to My voice, and kept My charge, *My commandments, My statutes, and My laws* [lit. "My Torahs, My bodies of instruction"].　　　　　(Gen. 26:5)

The Torah only mentions a single Commandment for Abraham to practice – that of circumcision. What was the rest of God's charge at the time? What other commandments, statutes, and laws are being referred to? They clearly refer to laws of an earlier Covenant between God and man.

The only clear mention in Torah of man receiving such a covenant before Abraham's time, with a terse reference to its laws, is Genesis 9:1-17: the Covenant with Noah following his descent from the Ark. In retrospect, verse 26:5 clearly points to the *Noahide Laws in all their detail, which Abraham loyally kept.* According to the Oral Tradition, this ancient legal tradition had been long-abandoned and forgotten by the rest of humanity by Abraham's time, except for a few righteous individuals such as Noah's son, Shem, and his descendant, `Ever (M.T. Laws of Kings and Wars 9:1-3 cf. Laws of Idolatry 1:7-8).

Once the Written Torah was given at Sinai, this tradition of Oral instruction did not cease. On the contrary, only then did it become fully-known. It was entrusted to the newly-ordained Great Court of Moses, becoming permanently established among God's "nation of priests." (Ex. 19:6)

3.
בית דין הגדול דן את ירמיהו הנביא
THE SANHEDRIN IN ACTION IN THE BOOK OF JEREMIAH

According to Oral Tradition, the Sanhedrin, the nation's high court and judiciary, is the very "pillar" or bastion of the Oral Law (M.T. Laws of Rebels 1:1). One of the weak claims by those who reject the Oral Law, is that the Commandment to hearken to the rulings of "the judge who will be in those days" (Deut. 17:9), actually refers to the nation's ruler —its "Judge" *(shofet)*— which happens to be the same word in Hebrew for a justice on the Great Court. Pointing out that *ha-shofet* ("the judge") in Deut. 17:9 is in the singular form, they claim that the Torah is commanding that Israel hearken to a national chieftain such as Gideon and Samuel, who ruled over the tribes of Israel successively from the time of the death of Joshua until the anointing of Saul, Israel's first king. In doing so, they contradict the

Oral Tradition on that verse, that *ha-shofet* here is referring to the plural judiciaries of the Great Court.

From the outset it seems logical. But like so many claims of this kind, this one, too, can be debunked simply by studying the verse in its wider context:

> And you shall come to *the Levite priests* and to *the judge* that will be in those days; And you shall inquire; and they will declare to you the sentence of judgment. And you shall observe to do according to all that they will teach you from that place which *HaShem* will choose, and you shall observe to do according to all that they will teach you. According to the law that they will teach you, and according to the judgment which they will tell you, you shall do; you shall not turn aside from the sentence that they will declare unto you, to the right, nor to the left. And the man that acts presumptuously by not hearkening to *the priest* who stands to minister there before *HaShem* your God, or *to the judge*, that man shall die; and you shall extirpate the evil from Israel.
>
> (Deut. 17:9-12)

If the singular form of "the judge" were significant, then so would the plural form of "the Levite priests." But if the verse speaks of the authority of the *single* national Judge/chieftain and the *plural* Levite priests, then why do we see only three verses later that "the Levite priests" (originally in the plural form), is now expressed in the singular form "the priest," alongside "judge" in the singular form? Just as "the priest" in 17:12 clearly refers to a plurality of Levites, likewise "the judge" refers to a plurality of judges.

This is but one example a common figure of speech in the Torah. Throughout the Torah, we find nouns that refer to a plurality being expressed in the singular form. See Gen. 4:19, 13:7; Ex. 14:7, Ex. 15:1; Deut. 11:4 and Deut. 32:25, just to cite a few examples.

The real "giveaway" to the true meaning of the verse is that both "judge" and "priest" in the verse speak with one voice, as it is written: *"and they will declare to you the sentence of judgment."* (Deut. 17:9) The verse is clearly referring to members of the Great Court, highlighting its most distinguished members – the Levite priests. They are mentioned separately to teach that, while judges are chosen from all the tribes of Israel, there is a special Commandment to appoint Levite priests to the Great Sanhedrin (M.T. Laws of Sanhedrin 2:2).

How fortunate we are that, thanks to the account of the prophet Jeremiah, *we have a glimpse of a First Temple-era Sanhedrin in action* (Jer. 26:8-24, see below). A careful reading yields another vindication of the Oral Tradition: Rather than analyzing the relevant Torah verses anew, as if no previous court's decisions had any lasting legal import, we find the Sanhedrin in Jeremiah's day most concerned with legal precedents made by previous kings and courts. *It is an example of legal decision-making precisely in the manner of the Talmudic sages, about 1,000 years before the last Sanhedrin was dissolved and the Babylonian Talmud compiled.* The court feels bound to the previous legal precedents set by earlier judges.

NOTE: the legal precedents mentioned below are the rulings of kings, according to an Oral Law principle: The kings of the Davidic line may sit together with the Great Court in judgment, or even judge the people individually. [M.T. Laws of Sanhedrin 2:4[5]] To my understanding; the decisions being referred to were rendered by Hezekiah and Jehoiakim when they sat in judgment with the court.

Now it came to pass, that when Jeremiah had finished speaking all that *HaShem* had commanded him to speak to all the people, the priests and the prophets and all the people laid hold on him, saying: 'You will surely die. Why have you prophesied in the Name of *HaShem*, saying: This house will be like Shiloh, and this city shall be desolate, without an inhabitant?' And all the people were gathered against Jeremiah in the house of *HaShem*. When the princes of Judah heard these things, they came up from the king's house to the house of *HaShem*; and they sat in the entry of the new gate of *HaShem*'s house.

Then the priests and the prophets spoke to the princes and to all the people, saying: 'This man is worthy of death; for he has prophesied against this city, as you have heard with your ears.' Then Jeremiah spoke to all the princes and to all the people, saying: ' *HaShem* sent me to prophesy against this house and against this city all the words that you have heard. ... But as for me, behold, I am in your hand; do with me as is good and right in your eyes. Only know you for certain that, if you put me to death, you will bring innocent blood upon yourselves, and upon this city, and upon its inhabitants; for in truth *HaShem* has sent me to you to speak all these words in your ears.'

Then the princes and all the people said to the priests and to the prophets: 'This man is not worthy of death; for he has spoken to us in the Name of *HaShem* our God.' Then certain of the elders of the land rose up and spoke to all the assembly of the people, saying: 'Micah the Morashtite prophesied in the days of Hezekiah king of Judah; and he spoke to all the people of Judah, saying: Thus says *HaShem* of Hosts: Zion will be plowed as a field, and Jerusalem shall become heaps, and the mountain of the house as the high places of a forest. Did Hezekiah king of Judah and all Judah put him at all to death? Did he not fear *HaShem*, and entreat the favor of *HaShem*, and *HaShem* repented of the evil which He had pronounced against them? Thus might we bring great evil against our own souls.' And there was also a man that prophesied in the name of *HaShem*, Uriah the son of Shemaiah of Kiriath-jearim; and he prophesied against this city and against this land according to all the words of Jeremiah; and when Jehoiakim the king, with all his mighty men, and all the princes, heard his words, the king sought to put him to death; but when Uriah heard it, he was afraid and fled, and went into Egypt; and Jehoiakim the king sent men into Egypt, Elnathan the son of Achbor, and certain men with him, into Egypt; and they fetched forth Uriah out of Egypt, and brought him to Jehoiakim the king; who slew him with the sword, and cast his dead body into the graves of the children of the people. Nevertheless the hand of Ahikam the son of Shaphan was with Jeremiah, that they would not give him into the hand of the people to put him to death.

(Jer. 26:8-24)

NOTE: *This is an assembly of prophets, priests, and princes sitting together in judgment. The king is noticeably absent from this legal assembly. Where is the single "Judge"-chieftain to whom one must supposedly ascend for judgment, according to the erroneous interpretation of Deuteronomy 17:9, refuted above? Clearly, judgment is being decided here by a plurality of judges.*

Jeremiah's trial does not take place in the King's court, and not inside the Temple, but in the gate – the traditional place of judgment, as we see in the Book of Ruth (Ruth 4:1-12).

Note how Jeremiah honors and complies with the institution that is judging him. It is evident that this is the means by which the Torah commands that judgment be made.

I hope the reader can begin to appreciate how the Great Sanhedrin and its Divinely-mandated role according to the Oral Tradition, was no later development, but part of ancient Biblical reality.

4.

מניין דיני המלוכה של ישראל בתורה?
WHERE IN THE LAW DO WE FIND THE POWERS OF AN ISRAELITE KING?

On his death bed, the ailing King David gave his final words of wisdom and made his final requests of his heir, the young King Solomon. The aged king reminds the budding monarch how Shimei ben Gera had cursed him and thrown stones and dust at him at the time he was fleeing from his seditious son, Absalom. He exhorts Solomon to put Shimei to death for his crime. Solomon finds a clever way to do this. He quarantines Shimei to the borders of Jerusalem by order of the king. Shimei eventually breaches the king's order, when his pursues his servants, who had fled beyond the city limits. The wise son of David then promptly has Shimei put to death (I Kings ch. 2).

While the Bible holds King Solomon to the full measure of his guilt for his sins later in life, he is unchallenged by the prophets for his actions here. Where in the Written Torah is a king permitted to put anyone to death for rebelling against his decree? While we see this principle in the words of the people to Joshua (Joshua 1:18)**,** no such law is written explicitly in the Name of *HaShem*. *Where in the Law are the details of the powers of an Israelite king?*

Although absent from the Five Books of Moses, it is clearly one of the tenets of an Oral component of the law called *mishpat ha-melekh* – literally "The King's Code." Without it, an Israelite king would have free reign to act however he sees fit as ruler – even to the point of placing himself above Torah Commandments to which all Israelite men are obligated. This code for kings is briefly mentioned for the very first time when God commands that the prophet Samuel recite it to the nation *as an existing body of law* (I Samuel 8:9), and the prophet faithfully complies (Ibid. 8:10-18).

These laws are absent in the Written Torah. Moreover, the above verses describing the Torah protocol for a king lack any mention of the king's power to execute another human being for disobeying him. If they were derived by logic from the Torah and legislated by Samuel and the nation's Great Court of the time, but by what authority could they do this: would it not be "adding" to God's Word, *HaShem* forbid?

Clearly, righteous Biblical Israelites operated according to laws that are not explicit in the Written Torah, yet were recognized by HaShem. We know them to be the teachings of the Oral Law from Sinai entrusted into the hands of the Great Court.

5.

הוסיפו את פורים וימי צום בנוכחותם של נביאי ישראל
PURIM AND FAST DAYS ADDED IN THE PRESENCE OF PROPHETS

Whoever rejects the Torah's empowerment of the rabbis of the Great Court (Sanhedrin) to create and enforce rabbinical law —original, new decrees and ordinances to safeguard *HaShem*'s Laws and rectify the world— must contend with the fact that such additions, made in the presence of true biblical prophets, are boldly mentioned in the Bible.

Consider the new, rabbinical holiday of Purim, which was established to remember the annulment of the genocidal decree of Haman, and Israel's military victory over her enemies throughout the Persian Empire. It was added into the official biblical canon in the days of Mordecai by the Men of the Great Assembly in Jerusalem, an act mentioned at the end of the Scroll of Esther:

> Therefore they called these days Purim, after the name of *pur*. Therefore because of all the words of this letter, and of that which they had seen concerning this matter, and that which had come upon them, *the Jews ordained* and took upon themselves and upon their seed, and upon all who had joined themselves to them, *so it could not be transgressed*, that they would keep these two days according to what was written about them, and according to their appointed time every year.
> (Esther 9:26-27)

Lest the distinction become blurry for some as to the total distinction between Queen Esther's royal decrees and the Jews' own legislative action for themselves, the Scroll continues and clarifies the matter:

> Then Esther the queen, the daughter of Abihail, and Mordecai the Jew wrote down all the acts of power, *to confirm* this second letter of Purim. And he sent letters to all the Jews, to the 127 provinces of the kingdom of Ahasuerus, with words of peace and truth, *to confirm* these days of Purim in their

> appointed times as *Mordecai the Jew and Esther the queen had enjoined them, and as they had ordained for themselves and for their seed, the matters of the fasts and their* [days of] *crying out.*
> (Esther 9:29-31)

First the holiday was ordained as law by the Jewish Sages. Afterwards Esther and Mordecai used their royal positions to promulgate the ruling by royal decree.

Now how did the Jews ordain these matters? What Jewish body represented the divided, far-flung communities of Israel, and could make such a judicial act that would be widely accepted? *None other than the Great Court in Jerusalem.* In fact, the close relationship between Mordecai and the Jewish leadership that had returned from the exile to Jerusalem is established in the Book of Ezra. Before his *return* to Shushan, capital of the empire, during the reign of Ahasuerus, Mordecai is listed alongside Nehemiah among the Sages who returned to Zion during the reign of Cyrus the Great, predecessor of Ahasuerus:

> Now these are the children of the province that went up out of the captivity of those who had been carried away, whom Nebuchadnezzar the king of Babylon had carried away unto Babylon, and returned to Jerusalem and Judah, every one unto his city. [Of those] who came with Zerubbabel: Jeshua, Nehemiah, Seraiah, Reelaiah, Mordecai, Bilshan, Mispar, Bigvai, Rehum, Baanah.
> (Ezra 2:2)

In order to clarify *how* the Jews ordained those matters for themselves, the Book of Esther compares the rabbinical ordinance of Purim to the Jewish ordinances of public fast-days: *"...as they had ordained for themselves and for their seed, the matters of the fasts and their* [days of] *crying out."* (Esther 9:31) These are the fasts mentioned in the prophecy regarding the Messianic era, by the mouth of the prophet Zechariah:

> And the Word of *HaShem* of Hosts came unto me, saying: 'So says *HaShem* of Hosts: The fast of the fourth month, and the fast of the fifth, and the fast of the seventh, and the fast of the tenth, shall be to the house of Judah joy and gladness, and cheerful festivals; therefore love ye truth and peace.
> (Zech.8:18-19)

These fasts together with the holidays of Purim and Hanukkah have something special in common: none of them are to be found in the Written Torah *as none of them existed at the time of Moses*. With the exception of Hanukkah (which has its own book in the Apocrypha), not only are they mentioned in the latter books of the Bible, but they were added to Torah observance by rabbinical decree (not in the Name of *HaShem*) in the presence of the prophets. As I quoted in the above section on Jewish identity, Ezra and Nehemiah both make reference to the prophets among the returnees to Zion, *mentioning the prophets Haggai and Zechariah by name*:

> Now *the prophets, Haggai the prophet, and Zechariah the son of Iddo,* prophesied to the Jews that were in Judah and Jerusalem; in the name of the God of Israel they prophesied to them.
> (Ezra 5:1)

What are those fasts? One, *"the fast of the fifth [month],"* is widely known. It is none other than the Ninth of Av, the day of mourning over the destruction of the Holy Temple. That and the other three are still kept fastidiously by Torah observant Jews to this day: the *17th of Tammuz* ("the fast of the fourth"), the *Fast of Gedaliah* ("the fast of the seventh"), and the *Tenth of Teveth* ("the fast of the tenth") (M.T. Laws of Fasts 5:4). What they all have in common, is that —besides other calamities that occurred before and after— they all mourn events connected with the Babylonian destruction of the First Temple and the original Kingdom of Judah. (Ibid. 5:2-3) *These fasts were clearly ordained in the days of Zechariah and Haggai by the same Court that ordained the holiday of Purim, all in the presence of true prophets.*

There can be no remaining doubt. *Authentic Rabbinical decrees do not constitute unlawful "adding" to Torah Law, per Deut. 4:2 and 13:1.* That prohibition can only mean not adding laws in God's Name, as if *HaShem* Himself had Commanded thus. For the Great Court had the full right and responsibility to make its own original decrees and ordinances to safeguard the Torah's laws, to preserve the nation, and mend the world.

6.

יסור טלטול בשבת ברשות הרבים וברשות היחיד
THE PROPHETS ENFORCE SABBATH LAW DETAILS ABSENT IN THE TORAH

Like the brief reference to the laws of kosher slaughter, the Torah commands Israel to keep the Sabbath "as I've commanded you." (Deut. 5:11) How did *HaShem* command that the Sabbath be kept? What actually constitutes "any manner of work?" (Lev. 23:21, Num. 28:26) Considering that desecrating the Sabbath by performing forbidden labor is a capital crime, there had better be an accompanying oral body of instruction to these undefined, cryptic verses.

The Sages of the Talmud recorded the ancient Torah tradition that there are 39 categories of forbidden labor, corresponding to the labors that were done for the construction and maintenance of the Tabernacle. Accordingly, rising up early Sabbath morning, walking a good distance to synagogue and praying for two to three hours —all before the morning meal— is not considered "labor." Carrying even a small object in a public domain, on the other hand, is a severe Sabbath desecration.

Since this does not sit well with many people (who insist that *HaShem*'s Torah operate according to their own logic), they create theories that such laws were invented by those "cold," "legalistic," "hair-splitting" Talmudic rabbis. *Yet the same people would not dare say the same thing about a biblical sage. How surprised many of these people would be to know that Nehemiah, no less, warned the people of this very sin:*

> And it came to pass that, when the gates of Jerusalem began to be dark before the Sabbath, I commanded that the doors should be shut, and commanded that they should not be opened till after the Sabbath; *and some of my servants set I over the gates, that there should no burden [massa'] be brought in on the Sabbath day.*
> (Neh. 13:19)

They might reason that Nehemiah was speaking of a "burden," according its connotation in English as something heavy, being brought into the city gates from afar. This is an error that results from studying the Bible in English, and not in the original Hebrew. *The Hebrew word is* massa', *which refers to any carried object; it has no special connotation of being a "heavy burden."*

The issue here is *melakhah* – labor forbidden to Israelites by God on the Sabbath (Ex. 20:9, 35:2, Lev. 23:3, Deut. 5:13). Consider the *melakhah* of bringing small donated objects in the construction of the Tabernacle. In the desert, the Israelites gave so generously of their gold and silver jewelry and precious stones, there was a surplus. In Ex. 6:10, Moses ordered the people to stop this "labor" *(melakhah)* on behalf of the project. The verse explicitly states, per Moses' command, "the people were restrained from bringing," i.e. even such small donated articles. When God originally commanded Moses regarding the Tabernacle's construction to begin with, He forbade all manner of "labor" (the same word *melakhah*) on behalf of the project during the Sabbath (Ex. 31:12-15). This obviously included the outpouring of donations of objects, large and small, by the common people to the priests overseeing of the project. *Massa'* or "burden" *includes any useful carried object, no matter how small.*

This is all the more obvious when Jeremiah warns the people in the Name of *HaShem* that even *carrying articles within the city walls of Jerusalem was a desecration of the Sabbath:*

> Thus says *HaShem*: beware of your souls, and do not carry a burden on the Sabbath day and bring them into the gates of Jerusalem. *And you shall not bring a burden [massa`] out of your homes on the Sabbath day;* and you shall do no [other] manner of labor [*melakhah*]; and you shall [thereby] sanctify the Sabbath day *as I Commanded your forefathers.* (Jer. 17:21-22)

Note how the prophet uses the above-mentioned, key technical term used throughout Torah —*melakhah* (forbidden Sabbath labor)— as parallel to carrying. He did not speak out specifically about moving heavy furniture. Neither of the above sources mentions the size or weight of the article forbidden to be carried. *In both situations, carrying was forbidden on the Sabbath – period.*

Revealing the Oral Tradition in the Written Word

What is fascinating is that according to Torah law, a walled city with guarded gates (like Jerusalem at the time) is a *private domain*... the Torah fully permits carrying within such a city! It was a later *rabbinical decree* from the Great Court under the reign of King Solomon that forbade carrying on the Sabbath even in an enclosed, private domain that is publicly or jointly-owned. Otherwise, people would get accustomed over time to carrying outside their homes, and forget the Torah prohibition to carry in a true public domain. However, carrying in such a private domain becomes permissible if the community creates an `*eruv*. This is a rabbinical legal invention, by which an amount of food is symbolically set aside to remind all that they may carry only because the space they share is jointly-owned and private; it is not a public domain. However, in a case where non-Jews, idolaters, public Sabbath breakers, or apostates live within the city walls —as was the case in Jeremiah's day and most Jewish communities in our own day— the city's `*eruv* is invalidated (M.T. Laws of `*Eruvin* 1:1-6).

If such rabbinical decrees were considered a perversion of, or an illegal later addition to the Torah, *how could this legislation be defended in God's Name by a true prophet of Israel, and his defense enshrined in the prophet's book forever?*

Nehemiah Mentions Sabbath Times Left Undefined in the Torah

One point that is easy to miss in the above quote from Nehemiah, is how *the Sabbath in Jerusalem clearly began at sunset on the Sabbath eve – not from Sabbath morning:*

> And it came to pass that, *when the gates of Jerusalem began to be dark before the Sabbath,* I

commanded that the doors should be shut...
(Neh.13:19)

Where is that point explained in the Five Books of Moses? *Nowhere.* The Torah gives no clear indication as to when the Sabbath day begins; it is Oral Tradition based on the wording of the verses of Creation that state: *"and there was evening and there was morning...."* (Gen. 1:5) It is yet another perfect example of how the ancient Israelites conducted their Torah observance according to the same oral details of the Law as Torah observant Jews throughout the ages.

7.
"ושחטתם בזה ואכלתם"
SAUL ENFORCES LAWS OF KOSHER SLAUGHTER ABSENT IN THE TORAH

In their 40-year sojourn through the desert, the Israelites were forbidden from slaughtering meat for food, without offering it up on the altar first (Lev.17:1-5). Once they would enter the Promised Land, *HaShem* gave the Israelites permission to slaughter meat for sacrifice "as I have commanded you," with no further comment (Deut. 12:21). How did He command that meat for offerings be slaughtered? Where is that information contained?

According to Oral Tradition, when these Oral Laws were widely forgotten in the days of King Saul, the king re-taught them to the masses, saving his ravenous army from the sin of "eating over the blood." (I Samuel 14:32 cf. Lev. 19:26) The reference to King Saul's educational efforts is his command, *"ush'hhat'tem **ba-zeh** wa-akhaltem"* – "Slaughter *with this*, and you shall eat." (I Samuel 14:34) What was "this?" What was the king pointing to? *Outside of the teachings of the ancient Oral Tradition, it makes little sense.*

The Talmud teaches that King Saul was referring to a knife that was properly checked for its sharpness (Tr. *Hhullin* 17b). Although the law was maintained orally, it is from the Torah: Only meat from an animal that was slaughtered with a knife properly checked for its sharpness is kosher. Otherwise it has the judgment of a possible *nevelah* (a carcass of an animal that died from any cause other than proper slaughter), which is strictly forbidden by the Torah for Jews to eat (M.T. Laws of Slaughter 1:19-20 [23-24]).

Why the Oral Tradition Makes Perfect Linguistic Sense

Is there another possibility for the meaning of *ba-zeh?* Rather than "slaughter *with* this," perhaps Saul's words should be translated "slaughter *upon* this," in reference to the large stone mentioned in the previous verse? (I Samuel 14:33) *Was King Saul commanding his soldiers to slaughter upon the large rock?* Besides the pointlessness of the Bible recording that Saul command that his soldiers slaughter on a particular, generic spot as a prerequisite for eating (they were not in the Temple), a short check with a Hebrew concordance reveals as follows:

The Hebrew word nearly always used in the Torah for "upon" (i.e. a surface) is `al, especially the construct `al ha-. For example, search for `al ha-areS ("upon the earth", Gen. 1:11,15), `al ha-adamah ("upon the ground", Gen. 7:8), `al rosho ("upon his head", Num. 6:5), or `al ha-mizbeahh ("upon the altar", Gen. 22:9, Ex. 24:6). Most pertinent to the question, is the verse in which Jacob pours oil upon a raised stone, the wording is `al roshah ("upon its head" [Gen. 28:18]).

In other words, not only is there no Torah significance as to where in the field an animal is slaughtered, the wording does not imply in any way that the king was referring to a place. What *does* have major significance in the laws of slaughter, however, is the implement used for slaughter. It must be a specially sharpened blade, providing as smooth and painless a death for the animal as possible.

Indeed, the prefix *be-* or *ba-* is used for "with" in the context of use of an implement, such as a staff or weapon. In his prayer, Jacob exclaimed that he had crossed the Jabbok River ***be**-maqli* – "with my staff." Later, upon his death bed, he told Joseph that he had taken the city of Shekhem ***be**-hharbi u-**ve**-qashti* – "*with* my sword and *with* my bow."

NOTE: 'be-' and 've-', written with same Hebrew letter 'beth' [only being pronounced harder one account of its 'daggesh'- point], have the same meaning.

Besides being Oral Tradition, it makes the most linguistic sense that the term *ba-zeh* in King Saul's command *"ush'hhat'tem **ba-zeh** wa-akhaltem"* refers to the implement to be used for slaughter.

An important point to ever bear in mind is as follows: The Bible makes it clear that the nation of Israel was intended by *HaShem* to be a "light unto the nations" (Isaiah 60:2-3), "a kingdom of priests [to the rest of the world] and a holy nation" (Ex. 19:6), and "a blessing to all the families of the earth" (Gen. 28:14). How can anyone who believes in the Divine authorship of those verses entertain the notion that His Chosen nation would lose the laws of kosher slaughter without a trace, so that its early Sages from 2,000 years ago would need to invent new ones? The ancient laws were never forgotten. They were maintained by Israel's Sages until they were ultimately recorded by the Talmudic sages.[2]

8.

בזמן שמד, דניאל איש חמודות מוכן למות
על דיני כשרות מדבריהם
DANIEL RISKS DEATH TO KEEP RABBINICAL DIETARY RESTRICTIONS

From the beginning of his captivity along with the inhabitants of Jerusalem, Daniel refused to eat the bread or drink the wine offered them in the king's palace:

> But Daniel purposed in his heart *that he would not defile himself with the king's food, nor with the wine which he drank;* therefore he requested of the chief of the officers that he might not defile himself. ... Then said Daniel to the steward, whom the chief of the officers had appointed over Daniel, Hananiah, Mishael, and Azariah: 'Try thy servants, I beseech thee, ten days; and *let them give us pulse to eat, and water to drink.* ...
> (Dan. 1:8-12)

Unless the wine given to Daniel and his fellow captive Jews was wine offered or consecrated as an offering or libation to the Babylonian idols, *where is the prohibition of regular gentile wine even hinted at in the Written Torah?* Moreover, unless the loaves of bread or the flour was offered or consecrated thus, *where is regular bread baked by gentiles forbidden in the Five Books of Moses?* [3] *Neither prohibition exists, because they are later enacted rabbinical fence-laws ('siyyagim')* intended to keep Israelites from close social contact with idolaters (in this case dining with them on their premises), in order to distance them from violating Torah prohibitions. This is, of course, as explained in Part I, according to *HaShem*'s own Commandment in Leviticus 18:30: "and you shall 'guard my guarding'" (meaning: "you shall put additional legal fences to fortify My decrees").

It is important to mention that the Torah does not generally permit a Jew to sacrifice his life rather than break the Torah's Commandments. On the contrary, the Torah teaches "And you shall keep My decrees and My Laws which by doing them, a man will truly live..." (Lev.18:5) According to Oral Tradition, this means that we are not to die by them. Far greater is it to *live* for the sanctification of God's Name every day of our lives, than to die for it in at a single moment. In principle, if a Jew is forced with no choice but to transgress God's Law, he is not merely *allowed* to transgress; he *must* transgress in order to preserve his life (M.T. Laws of Foundations of Torah ch.5).

However, there are notable exceptions, which the book of Daniel proves. Torah Law requires that, in certain extreme situations, a Jew must indeed be willing to die for the sanctification of God's Name rather than transgress the Commandments of the Creator, our King (Ibid.). They are as follows:

> (1) If one is being forced to commit idolatry, murder, or forbidden sexual intercourse, under any circumstance.
>
> (2) If he is being forced by the wicked to transgress a Commandment, biblical or Rabbinical, *in public* (in the presence of ten Jews) and for a *religious* motive; i.e. that he cease to obey the Law.
>
> (3) In a time of religious persecution (where the Commandments have been outlawed by a tyrant who seeks to wipe out the Jewish faith), one must be willing to be martyred rather than transgress *any*

Commandment: biblical or rabbinical, whether in public or in private. This indeed was the situation in which the young Daniel and his friends found themselves when they were taken into Babylonian captivity. That is why, according to law, Daniel would risk his life to keep every detail of the Law —even the most minor rabbinical edicts— in the palace of the very tyrant who had burned Jerusalem to the ground.

Again, if this were not the case —if adding and observing rabbinical fences to the Torah were improper in God's eyes— would the only man in the Bible known as "the greatly-beloved man" (10:11,19), gifted with prophecy, not have known better? Would *HaShem* not have rebuked him for being reckless with his soul? *Would He not have rebuffed the prophet, saying: "I am not to be served thus," "Do not dare add to what I Commanded," or "Why do you risk the life I gave you because of legal inventions by human beings?"*

On the contrary, *HaShem*'s silence here and His miraculous preservation of Daniel, raising him up to the heights of honor at the hands of perversely wicked tyrants, are a resounding affirmation of the Holy One's approval of the Torah observance of His prophet.

9.

"והיו לטוטפות בין עיניך": תפילין בתנ"ך
OTH (SIGN) AND *TOTAFOTH* (ORNAMENT): *TEFILLIN* IN THE BIBLE

In the Written Torah, *HaShem* commands that we tie words of the Torah as a "sign" (*oth*) on our arm, and that they be an "ornament" (*totafoth*) or a "reminder/memorial" (*zikaron*) between our eyes (Ex. 13:1-10, 13:11-6, Deut.

6:4-9, 11:13-21). Karaites insist that this commandment is figurative and not to be fulfilled literally. But such an interpretation is out of character with the rest of the Bible. Where else does the Bible speak of an *oth* – "a sign" that is not seen? Signs called *oth* in the Torah include the visible mark on Cain, the rainbow, God's visible miracles in Egypt, the letter *tau* (letter is *oth* in Hebrew) to be marked on the heads of the righteous by Ezekiel, etc. *As far as the Bible is concerned, an* oth *is always seen.* How figurative can an action-based command to tie such a sign to the arm or hand be?

If the *totafoth* —the head ornament— were a figurative one, why would a peculiar, non-Hebrew word be used? (Ex. 13:16, Deut. 6:8, 11:18) It suggests a known, tangible object known to the generation that left Egypt. Indeed, from Africa to the Far East, ancient cultures placed various signs, amulets and ornaments on their foreheads, between their eyes. How much sense does it make that the Commandment that Israelites have such an ornament between their eyes as a memorial piece of the Exodus from Egypt, is actually fulfilled with nothing tangible between the eyes?

The key verse states: "and you shall bind them for a sign upon your arm and *they shall become* [or "they shall be for"] *an ornament* between your eyes." *(Deut. 6:8)* The Hebrew wording, *wa-hayu la-totafoth,* means "and they shall *become* an ornament" (or "and they shall be *for* an ornament). If the meaning were figurative, the wording would be *wa-hayu ka-totafoth,* meaning "and they shall be *as* an ornament…." A difference of only one letter, a *lamed* instead of a *kaph*, gives the wording a clearly practical meaning rather than a figurative one.

Ironically, if the counter-intuitive Karaite interpretation was the correct one, it would require an authoritative Oral

Tradition to preserve it for over 3,300 years ago until today. In order to prevent endless argument by equally-qualified Bible interpreters, such a tradition could only have only faithfully preserved by a society of specially-ordained scholars begun by Moses for that purpose. However, one of the defining hallmarks of Karaite faith is the denial of such an Oral Tradition.

They cannot have it both ways: Either the Torah means what it says according to what its simple meaning suggests (which in this case points to a practical Oral Tradition as to how the "sign" and "ornament" are made and placed), or the Karaites produce their own proof of a rival Oral Tradition. They would also need to reveal their own unbroken chain of ordained tradition bearers going back to Sinai. Being that they recognize no Oral Tradition literature (not even claiming their own), they would have nothing to stand on.

Besides the Oral Tradition implied in the wording of the Torah's commandments concerning the *oth* and *totafoth*, there appears to be passing reference to them in the book of Kings.

The Phylacteries of Israel's First King

According to ancient rabbinical tradition from the 1st century BCE, there is a direct reference in the Bible to the *tefillin* boxes (at least to the arm-phylactery) worn by Israel's first king, hardly 400 years after the Revelation at Sinai. It is found in the Aramaic translation of the Second Temple-era sage Yehonathan ben 'Uzi'el (Targum Yehonathan) on the verse II Samuel 1:10.

They are the words of the Amalekite servant who slew the mortally-wounded King Saul, upon the monarch's order. Imagining that David would be relieved at the news of the king's death and perhaps even reward him, the servant removed two tokens from the dead king's person and brought them to David. The opposite occurred: As a loyal servant of King Saul (despite the king's envy and hate for the young, anointed warrior destined to replace him as king), David was shocked by the news and outraged by the audacity of the Amalekite. He promptly had the Amalekite put to death.

The Amalekite's words, as he recounts to David what had transpired on the battlefield, were as follows:

> So I stood beside him, and slew him, because I was sure that he could not live after he had fallen; *and I took the crowning ornament [nezer] that was upon his head, and the bracelet [eS`adah] that was on his arm,* and have brought them here to my lord.   (II Samuel 1:10)

What were these tokens? To understand the wording, consider the following:

- The word for "bracelet" *(eS`adah)* is translated as *"totefeth,"* meaning "phylactery" in the Aramaic translation of Yehonathan ben Yomah.

- The word for "crown" in Hebrew is *kether* —not *nezer*— and it is only mentioned in Scripture in the context of non-Jewish monarchs (Job 36:2, Esther 2:17, 6:8); never in the context of Israelite kings. The only tokens of the Jewish monarchy mentioned in the Bible are the king's throne and his mule. (See I Kings 1:33,38,44. Note how, among the symbolic actions taken by Absalom and Adonijah to be crowned king, followed by the successful coronation of Solomon, *there is no mention of a royal crown*.) The servant clearly did not have a regal crown from Saul's head.

- The word used here, *nezer*, is used throughout the Torah to describe the golden plate on the head of the High Priest. Like the head-*tefillah* (singular for *tefillin*), the golden plate was an ornament for the front of the head, held on either side by protruding cords, and wrapped around the back of the head. From the mouth of a non-Jew (who was likely not to have known the proper name) *nezer* is an ideal synonym for the crown-like head-*tefillah*.

In summary, the Amalekite was bringing David the arm-phylactery removed from the slain King Saul, with his head-phylactery.[4] We can now understand the context for David's emotional reaction to the servant's account: He had just beheld tokens of King Saul's enduring righteousness.

This scenario fits well with the Talmud's historical account of the *tefillin* gathered from the bodies of the fallen Jewish soldiers in the war of Beitar (Talmud Tr. *Gittin* 57b-58a). *Tefillin* were part of the battle dress of a righteous soldier of Israel from ancient times.

Another possible reason the servant referred to the arm *tefillah* as a "bracelet" (*eS`adah*) is as follows: Given the precious value of tefillin and how, during prolonged use, they naturally slip out of place from atop the bicep, an Israelite warrior would certainly have worn a special padded bracelet or band to protect and keep the phylactery in place, on his arm during war. This may well be the *eS`adah* referred to in the verse. After all, if the Amalekite had merely brought a non-descript arm *tefillah* to David, he would not have recognized the owner, eliciting his emotional reaction. But if the Amalekite brought the king's royal arm-*tefillah* together in its protective bracelet —the king's *eS`adah*— *David would have recognized King Saul to have been their unambiguous owner.*

Where Tefillin are Placed: The Meaning of "Between The Eyes"

As mentioned above, the Torah commands that Jews bind and wear phylacteries (*tefillin*) daily, one *tefillah*-box is bound to the arm, while the other is placed upon the head between the eyes, as it is written:

> And it shall be for a sign for you upon your hand, *and for a memorial between your eyes, that the Law of HaShem may be in your mouth; for with a strong hand HaShem brought you out of Egypt.* (Ex. 9:13) See also Ex. 3:16, Dev. 6:8, 1:18 and Proof #16

According to Oral Tradition, the precise place where the head *tefillah*-box is placed is above the forehead, along the central line that runs down between the eyes. It is described in the ancient sources of the Oral Law as the soft spot on a young baby's head. While it is no proof in itself of the origin of *tefillin*, it is fascinating that science has discovered that this precise place on the head marks the location of the prefrontal cortex (PFC), which is responsible for higher cognitive skills:

> …humans have acquired 'higher' cognitive skills —such as language, reasoning and planning— and complex social behaviour. Evidence from neuropsychological and neuroimaging research indicates that the prefrontal cortex (PFC) underlies much of this higher cognition.[5]

The cubic leather *tefillah*-boxes contain select passages from Scripture declaring *HaShem*'s Oneness, the Commandments to love Him by obeying all of His

Commandments, and training one's children accordingly. The head-*tefillah* is placed precisely above the center of man's higher thinking – above his center of logic. *This translates into placing a symbol of HaShem's Kingship above one's rational core.*

It is recorded that the Sadducees, notorious rejecters of the Oral Law, were well-known for placing their phylacteries *(tefillin)* literally "between the eyes" per their literal interpretation of the wording of the Torah Commandment. Besides the inspiring hints revealed by science, *the Written* Torah itself reveals the true meaning of "between your eyes." In Deut. 14:1, we are bidden never to make a bald spot for the dead *"between the eyes."* What hair is being referred to?

Donning the tefillah-box in its precise place "between the eyes" according to the Oral Torah tradition.

With the exception of certain individuals from Eastern European/Central Asia, there is hardly any hair to speak of on the brow ridge between the eyes. No race of man has easily removable hair growing between the eyes on the forehead. Yet even the popular phrase "don't tear your hair out" harks back to the ancient mourning rite of tearing hair out of the head, creating a bald spot. *Ancient idolaters would tear hair out from that specific place on the head which is between the eyes, albeit from a higher point on the head.*

When the Karaites relate to *tefillin* as a ritual invented by "the rabbis," one should ask: did they also possess knowledge of the structure of the brain as we do today, or the science of acupuncture? Did the Rabbis invent the *tefillin* that King Saul died in, the *tefillin* in the ancient Egyptian depiction of Israelites from the period of the Judges or early monarchy, or the ancient *tefillin* found at Qumran? (See the evidence in Part III Point 16) In truth, all that need be asked is, "by what Oral Tradition of theirs should we ignore what is suggested by the simple understanding of the text?"

10.
זהות ישראל דרך האם בלבד
JEWISH IDENTITY PASSES THROUGH THE MOTHER ONLY

One of the most common attacks on rabbinical tradition is the claim that matrilineal descent (that Jewish identity passes through the mother only) was either an invention by the Rabbis or a revolution led by Ezra the scribe, while originally, one's Jewish identity supposedly passed through the father.

As elaborated further below, and as anyone who has read the Bible in any language should know, the Book of Ezra clearly describes how the returning Jewish exiles from Babylonia were forced to give up the non-Jewish women they had married and send them back *with their children*. If the father alone determined Jewishness, the erring nation would never have agreed to send away such women with their children. The latter would have been Jewish from their father and remained with the Jewish people.

Clearly the argument that it is an invention by the *Pharisaic Rabbis* is not even worthy of a response.

Understanding Samson And Solomon

Proponents of patriarchal-descent point to well-known Israelite leaders, namely Samson and King Solomon, who married women from foreign nations. If Jewish identity passed through the mother, they ask, then why would those men openly pursue and officially marry gentile wives?

What they cannot find, however, is a source in Scripture or elsewhere to *disprove* the Oral Tradition on the matter: During the reigns of King David and Solomon, the official courts would not approve conversions. The official channels of entry into the Jewish People were blocked for a simple reason: Like so many who convert to Judaism for material benefits today, potential converts of the day were suspected of ulterior motives. Nevertheless, *these otherwise great men converted their wives in private courts of three Torah-observant individuals before marrying them, without taking pains to be certain they were converting for the sake of Heaven.*[6] It is for this reason that Scripture refers to them as gentile women. Indeed, in the Biblical accounts of both men, the corrupt intentions of these women were proven: Samson's wives remained loyal to the Philistines, and Solomon's wives reverted to idolatry (M.T. Laws of Forbidden Sexual Relations 13:13[16]).

Neither the Prophets nor the Sages ever whitewashed Samson's failure to heed the Torah's warning against lusting after the eyes (Num. 15:39), which resulted in his own eyes being destroyed. They never condoned

Solomon's open transgression of the Torah laws forbidding a king from taking too many wives or from taking foreign wives who were not genuine converts (I Kings 11:1-2 cf. Deut. 17:17 and Deut. 7:1-4). On the contrary: the Bible clearly reveals how, in their relationships with women, these men —who were both righteous heroes and fallible human beings— acted with carelessness in regards to these Torah Commandments, for which they were both sorely punished. *To claim that these stories provide proof of patrilineal Jewish descent in ancient Israel, is plainly dishonest.*

In fact, in regards to Jewish descent in ancient Israel, the truth is written in black and white in the Written Torah for those who are open-minded and sensitive enough to its wording:

Israelite Punishment for the "Son of an Israelite Woman"

We find it in the Torah's account of the man who cursed *HaShem*'s Name in the desert, and his means of punishment:

> And *the son of an Israelite woman, whose father was an Egyptian,* went out among the children of Israel; and *the son of the Israelite woman* and a man of Israel fought together in the camp. And *the son of the Israelite woman* blasphemed the Name, and cursed; and he was brought to Moses. And his mother's name was Shelomith, the daughter of Dibri of the tribe of Dan. ... And *HaShem* spoke to Moses, saying: 'Remove the one who has cursed from the camp; and let all who heard him lay their hands upon his head, and *let all the congregation stone him.* And you shall *speak to the children of Israel*, saying: Whosoever curses his God shall bear his sin.' (Lev. 24:10-15)

The man is first introduced as the son of an Israelite woman and an Egyptian father. But from then on, after that one-time introduction, *his Egyptian father is not mentioned;* he is only called "son of the Israelite woman." He is then slated to be put to death by stoning: a punishment that is, as explained below, befitting a true Israelite *only*. He is then made an example before all the children of Israel as to what will occur to any of *them* who curse *HaShem*'s Holy Name.

Note how the Torah goes out of its way to inform us that the man's identity was defined by his mother's lineage, and that his mode of execution was pronounced accordingly. The Oral Law clarifies what we find time and again in Scripture: *Torah justice for non-Jews convicted of breaking the Seven Laws, means death by the sword* (M.T. Laws of Kings and Wars 9:17[14]).

Indeed, from the execution of Hamor and Shechem who were guilty of kidnapping (Gen. 34:26), to the execution of the wicked prophet Balaam (Joshua 13:22), and the holy wars waged against the Midianites (Num. 31:8) and the Canaanites (Joshua 10:11, 11:10, etc), we find Noahide justice being carried out by the sword only – not by any other means of execution.

The prohibition of cursing *HaShem*, one of the Seven Laws of Noah, is a capital crime for non-Jews as much as for Jews; only the mode of execution differs: *If the "son of the Israelite woman" was defined as a non-Jew according to his father's line, he would have been put to death by the sword.* Lo and behold – he is not beheaded, but stoned to death. *On account of his mother's lineage, he is an Israelite through and through.*

Understanding the Core Torah Source for the Oral Tradition

The Written Torah source that rules out patrilineal descent for children born out of intermarriage, which was quoted by the Talmudic Sages (Bab. Talmud Tr. *Yevamoth* 23a, Jerusalem Talmud *Yevamoth* 13a, ch.2:6) is indeed unclear at first glance. The key to understanding is a well-known principle in Biblical scholarship that *ben,* Hebrew for "son," connotes "grandson" in certain cases[7] – as it does here:

> Neither shall you marry into them [idolatrous peoples]: you shall not give your daughter to his son, nor shall you take his daughter for your son. For he [your son] will remove your [grand]son from following Me, that they may serve other gods; so that the anger of *HaShem* will be kindled against you, and He will destroy you quickly.
> (Deut. 7:3-4)

Obviously the simple act of marrying a non-Jewess does not condemn a Jew to a life of idol-worship. There are plenty of Jews who leave a mixed marriage, because at a certain point they can no longer stand the foreign beliefs and practices of their non-Jewish spouse. Despite a limited-time stint with intermarriage, they have remained believing Jews all along. It is therefore clear that the second "son" here is not the young man himself, but the father's other "son" in this case is *the grandson born from the inter-marriage.*

Now how can an Israelite son turn his own son into an idolater, simply by fathering him through a non-Jewess? How has the grandson been "removed from following *HaShem?*" In Hebrew society, from ancient times to the present, the father is most responsible for his son's religious education. According to that father-dominated role, couldn't he dictate how his son is taught? It clearly does not matter how the grandson is raised: Unless he converts, the child is not an Israelite. *The Torah is referring to the fact that, by marrying a non-Israelite, the Israelite son is effectively removing the children born to that wife from the Covenant.*

Given this rule from Sinai —even from a purely social perspective— who can honestly believe that the children born to a sinner who broke that law with his non-Jewish wife would be regarded with the same status in Israelite society as a son born to a genuine Israelite mother?

Unfortunately, when it comes to de-legitimizing authentic Torah tradition, genuine objectivity, fairness, and academic honesty tend to take a back seat.

Ezra & Nehemiah Reject Patrilineal Descent Before The Prophets

So far, the proofs I have brought, however rational, require a degree of interpretation. As explained briefly above, in the context of Ezra and Nehemiah, Jewish patrilineal descent is revealed to be one of the easiest anti-Torah arguments to falsify. For those books describe a dramatic episode in which Ezra the High Priest, and Nehemiah (a key civil leader) use their leadership to bring the Israelites to repent for having taken non-Jewish wives – which all the people recognize to be a real sin. In fact, as noted above, rather than convert those wives and their children, the men separate from those wives entirely *as well as the children born to them*:

When Ezra first learns of how widespread the sin was, he was in utter horror and shock. He goes into deep mourning, tearing his clothes, plucking out hair from his head and beard, fasting and weeping. He falls on his knees, raising his hands up before *HaShem*, crying:

> And now, our God, what will we say after this? For we have forsaken Your Commandments, which You have Commanded by Your servants the prophets, saying: "… you shall not give your daughters to their sons, neither take their daughters for your sons…" And after all that has come upon us on account of our evil deeds… shall we again break Your Commandments and make marriages with the peoples that do these abominations? Would You not be angry with us to the point of consuming us, so that there should be no remnant, nor any to escape?
>
> Now while Ezra prayed and confessed… a very great congregation of men and women and children out of Israel gathered to him, *for the people wept very bitterly.* And Shecaniah the son of Jehiel, one of the sons of Elam, answered and said to Ezra: 'We have broken faith with our God and have married foreign women of the peoples of the land; yet now there is hope for Israel concerning this matter. *Let us now make a covenant with our God to put away all the wives and those born to them, according to the counsel of HaShem, and of those who tremble at the Commandment of our God; and let it be done according to the law.* (Ezra 9:10-10:3)

Nehemiah's response to the crisis —no less severe— is found in Nehemiah 13:23-31.

Is there any hint here that the High Priest was adding a "new concept" to Judaism – or imposing a novel concept to replace an earlier understanding of Torah? *Note the emphasis on the people having broken the Commandment of HaShem, and none other than Deut. 7:3-4, as explained above.* What could bring the stubborn nation of Israel to weep bitterly, if they had not transgressed a law that was already known to them? Note the solution that is arrived at: to establish a new Covenant with *HaShem*, in which the guilty men would separate from their non-Jewish wives *and their children* – and that it "be done according to the law." Moreover, that is called acting "according to the counsel of *HaShem*."

Does this sound like a revolutionary rewrite of an original policy in the Torah of Moses that Jewish identity is purely through the *father*? If that were so, Ezra the High Priest and Nehemiah would not only be guilty of cruelly breaking up families; *they would be guilty of robbing truly Jewish children of a Jewish upbringing*. Most fortunately for us, there were living prophets of *HaShem* at the time who witnessed these events, and, according to Oral Tradition, sat on the very Court that enforced these laws:

> Now *the prophets, Haggai the prophet, and Zechariah the son of Iddo,* prophesied to the Jews that were in Judah and Jerusalem; in the name of the God of Israel prophesied they to them.
> (Ezra 5:1)

> Now therefore, our God, the great, the mighty, and the awesome God, who keeps covenant and mercy, let not all the travail seem little before You, that has come upon us, on our kings, on our princes, and on our priests, *and on our prophets*, and on our fathers, and on all Your people, since the time of the kings of Assyria *to this day*. (Neh. 9:32)

The prophets Malachi and Daniel were present on the Court as well (M.T. Preface 7).

Understanding the Significance

All the above prophets left behind books of their prophetic teachings and narratives of their times, which became enshrined and sealed in the Bible to this day. True prophets of *HaShem* throughout the Bible did not hesitate to give scathing rebuke or even depose powerful, sinful rulers in the Name of *HaShem* at the greatest risk to their own lives. Their lives were given over entirely to *HaShem*; they feared nothing but His Word. *If HaShem were opposed to the actions of Ezra and Nehemiah, they would have been sorely rebuked by the prophets. Indeed, they were not rebuked in the least.*

The prophets' silence in regards to the breaking up of intermarried families is deafening. If the purge of Ezra and Nehemiah was a "reform," it was a reform with *HaShem's* consent, to bring the nation back under Torah Law. The only "reform" here was a decision by Israel's leaders to reform the hearts of the nation to follow the eternal laws of the Torah.

11.

כניסת רות המואביה לכנסת ישראל
HOW COULD RUTH THE MOABITESS MARRY INTO THE PEOPLE OF ISRAEL?

An excellent example of Oral Torah in action is when Ruth was regarded as a full convert by the sages of Bethlehem, and was married to Boaz. According to the Written Word, Moabites and Ammonites (who converted into the Jewish People) would forever remain prohibited from marrying into Jewish families. (This law has no longer applied for thousands of years already, *since the nations of the Middle East have so thoroughly mixed.* [M.T. Laws of Forbidden Sexual Relations 12:9<25>])

> An Ammonite or a Moabite shall not enter into the congregation of *HaShem*; even to the tenth generation none of them shall enter into the congregation of *HaShem* forever. (Deut. 23:4)

However, one of the most well-known and moving stories from the Bible is that of Ruth, the Moabite woman who left her native people to join the nation of Israel as a righteous convert. After marrying Boaz, a respected judge of the tribe of Judah, she becomes the great-grandmother of King David. *Not only was David chosen by HaShem to be king for his generation, but his family line was blessed with kingship forever.* HaShem actually made a solemn promise to David that even though his progeny would sin, the right to the throne would never be removed from his descendents as it was removed from King Saul and his line (II Samuel 7:15-16). *Considering David's root from the accursed nation of Moab, how could this be?*

Without the Oral Law of the Torah, this would remain a very disturbing mystery, for there exists an Oral law going all the way back to Moses at Sinai, that that verse refers exclusively to the Moabite and Ammonite men, and not the women (Laws of Forbidden Sexual Relations 12:14[18] cf. Talmud Tr. *Yevamoth* 76b-77a).

It is yet another example of how the most righteous characters of the Bible —even *HaShem* Himself— operate according to principles of Law that are not written down in Scripture. For thousands of years, despite the factions of rebels who create havoc in every generation, the sages of Israel have faithfully and stubbornly maintained records of those laws. In spite of my efforts in this book, the burden of proof lies on the newer religious groups that arose later to reject that tradition – not on those who have maintained the tradition all along.

12.

לא עין תחת עין ממש
THE ORAL TRADITION OF "AN EYE FOR AN EYE"

HaShem Commanded in His Torah that one who wounds or maims his fellow be punished according to the principle of "an eye for an eye, a tooth for a tooth". (Ex. 21:24, Lev. 24:19-20)

> And if a man maims his fellow; as he did, thus shall it be done to him: a break for a break, an eye for a eye, a tooth for a tooth; as he maimed a human being, thus shall it be done to him.
> (Lev. 24:19-20)

According to Oral Torah tradition, the Torah actually demands here that the one who maimed *pay full monetary compensation* to his victim, according to the loss incurred by the wound. Rejecters of the Oral Law, on the other hand, relate to this as a later, more benevolent interpretation by the Rabbis, which came to replace a simpler, harsher Biblical system of punishment.

At first, this might seem quite reasonable. However, closer scrutiny reveals how weak it is:

Firstly, there is not a single example throughout the Bible of Israelite courts or kings punishing guilty parties in this way – poking eyes out and yanking teeth. The closest thing we find to this is a single act by the warriors of Judah in Judges 1:6-7. After capturing the wicked king of Bezeq, they amputate his thumbs and big toes. At a closer glance, however, it seems clear the Judeans did thus to him not as a legal judgment, but in order to prevent the enemy warrior from ever being able to run or hold a weapon again.[8]

Secondly, the injustice of the literal interpretation of "an eye for an eye" is appalling. What if one who digs graves for a living maliciously takes out the eye of one who makes his living as a professional diamond cutter? While the family of the one-eyed diamond cutter (who depends on both his eyes) is deprived of their livelihood, the grave digger and his family will remain well fed: Their breadwinner can continue his work with only one eye! Where is the justice in this? "Shall the Judge of all the earth not act justly?" (Gen. 18:25) Not only has full justice not been done by removing the grave-digger's eye, but no good has been done to the victim. Does *HaShem* truly desire that more wounds be created while the victim becomes impoverished?

Moreover, what if the eye of the victim was only partially blinded by his fellow? In order to execute proper justice, the court would need to inflict the guilty party with the same partial blindness in his eye – a condition that is impossible to replicate! Unless one imagines that the One Who commanded "justice, justice shall you pursue" (Deut. 16:20) does not care that true justice be done in such cases, Torah justice clearly does not involve blinding the perpetrator.

Fortunately, there is no need to rely on the above moral logic with no hard textual evidence: *The true meaning of "an eye for an eye" is found in Written Word itself, by studying the use of the same expression elsewhere:*

> He who mortally strikes down any human being shall be put to death. *And he who mortally strikes down a beast shall make payment for it: a life for a life.* And if a man maims his fellow; as he did, thus shall it be done to him: a break for a break, an eye for an eye, a tooth for a tooth; as he maimed a human being, thus shall it be done to him. *And he*

> who strikes down a beast shall make payment for it; and he who strikes down a man shall be put to death. (Lev. 24:17-21)

We see that the punishment for maiming another person — "an eye for an eye, a tooth for a tooth" — immediately follows the penalty for killing a beast, which is called a "life for a life," yet involves monetary payment for the value of the animal's life. The Oral Tradition that *HaShem* demands monetary restitution for a lost limb is no "rabbinical softening" of "Biblical justice"; it *is* Biblical justice.

So why, then, is the Torah written in such harsh, physical terms as "an eye for an eye?"

The Law is worded thus to be a deterrent. The reader is made to understand that one who takes out his fellow's eye *deserves* that the same be done to him. But practically speaking, the criminal is to pay his victim for the loss incurred by the broken bone, the lost eye, the lost tooth, etc. *That* is true "Biblical justice," and it is there in the text, waiting to be discovered by the careful, humble Torah student. That is one who desires not to fit the Torah into his own preconceived notions, but to nullify his own preconceptions before the over 3,300 year-old Oral Torah tradition from Sinai.

13.

בזמן שמד, דניאל מסכן את חיי נפשו על שמירת
דיני תפילה מדבריהם

**DANIEL RISKS EXECUTION TO PRAY
ACCORDING TO ORAL TRADITION**

"Biblical"-types who looks askance at modern Jews who *daven* (Yiddish for "pray") thrice daily may be shocked to

Revealing the Oral Tradition in the Written Word

know that this practice reveals observant Jews to this day to be students of Israel's prophets of old. None other than Daniel, *ish hhamudoth* –"greatly beloved man of God" (Daniel 10:11, 10:19), had a regular practice of bowing down on his knees in prayer towards Jerusalem three times daily, as it is written:

> And when Daniel knew that the writing was signed, he went into his house *–now his windows were open in his upper chamber toward Jerusalem– and he kneeled upon his knees three times a day, and prayed,* and gave thanks before his God, as he did aforetime. (Ibid. 6:11)

QUESTIONS

Where in the Five Books of Moses is there any clear Commandment to pray, much less three times a day?

In the absence of any clear mandate to pray, from where did Daniel derive that prayer should be done in any particular place, in any special direction, or in any specific position?

If he had merely developed his own individual custom, by what obligation or right did he have —based on Written Torah Law only— to put himself in danger of execution for something *HaShem* had never Commanded in the first place?

What did Daniel know that was hidden from the future Sadducees, Karaites, and other deniers of the Oral Tradition?

- The Oral Tradition known to the Sages that the Torah Commandment "to serve *HaShem* with all one's heart" (Ex. 23:25, Deut. 11:13) is a

Commandment *to pray* – a "service of the heart" (M.T. Laws of Prayer and the Priestly Blessing 1:1).

- The Oral Tradition that even from before the birth of the nation, Israel's patriarch Abraham had instituted the Morning Prayer *(Shahharith)*, Isaac the afternoon prayer *(Minhhah)*, and Jacob the Nighttime Prayer *(`Arvith)*. The tradition of these three daily prayers was known to and maintained by King David in his day (Psalms 55:18).

- The Oral Tradition known to the prophet Hosea as well (Hosea 14:3), that in the absence of a Temple, prayers substitute for offerings. The Sages regarded them as such, and wrote them into law to correspond to the number and timing of the daily Temple offerings (M.T. Laws of Prayer and the Priestly Blessing 1:7[5]).

- The Oral Traditions that became rabbinical laws: (a) that one pray the standing prayer facing the direction of Israel, Jerusalem, and the Holy Temple (Ibid. 5:3); (b) that one establish a set place for his prayers, and open windows or doors towards the direction of prayer (Ibid. 5:7[6]), and (c) that one descend to one's knees to bow down at appointed places in the prayer (Ibid. 5:11[10], 14[13]).

- The Oral Tradition that the Commandment "and you shall love *HaShem* your God… with all your *soul*" is a Commandment to be willing, under certain extreme circumstances, to give up one's life rather than to transgress the Torah. As taught above in Point 8, one of those circumstances is during a time of religious persecution, such as the one suffered by the Jews in Persia at the time of Daniel's prayer above (Ibid. Laws of Foundations of Torah 5:4[3]). *(At such a time, one must willing to be martyred rather than transgress even one of the Torah's minor commandments, such as prayer (which carries no penalty by a human court for transgression.)*

In Conclusion: Repeating Our Key Message to the World

When one considers the rabbinical fences honored by the prophets of *HaShem*, for those who believe in God and the truth of the Bible, there is no room left for doubt: When *HaShem* wrote in His Torah, "And you shall observe to do according to all that they will teach you from that place which *HaShem* shall choose, *and you shall observe to do according to **all** that they will teach you*" (Deut. 17:10), **He meant exactly what was written.** Even after 3,300 years since Sinai; while their manner of observance evolved, His Laws remain the same. Although rabbinical law developed as it should have under the leadership of the Sanhedrin of old until the last Great Court disbanded, the system remains unchanged to this day; neither will it cease forever.

I re-emphasize what was expressed in Part I: Bible believers of all other faiths will only arrive at the truth found in their own spiritual traditions when they internalize that the Commandments of the Torah, according to the Oral Tradition maintained by the Jewish People –the 613 for Israel and the Seven Laws of Noah for the rest of humanity— were Given *for all time*, as it is written:

> "an eternal law for all your generations"
> (Lev. 3:17 and another 7 places)

> "and the things that have been revealed belong to us and our children for eternity, that we may execute all the teachings of this Torah"
> (Deut. 29:28)

These are the words of the Living God from the same Torah that includes prophecies of future times, taking it well into account that Israel would sin and be thrown into exile, only to be brought back to our Land (Deut. 30:1-5).

No one can say that *HaShem* "changed His mind" at any point to choose another people, or to change or replace his Commandments with others – unless the deity he refers to is not the God who said: *"I, HaShem, do not change."* (Malachi 3:6) He could not be referring to the God of David who confirmed in his prayer, "And You established for Yourself Your people Israel to be Your people ["a people unto You"] *forever*, and You, *HaShem*, became their God." (II Samuel 7:24)

Neither can anyone imagine (as many Christians do) that *HaShem* Commanded what He did with the hidden intention of proving that His Word could never be kept – unless the deity in mind is not the God Who said through Moses, *"God is not a man that He should deceive."* (Num. 23:19)

One of the 613 immutable Commandments of His Torah — and the foundation of the Noahide Covenant as well— is to observe *"all that they will teach you."* This can only refer to the Oral Torah taught by the ordained sages of the Great Court (Sanhedrin), which were preserved and clarified by the Talmudic Sages, and codified succinctly in RaMBaM's *Mishneh Torah* until the day when the Great Court is re-established according to Law.

Revealing the Oral Tradition in the Written Word

NOTES

(1) This tradition about the Vilna Gaon, learned from Rabbi Yoel Schwartz (senior lecturer at D'var Yerushalayim Yeshivah, Jerusalem), is rooted in established knowledge about the 18th century (C.E.) Torah giant. (See: Schechter, Solomon and Seligsohn, M., "Elijah ben Solomon," article at Jewish Encyclopedia.com)

(2) This is hinted in the blessing Jacob gave to the tribe of Yehudah (Judah, Judea). Yehudah would maintain its autonomy the longest, and Israelites of the other tribes come to identify with his name until this day as Jews (or Judeans). His father prophetically blessed Yehudah as follows: "The sceptre shall not depart from Judah, nor the scribe [lit. 'the engraver' from between his feet." (Gen. 49:10)

(3) Let not Daniel's abstinence from wine and bread for the king's table be confused with that of "the man of God" whom *HaShem* sent to the wicked King Jeroboam (I Kings 13:8). *HaShem* gave a special Command to that earlier prophet —for that instance— not to eat bread or drink water on his mission in that local area. On the contrary, *Daniel drank the local water in his locale.* Moreover, the verse indicates that the reason for his refusal to eat was not "the place," *but the fact it was fit for a king's table, having been prepared by idolaters.* He agreed, however, to eat simple food (being unfit for the king's table), precisely in accordance with the rabbinical law as it remains to this day: Food that is cooked or baked by idolaters is forbidden to a Jew, so long as it is fit for the table of a king. Simple foods that are *not* fit for a king's table *are* permitted (M.T. Laws of Forbidden Foods 17:9-15).

(4) There is another possibility that the *nezer* of the king's head here refers to his crown of nazirite locks (*nezer* is the root of the Hebrew word *nazir*, or nazirite). God's *mashiahh* ("messiah" means "anointed one" and all properly-anointed kings and high priests were referred to as such) would most likely have been a *nazir*. A *nazir* is one who took a vow neither to cut his the hair on head, nor to taste any product of the vine *(wine, grapes, raisins, grape-skins)*. *Nezer* in II Samuel 1:10 could be referring to a hair lock that wrapped around the head like a wreath to keep the king's sacred locks out of his face in battle. This, too, would fit the

Aramaic word *alilah* (meaning "crown" or wreath") – the translation for *nezer* in *Targum Yehonathan*.

If this is the correct interpretation, then either: (1) the Amalekite forwent the king's head-phylactery to cut off a lock of hair from his sanctified head, or (2) the king was only wearing his arm *tefillah*-box – which is a distinct, independent Commandment from donning the head *tefillah*-box (M.T. Laws of Tefillin, Mezuzah, and Torah Scroll 4:4).

(Special thanks to Yehoshua` Sofer-Ma`atuf Dohh for this original Torah insight.)

(5) Jacqueline N. Wood & Jordan Grafman. "Human prefrontal cortex: processing and representational perspectives." *Nature Reviews Neuroscience* 4, 139-147 (Feb 2003). Found at: *www.nature.com/nrn/journal/v4/n2/full/nrn1033.html*

(6) Indeed, although not impossible, it is improbable that Samson, a man looked up to as the judge of all Israel (in a line of national Judges stretching back to Moses and Joshua) would marry a foreign woman while she remained a gentile in the eyes of all Israel. All the more so King Solomon, prophet-king of Israel, whom *HaShem* called *Yedidiyah* ("friend of God" – see II Sam. 12:24-25). The tradition of the Sages, that ceremonies were indeed held marking these women's "entrance" into the Covenant of Israel (however ineligible they were proven to be), is the most plausible.

(7) For example, the Scroll of Esther relates that Mordechai was "son of *(ben)* Yair, son of *(ben)* Shimei, son of *(ben)* Kish the Benjamite." (Esther 2:5) However, while Mordechai was active circa 350 B.C.E., his ancestor Shimei disgraced King David, while Kish —father of King Saul— was active as early as 900 B.C.E. (see footnote 1 of Part I). Even according to the common academic dating, they are separated by over five centuries. How then could Kish have been merely the great-grandfather of Mordechai? Clearly *ben* can mean "grandson" or "descendant" as much as an actual son.

(8) Conquered and humbled, the Canaanite monarch *himself* comes to understand that his punishment, measure for measure, must be from God Himself: Just as he would sadistically humiliate the kings whom he conquered by cutting off their thumbs and big toes, such was now being done to him. Since the king of Bezeq himself attributed this to the judgment of God and not man, it seems clear the Judeans did thus to him not as a legal judgment, but so that this cruel enemy warrior would never be able to run or hold a weapon again.

Oral Torah from Sinai

PART III: SCIENTIFIC PROOF

Hard Science Reveals the Antiquity of the Oral Tradition and Hints of its Divine Origin

אֱמֶת, מֵאֶרֶץ תִּצְמָח; וְצֶדֶק,
מִשָּׁמַיִם נִשְׁקָף.
(תהילים פה:יב)

Truth springs forth from the earth; and righteousness is looked upon from heaven. (Psalms 85:12)

Oral Torah from Sinai

INTRODUCTION TO PART III

Besides those who are rightfully satisfied with internal proofs from the Bible, there are others who will still remain not fully convinced. Wary of all those who, over the course of time, have twisted the Written Torah's words to fit their own agenda, they wish for some proof that could ground the Torah in empirical, quantifiable reality. Such truth-seekers must not be left with the impression that the only real proof is internal Biblical analysis. *Actual hard evidence exists that the Torah was indeed understood and practiced in the deep ancient past largely as it was preserved by the Talmudic sages.* The following evidence is derived from the diverse fields of ancient literary analysis, world history, archaeology, marine biology, astronomy, embryology, and cultural anthropology.

Again, the purpose of this book is not to provide proof for the antiquity and Divine authorship of the Written Torah – the Five Books of Moses. Due to its importance to other "Bible-based" faith communities, much work has been done in that field. Moreover, there is no attempt to present these proofs as utterly incontrovertible, or as the reason why we believe and live as we do. Rather, it is to show the world that rational proof exists for belief in the Oral Torah Tradition. It exposes the notion of the Oral Tradition as an "invention" by the Pharisaic Rabbis of 2,000 years ago to be weak at best; a hateful libel at worst.

As was noted in the introductory words to Part II, let the reader again be reminded that people's perspectives vary widely. It is impossible for every point to impress and convince every type of reader. However, all that is necessary to demonstrate the deep antiquity and accuracy of the Oral Tradition is one single strong line of evidence or proof. *I do not believe it far-fetched to expect every intelligent reader to find at least one point that establishes for him the rational basis for belief in the authenticity of Israel's Oral Tradition.*

14.
זכויות שבט נפתלי בים כנרת עדיין בתוקף
NAFTALI'S FISHING RIGHTS STILL IN FORCE

Imagine if a law was discovered in the writings of the Talmudic Sages, hailing back to a bygone era, discussing the property rights of a particular tribe that had been exiled by Assyria in 556 BCE? *That is nearly 750 years before the Mishnah —the oldest of rabbinical writings— was put down in writing in 189 C.E.*

The fateful year of 556 BCE saw the tribe of Naftali, along with its brother Northern Israelite tribes, uprooted by the wicked Assyrian forces of Sanhheriv (Sennacherib). While many Northern Israelite tribesmen of Asher, Manasseh, Ephraim, Issachar, and Zebulon returned in body and spirit to rejoin the Jewish People (II Chronicles 30:11,18), we have no written evidence or oral tradition about the Naftalites ever returning home – not before the prophesied ultimate ingathering of the exiles in the 'End of Days'. In fact, the pre-eminent legal force in the Mishnah, Rabbi Akivah, was of the opinion that the ten Northern tribes would *never* return – not ever (Mishnah Tr. *Sanhedrin* 10:3).

Yet, incredibly, the Rabbis maintained the ancient law that upheld the exclusive fishing rights of the tribe of Naftali at the Sea of Galilee,[1] even along the southern shore of the small inland sea. From the original written sources of the Oral Law down to its final compilation in the *Mishneh Torah*, the law remains in full force to this day:

Hard Science Reveals the Antiquity of the Oral Tradition

> The [other] tribes may not harvest fish from the sea of Tiberius because it belongs to Naftali. Furthermore, they [Naftali] are given the strip [of land] on the southern shore of the sea, as it is written "possess thou the sea and the south" [Deut. 33:23]. (The words of Rabbi Yose HaGalili (Tosefta, Tr. *Bava Qama* 8:6 [Compiled in the Land of Israel by Rabi Hhiyya bar Abba circa 300 C.E.] cf. Talmud Tr. *Bava Bathra* 122a.)

> And Naftali is to be given to possess the strip [of land] on the south of the sea...(Jerusalem Talmud, Tr. *Bava Bathra* 16b [Compiled in the Land of by Rabbi Yohhanan, circa 350 C.E.])

> Likewise he legislated that any man may harvest fish in the Sea of Tiberius. But that is on condition that one fish with a pole only; however, one may neither cast a net, nor station a boat there – except for members of the tribe in whose inheritance the Sea came.
> (M.T. Laws of Monetary Damages 5:8[6])

It is written, "He legislated..." Who does this refer to; who made this legislation? What is the source of this ancient legal remnant from well before the Assyrian conquest of the Northern tribes? When we study the fuller context of the above chapter in *Mishneh Torah*, we discover that *it is but one of ten legal enactments from Joshua —student of Moses— and his Great Court of 70 Elders* (Ibid. 5:3[1]).

Incredibly, we find this law in *Mishneh Torah* remains practical law to this day, for the simple reason that no Sanhedrin ever acted to change it. Although there is no one to enforce it, it remains *halakhah* (practical Torah law) *even in our times, for all those who desire to fish the waters of the small inland sea*. It is no less binding than later rabbinical prohibitions which were decreed by the great Sanhedrin throughout the ages, such as the laws of `eruv (from the times of King Solomon and his Court [M.T. Book of Times, Laws of ``Eruvin 1:2]) and the well-known rabbinical additions to Israel's *kashruth*-dietary laws, many of which are also of great antiquity.

Who would zealously preserve the property laws of a long-exiled Israelite tribe – a tribe believed by the greatest of the Rabbis of the Mishnah would never return? Is this the mark of "Johnny-come-latelies," of inventors, of revolutionaries? *Heaven-forbid! This and other proofs reveal that the rabbis of the Talmud received from their forebears, preserved, and passed forward legal traditions as old as the Torah itself.* It is an Oral Tradition that has accompanied the Written Word from the time it was given to the nation by *HaShem* at Sinai.

In our times when so many lies are promulgated regarding the ties of the Jewish People to their ancestral land, the preservation of the rights of a long-disappeared tribe of Israel to Lake Tiberius by their Israelite brothers is testimony to the unbreakable bonds between the Hebrew nation and their native land, and between one another.

15.

סודות עתיקות-יומין במדרשי
חז"ל מנבאות על עידן הנוכחי
**OBSCURE TALMUDIC TRADITION REVEALS
PROPHECY OF MODERN TIMES**

One of the proofs for the truth of the Oral Tradition is found in teachings of the Talmudic sages that are revealed to be prophetic from the vantage point of history. To the uninitiated, secular scholar, such teachings often appear to be primitive, out-dated, and medieval. Other times they are relegated to simplistic pedagogical devices for instilling Torah values. Indeed, any rabbinical teaching that is not a legal ruling *(halakhah)* is in the realm of non-legal, legendary teaching *(aggadah* or *midrash)*. Of this, a Jew is only expected to accept that which makes sense to him (HaRav Shemuel HaNaggid, 993-c.1056). To be honest, as much Divinely-originating wisdom as the Talmudic literature contains, beliefs based on outdated science and medicine exist there as well (*Discourse on the Sayings of the Rabbis* by Rabbi Avraham ben ha-RaMBaM, 1186-1237).[2]

However, unlike an old-school Western academic who feels compelled to debunk anything that would lend support to the belief in Divine wisdom (much less Divine commands), it behooves an honest truth-seeker to look deeper.

The Torah Verse

Consider a mysterious verse in the Torah, the ancient Talmudic tradition on its meaning, and its layers of coded, prophetic content. After the account of the Six Days of creation, the Torah concludes:

> And God blessed the seventh day, and made it holy; because on it *He ceased from all His labor which God created to do*. (Gen. 2:3)

What does *"His labor which God created to do"* mean? In his classical Torah commentary, RaMBaN (Rabbi Moshe ben Nahhman [Nachmanides], 1194-1270) explains the verse as follows: God completed all that He had made in the six days of Creation, with the purpose that —from the all He had made (the world and all it contains)— the very same deeds mentioned in the Six Days *would be done once again* over the course of history.

The Ancient Tradition Of Its Meaning

RaMBaN brings the Talmudic teaching on the verse, and decodes it further:

> The *Tanna de-be Eliyyahu* teaches: *The world is to exist six thousand years.* In the first two thousand there was tohu [desolation or chaos]; two thousand years the Torah flourished; and the next two thousand years is the Messianic era, but through our many iniquities all these years have been lost.
> (Talmud Tr. *Sanhedrin* 97a)

The source, *Tanna de-be Eliyyahu,* was regarded by the sages as wisdom learned from Elijah the prophet. While this brings a certain variant of rationalists to smirk, when they see the coded layers of future historical information embedded in it, their attitude may change. To begin with, the concept that *HaShem*'s day is like 1,000 years is found in Psalms 90:4:

> For a thousand years in Your sight, are like yesterday gone by, and as a watch in night.

The plain meaning, of course, is that *HaShem* —Who is outside of time and space— is unaffected by the passing of even 1,000 years; it is like a day or even less. However, the subtle concept of a 1,000-year-long "Day" is a key to unlock sealed Oral Tradition: *The new "days" in which the deeds of Creation are being replayed are 1,000 years each.* In his commentary, RaMBaN analyzes history from the creation of man to his own day according to the symbolic language of the Bible, and shows how accurate the Talmudic teaching is.

Hard Science Reveals the Antiquity of the Oral Tradition

But could it not be the product of rabbinical imagination? Can the order of history's main events and phases actually be fairly and convincingly linked to the order of Creation?

The Deeper Layer Revealed By RaMBaN

The following table, which includes additional historical data I found, will show that *even from a straight academic historical perspective, the order of reliably-dated events and phases according to the Biblical order of Creation cannot be denied.* When we see the further decoding by the Vilna Gaon, it will prove to be undeniably prophetic.

NOTE: Being that prophecy paints a general picture with broad strokes, the table below compares the main act of Creation of each of the Six Days with the most significant, salient historical event or phase in its corresponding 1,000 years of human history, from the Creator's perspective. Let's bear in mind that a day need not begin precisely at the turn of the millennium, but slightly before or after.

Act of Creation	Human History from Torah's Perspective[3]	Talmudic Description
DAY ONE: Light is created. (World is covered by water [RaMBaN])	**0-1,000 A.C. (After Creation)** The life of Adam. According to Oral Tradition, Adam chose to give 70 years of his life to King David, dying at the age of 930, instead of 1,000. *(Yalquth Shim`oni Bereshith 5:41 [Midrash])* Adam was "**the light of the world**," *[Midrash]* and "the soul of man [lit. "Adam"] is the **lamp** of *HaShem*." *(Proverbs 20:27)*	YEARS OF CHAOS There is no one publicly promoting the service of God; only righteous individuals as Enoch and Methuselah. Hence, these are considered to be years of *tohu* – desolation or chaos.
DAY TWO: The upper and lower waters are divided. *(World is covered by water [RaMBaN])*	**1,000-2000 A.C.** In the year 1056 Noah is born into a world spiraling down in violent sin. The **upper waters** (rain) and **lower waters** (geysers and well-springs of the deep) rejoin to destroy all human and animal life, and separate once again for Noah to replenish the earth.	YEARS OF CHAOS There is still no one *publicly* promoting the service of God; only private righteous men as Shem and Eber. The era of *tohu* only ends with the career of Abraham…

DAY THREE: Seed-yielding plant and tree life is Created.	2,000 A.C. Abraham, born in 1948 A.C., leaves with his father for Haran at 52, the year 2000. Thus begins his outreach to mankind, "making souls." Thus begins the age of Torah. He is God's **"righteous plant."** *[RaMBaN]* His enduring covenant with God is symbolized by the **burning bush** shown to Moses. This era continues until after the Temple is built. Now *all* the Commandments (the real **fruits** of this world) of God's Torah (likened by Solomon to a **Tree of Life** *[Proverbs 3:18]*) could be fulfilled.	THE TORAH FLOURISHES Abraham's career of publicly teaching the belief in God and His Commandments marks the beginning of the Age of Flourishing Torah. This 1,000 years continues until the Temple is built and all the Commandments can be fulfilled.

DAY FOUR:	3000-4000 A.C.	THE TORAH FLOURISHES
The heavenly lights, Sun and Moon, are made to appear in the sky.	The era of the two Temples. The first Temple, erected in 2935 (827 B.C.E.), was like **the Sun**, due to the intensity of its Divine Presence and open miracles. The Divine Presence in Second Temple was much diminished. Like a mere reflection of first, it is likened to **the Moon**. It was destroyed in 3829 (69 C.E.)[4]	Despite the Temple's destruction, the age of Flourishing Torah only ends after the Mishnah is composed and ratified in 3989. Rav left the Land in 3979 (219 C.E) in order to establish the Torah in exile. When this ordained student of Rabbi Judah the President established the first post-Second-Temple Torah center in Babylonia, whose non-ordained scholarship would later eclipse Israeli scholarship, it marked the end of the Era of Flourishing Torah.[5]

DAY FIVE: Fish, swarming sea creatures, and the sea-monsters are Created.	4000-5000 A.C. (240 to 1240 C.E.)	MESSIANIC ERA
	Exiled Israel suffers brutal oppression. Exiled en masse from land to land by wicked powers, they resemble **schools of fish** pursued by **sea-monsters** and large nets. RaMBaN links this time to Habbakuk's lament: *(1:14-15)* "*[Why do You, God] ...make men like **the fish of the sea**, like the swarming creatures that have no ruler over them? They* [the wicked] *take up all of them* [the righteous] *with a hook, they catch them in their net, and gather them in their dragnet; for which cause they rejoice and exult.*"	Christianity and Islam played a key role in bringing the awareness of Torah concepts (namely the general idea of one God, His Statutes, and concept of the Messiah) to the ends of the earth. (M.T. Laws of Kings and Wars 11:10-13) Therefore, the early seeds of the Messianic era ironically took root in the beginning of the 5th millennium, with the rise and spread of Christianity.

DAY SIX	5000-6000 A.C. (1240-2240 C.E.)	MESSIANIC ERA
Beasts of the earth are Created, followed by mankind. He is given the mandate to conquer the earth and rule over all its inhabitants in righteousness.	RaMBaN predicted the sixth 1,000 would be marked by the rise of *more powerful beasts* (wicked empires) than those of the last 1,000. Yet, just as *land animals* are closer to human beings than the creations of the Fifth Day, these will be closer to the truth. Indeed, in precisely the year 5000 (1240 C.E.) Muslim Arabs, a monotheistic "beast," acquire knowledge of gunpowder.[6] Empires with vast mechanized armies rise. Today they wield Weapons of Mass Destruction. Fired from the air or under the sea, they can wipe out an entire nation within minutes. Yet, in place of brute idolatry, these powers are ruled —at least in principle— with democratic, liberal-humanist values; making them closer to	From the messianic perspective, the 6th millennium begins with RaMBaM's *Mishneh Torah*, completed in 4940s (1180s C.E.). With a clear, comprehensive Torah guide to restoring the nation's judicial system and rebuilding the Temple, the bearers of Adam's faith can re-establish the reign of God's Law in the Holy Land. It also begins with the physical `aliyah (immigration) of RaMBaN and his followers in 5027 (1267 C.E.). It is the first successful establishment of a Jewish community and a new synagogue in Jerusalem since the Temple's destruction. The return culminates in the rise of a sovereign state in 5708 (1948 C.E.), facilitating a mass return. It will continue until the advent of the

the truth than their predecessors in the 5th millennium. The era will end when Israel –the *torch-bearers of Adam's faith*– will, with HaShem's miraculous aid, *subdue the final beast* when it attempts to annihilate them, (Zechariah 12 cf. Ezekiel 38-39) and entire world will recognize Torah truth. (Isaiah 11:9)	Messiah-King, who will usher in an era of world peace. Mankind will return to its original state in Eden, maximizing its positive potential.

The proof of the integrity of such a structure is when it withstands even a mistake by its discoverer: While the RaMBaN's miscalculated that the 1390 C.E. would see the advent of the Messiah-king, the *Chatam Sofer* (Rabbi Moshe Sofer, 1762-1839) showed how clearly out of sync this is with the very structure revealed by the RaMBaN:

In the Torah, a day begins with the night (see Point #6 in Part II). So, too, the 1,000-year "Day" begins with a "12-hour night," equivalent to 500 years, while the Sages likened the Redemption to the light of day.[7] Moreover, God created the beasts who ruled the earth earlier in the 6th Day, before Adam was created (a hint of the times of the future Redemption). Therefore, the 18th-century rabbi corrected, the Messiah-King will not arrive earlier than 5550 (1790 C.E.) This is the year, 500 years later than RaMBaN's date, that marked "the first light of morning" of the 6th "Day," the sixth milliennium.[8]

Indeed, that very year proved to be, according to Rabbi Hillel Rivlin of Shaklov (1758-1838) in *Qol ha-Tor* (Voice of the Turtledove),[9] the first ray of light in the slow, messianic rebirth of the Jewish People in the land of Israel. That year, his rabbi, the Vilna Gaon (Rabbi Eliyahu ben Shelomo Zalman 1720-1797), unveiled Torah secrets to his students, including the next layer in the Talmudic teaching from *Tanna de-be Eliyahu* which he decoded: the actual breakdown of the 6th millennium. Recorded in *Qol ha-Tor*, his teachings and energetic support for resettling the land became the impetus and inspiration for God-fearing Jews of Europe to begin returning to the land of Israel *en masse*.[10] Without it, it is doubtful if the resettlement enterprise would have gained the numbers of immigrant Jews required to launch the modern state, which —for all its shortcomings— holds such great significance, which I will discuss below.

The Next Layer Unveiled by the Vilna Gaon

Based on RaMBaN's teaching, the Vilna Gaon decoded the Talmudic teaching of the world's 6,000-year history further, by applying the following Talmudic teaching to the structure. R. Yohhanan ben Hhanina said:

> The day consisted of twelve hours. In the first hour, his [Adam's] dust was gathered; in the second, it was kneaded into a shapeless mass. In the third, his limbs were shaped; in the fourth, a soul was infused into him; *in the fifth, he arose and stood on his feet...* (Tr. *Sanhedrin* 38a)

Since we are in the middle of the 6th Day of world history, which indeed follows the pattern of Creation, and since the Talmud breaks down that 6th day into 24 hours and relates what occurred each hour; then our 6th millennium should follow that pattern as well. It can be broken up into 24 Godly "hours" of 41.667 years, or 41 years and 8 months:

$$1000 \text{ years} \div 24 = 41.667 \text{ years}$$

Furthermore, since this "Day" follows 12 "hours" of night," the messianic morning began in 5550 (1790 C.E.), as noted by the *Chatam Sofer*.

Embedded Prophecy of the Rise of the Modern State

Based on this, a beloved teacher of mine from my early years of Torah study, Rabbi Benjamin Blech of Yeshivah University *(may HaShem grant him swift healing in the merit of the Torah light he has spread)*, showed his fortunate students a final layer:

In the above Talmudic source employed by the Vilna Gaon, Adam "arose and stood on his feet" in the 5th hour of the day. This actually means the 17th hour (12 hours of night + 5 hours of day). In the context of the 6th millennium, 17 "hours" of 41.667 years (since the year 5,000 A.C.) is the year 5708 A.C., or 1948 C.E. *Indeed, in 1948 the People of Israel —the faithful sons of Adam, bearers of God's Torah— "arose and stood up on our feet" in our land before the whole world, and declared a sovereign state.*

On behalf of the Jewish People in their land, from within a building in Tel Aviv (a new city in the tribal territory of Dan, part of Israel's ancient heartland), David ben Gurion stood and delivered Israel's declaration of Independence. He broadcast to the world how, after a long, painful exile, the People of Israel had returned to our ancestral land *en masse,* and now declared a sovereign Jewish state, concluding with the phrase, *"Mitokh Bitahhon be-Sur Yisra'el"* – meaning "With faith in the God [lit. "Rock"] of Israel."[11]

Let the reader make no mistake: There is no attempt here to portray the shamefully-secular, anti-Torah establishment in Israel as the culmination of the Messianic Era, God-forbid. However, no one can deny that the rise of the state of Israel, with all its faults, marked the return and "standing up" of the Jewish People in our land before the world. *And it occurred precisely at the point in time concealed in the Talmud's prophetic glimpse of history's 6,000 years.* To this day in continues to facilitate a marvel that has no precedent in world history: the return of an ancient people to its native land after nearly 2,000 years. (See Appendix I: The Sixth Day Continues to Unfold)

16.
תפילין ב**ע**תיקות קומרן ומצריים
ARCHAEOLOGICAL EVIDENCE OF *TEFILLIN* FROM SINAI

Even Rival Sects Wore Them 2,000 Years Ago

As briefly mentioned in Part II Point 9, well-preserved, black *tefillin* cases (phylacteries) from the 1ˢᵗ century BCE – complete with four chambers and their parchment inserts– were discovered in 1955 in Qumran in the Judean Desert. This indicates widespread use of *tefillin* by the 1ˢᵗ century C.E., and already proves the Oral Tradition back to 2100 years ago. Note that that this covers nearly 2/3 the time span between our day and the Giving of the Torah at Sinai.[12]

But what is truly amazing is the scriptural content of the parchment inserts. Of the 30 tiny *tefillin*-scrolls discovered, many deviate far from the scriptural content mandated by rabbinical law – the traditional passages prescribed by the Sages. Deviations include the Qumran phylacteries containing the Ten Statements (Ten Commandments).

Hard Science Reveals the Antiquity of the Oral Tradition

Professor Norman Golb of the University of Chicago writes:

> This unusual feature of the Qumran phylacteries would be quite accurately described by Josef Milik in his 1977 edition of many of those from Cave 4. Some texts are much lengthier than others, taking in relatively long passages of the Pentateuch, including Exodus 12.43-13.16 and Deuteronomy 5.1-6.9 and 10.12-11.21; and to these lengthy sections the Song of Moses (Deut. 23) was also once added. Four additional texts are much shorter, approximately equaling the passages used eventually by the rabbinical Jews. *In four cases the admonition contained in the sixth chapter of Deuteronomy beginning with the familiar words "Hear O Israel, the Lord is your God" —universally considered to be at the very core of the content of phylacteries— is itself excluded.* The distribution of the various passages is, in Milik's words, "most capricious."[13]

The discovery of *tefillin* containing the Decalogue is hailed by Karaites as proof of "another stage in the development of phylacteries," further proof in their eyes that *tefillin* are an invention, God forbid.[14] What they are unaware of (or conveniently ignore), is that the Torah content to be written on the *tefillin*-scrolls is not claimed by rabbinical tradition to be a legal tradition harking back to Moses. The only aspects of phylacteries taught as legal tradition from Sinai are the following ten (M.T. Laws of Tefillin, Mezuzah, and Torah Scroll ch.1-3):

1. The scrolls must be written with sturdy, black ink.

Oral Torah from Sinai

2. The scrolls must be made of properly-tanned *qelaf* (the dermis of the hide of a kosher animal, written on the surface facing the flesh).

3. The *tefillin*-boxes and their stitches must be perfectly square.

4. The shape of the letter "shin" must be embossed on the right and left sides of the head *tefillah*-box *(tefillah* is singular for *tefillin)*.

5. The scrolls must be wrapped in cloth.

6. The scrolls must be bound with hair from a kosher animal.

7. The *tefillin*-boxes must be stitched with the sinew of a kosher animal.

8. A hollow "passageway" must be made in the *tefillin*-boxes for the straps to pass through.

9. The outer surface of the straps must be black.

10. The straps of the head *tefillah*-box must be knotted in the traditional square knot that forms the letter *dalet* (with the protruding straps).

The Sages knew fully well that the content of the *tefillin*-scrolls was a matter of rabbinical ordinance, not ancient tradition. In fact, although the Sages clearly ruled that *tefillin* with anything other than four compartments are invalid, *even the number of compartments* is not a tradition from Sinai. Therefore any attack on rabbinical tradition based on finds of variant *tefillin*-passages, or how many compartments *tefillin* may have contained in the ancient past, is a "straw man" argument.

Hard Science Reveals the Antiquity of the Oral Tradition

However it is greatly significant that, since the Qumran *tefillin* with variant scriptural contents stray so far from rabbinical *halakhah*, researchers have concluded that they belonged to non-Pharisaic Jews.[13] *The discovery that square, leather tefillin were being worn by non-Pharisees 2,100 years ago is significant proof of Oral Tradition rejected by the Karaites:* We find that even a rival group to the ordained Sages, while rejecting certain legal rulings coming from their Pharisaic opponents, still practiced this Torah Commandment in a way that honored the details of Oral Torah that came from Sinai.

A Picture Worth a Thousand Words

While the findings at Qumran are significant, what would we not give to behold actual visual evidence of *tefillin* on Israelites as early as the Davidic monarchy, or even the period of the Judges. In fact, although they do not realize its true interpretation, such evidence exists and is well known to Egyptologists.

Below is an image from a relic discovered in the tomb of King Tutankhamun. For decades, it was commonly accepted that this pharaoh ruled circa 1334 to 1323 BCE. However, five intrepid scholars from the highest echelon of the academia in the field of ancient history of the Near East, have recently exposed the deep flaws in conventional Egyptian chronology, turning it on its head. In their book, *Centuries of Darkness* (Rutgers University Press, March 1993), Peter James, Dr. I.J. Thorpe, Dr. Nikos Kokkinos, Dr. Robert Morkot and John Frankish contend that, due to faulty, unsupportable dating methodology, the Egyptian chronology could be off by as much as 200-250 years. This is extremely problematic because scholars have used this Egyptian time line to calibrate and cross-date archaeological finds from ancient cultures spanning the Middle East. This has played havoc with the chronologies of all peoples of the Near East. The result has played well into the hands of a secular establishment at war with Judeo-Christian belief, allowing them to relegate the Bible's description and chronology of events to the category of mythology.

The first world-class scholar to publicly challenge the establishment on this issue and present his own solution was Immanuel Velikovsky (of blessed memory). In his timeless classic, *Ages in Chaos* (Buccaneer Books 1952), he showed how, when the histories of Egypt and Israel are brought into synchronization, the conquests recorded in the Bible match the archaeological record with remarkable accuracy. *According to the rectification of Peter James et al., King Tutankhamon is moved forward centuries, falling neatly into the era of Israel's Judges (pre-Monarchy).*

Consider now an Egyptian image from what is likely to be pre-First Temple:

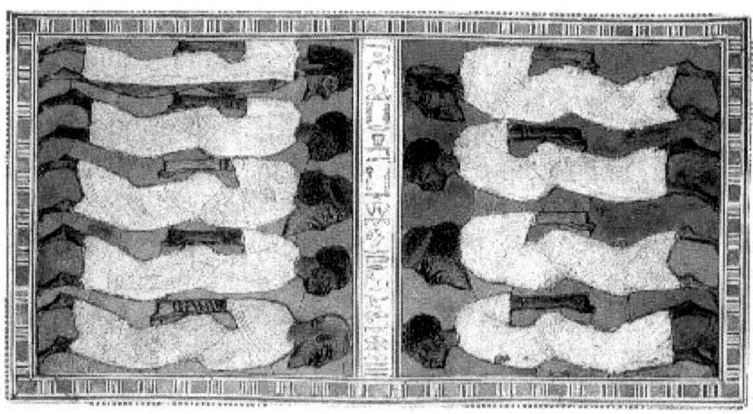

It is an image of the young pharaoh's footstool for him to symbolically place his feet on his enemies, the Ethiopians and Hebrews, who are depicted as bound captives.[15] One is struck by the realism of the image: It seems to be a snapshot depiction of nine actual individuals, each with his own distinct characteristics. The Israelites are clearly identifiable as such by their Semitic features, skin tone, and hair styles. We see one man sporting shorter hair and side-locks, two men with shaved or bald heads and side-locks, and two with the *nazirite* hairstyle of Habbani Yemenite Jewry. Notably, each one of these hairstyles remained among Yemenite Jews —the most ancient ethnic Jewish community— and that left the most untouched over the ravages of time.

Now notice their arms: While the visible arm of each captive is bound, *the visible arm of the elder man on the bottom right is wrapped with seven or eight windings of a black strap. They are not characteristic of the windings of a bound captive, but of the arm tefillah.* Being that arm and head *tefillin* are separate Torah commandments; according to authentic *halakhah* as recorded in the Talmud, a pious Jew wears his arm-*tefillah* even if he is unable to wear the head ornament (M.T. Laws of Tefillin, Mezuzah, and Torah Scroll 4:4). *It is not difficult to imagine a freshly-captured Torah-observant elder of those times, still wrapped in his arm tefillah.* This appears to have been the very case of the subject depicted.

From Ancient Writings Sacred to Non-Jews

Even the writings sacred to Christians (classical rejecters of the Oral Tradition) record Jesus' indirect recognition of the Commandment of *tefillin* amidst his tirade of insults against the very sect of Jews who preserved the Oral Law.[16] One barb is aimed at those Jews who were evidently trying to keep *HaShem*'s Laws of Jewish dress beautifully and proudly, and out of holy protest against the Hellenism and pagan Roman influence in Israel at the time:

> Everything they do is done for men to see: *They make their phylacteries wide* and the tassels on their garments long... (Matthew 23:5)
> New International Version ©1984,
> (See Footnote 5 to Introduction)

Note how this scathing rant against the Pharisees would have been the perfect place for Jesus to assail his Jewish brothers for having added to and replaced God's laws with human inventions, *HaShem*-forbid. In fact, according to the Christian Bible, not only does Jesus *not* brand phylacteries as an invention, he is cited later in the same chapter as encouraging Jews to keep such minutiae of the law, while practicing justice and mercy:

> Woe to you, scribes and Pharisees, hypocrites! For you tithe mint and dill and cumin, and have neglected the weightier provisions of the law: justice and mercy and faithfulness; but *these are the things you should have done without neglecting the others.* (Ibid. 23:23)
> New American Standard Bible [©1995]

Of course, to observant Jews and Noahides, the "New Testament" is not a reliable source, being a book of idolatry (M.T. Laws of Idolatry 9:4). NT has been exposed to be a set of confused texts and testimonies, with different gospel writers giving irreconcilable, contradicting accounts of the same events, such as Matthew 28:1-10 vs. John 20:1-18, conflicting dates as to when Jesus was supposedly crucified, and much more.[17] However, we learn above that for those who regard those verses to be the word of God — either the word of God Himself (Christians) or the word of a true prophet (Muslims)— *denying the authenticity of the Oral Torah tradition maintained by the Jewish People contradicts the founding document of their faith.*

Moreover, if one applies the method mentioned in the Introduction for discerning possible elements of truth in the New Testament, the fact that such verses pose an embarrassing challenge to the Church, increases their likelihood of being historically grounded.

17.
מסורת שנשתמרה על פה 1,500 שנה עד כתיבת המשנה
PROOF AT TEL SHILO OF TRADITION MAINTAINED ORALLY 1500 YEARS

According to *Seder `Olam Rabbah*, the great timeline of Jewish history written by Yose ben Halafta in 160 C.E., the tabernacle in Shilo stood for 369 years, from the year 2502 from Creation, until 2871 when it was destroyed. The year of its destruction corresponds to the 13th century B.C.E. – 1261 B.C.E to be exact. (See footnote 1 to Part I)

The Mishnah, written much, much later by Rabbi Yehudah HaNassi, was completed in roughly the year 189 C.E. – 3949 from Creation. *Between 1261 B.C.E to 189 C.E, is 1,450 years – one and a half millennia.*

Even when the *Mishkan* (Tabernacle) stood at Shilo, it was not as active a center of national worship as it should have been. According to Oral Tradition on the story at the opening of *Shemuel* (Book of Samuel), the pilgrimage of Israelites three times a year had all but ceased before Elqanah —righteous father of the prophet Samuel— inspired his brethren to resume the ascent to Shilo for the festivals. Considering how inactive it was at times even when the *Mishkan* stood, and how it was then re-established elsewhere, there can be little doubt: *When Shilo was destroyed, it was abandoned for many centuries,* becoming the very epitome of destruction in prophetic verse (Jer. 7:12, 7:14, 26:6, Ps. 78:60). This destruction and ensuing desolation until the Roman period has been upheld by archaeological excavation.[18]

During the next 1,500 years until the Mishnah was written down, the nation would suffer the collapse of three Israelite kingdoms and two exiles of nearly all its population. By that time, Shilo was a long-distant memory. It should go without saying that the way the *qodashim qallim* (offerings of light sanctity) were eaten at Shilo was long forgotten in Israel, since the rules had changed after the Tabernacle was re-established at Nov.

Yet, incredibly, the Sages maintained a fresh memory of minute details of the way the Hebrew pilgrims once ate of the holy offerings at Shilo – even though they had already been defunct for so long. All that time, the details of how the offerings were eaten at Shilo were taught orally from teacher to student so that 1,450 years later, the Sages remembered them as if Shilo were still standing just the day before.

The Mishnah teaches (Tr. *Zevahhim* 14:6) how, in Shilo — as opposed to later on— the *qodashim qalim* (offerings of light sanctity) were eaten *ba-khol ha-ro'eh* – within view of the Tabernacle. After the sacred offerings were consumed in their clay vessels, the Israelite pilgrim was not permitted to take the used clay vessels beyond that point; they needed to be smashed. Later in Nov, private altars were permitted, and such offerings were not even limited to the *Mishkan*, but could be eaten *ba-khol `are-Yisrael* – in all the cities of Israel. Finally, when the Divine Service reached its ultimate form with the building of the First Temple, those offerings could be eaten *lifnim min ha-hhomah* – anywhere within the walls of the city of Jerusalem, not necessarily within view of the Temple.

Indeed, the site of Tel Shilo today is found on its own small, central plateau, surrounded by high hills that form a natural amphitheater. Incredibly, as the author personally verified with a quality compass, the remaining base of the Tabernacle still stands aligned on a perfect East-West axis. The rocky remains of the holy structure's foundation, which supported the walls of stone and roof of animal skins, are clearly visible from the surrounding hills. *From the site of the sanctuary and outwards up to the perimeter of the surrounding peaks, are countless ancient shards of smashed pottery.* There can be no doubt: they hail back to the time when the Israelite pilgrims would smash their pottery after eating their offerings within view of the holy *Mishkan*.

In his podcast lecture series *P'shuto Shel Mikra* (traditional study of the Biblical text), in the segment on I Samuel ch.1, Rav Yitzchak Etshalom recalls his own observations hiking at Shilo. Explaining how pilgrims at Shilo needed to know just how far they could climb with their offerings while still being officially in sight of the Tabernacle, he describes the remains he saw of the ancient stone wall erected for that purpose. Discovered and maintained by a local friend of his, the ancient stone wall —still visible today— was clearly erected to mark the outer limits of where the offerings could be eaten. To this day, it runs along a good part of the hilly perimeter of the natural amphitheater.[19]

Many wonder why Israeli archaeologists do not appear interested in this incredible site. The author predicts that as long as Israel's political leadership refuses to recognize Shilo as an integral part of Israel's heritage —much less sovereign territory— it will continue to be snubbed by mainstream archaeology. After all, study of the area will reveal no finds justifying the Palestinian claim to Israel's biblical heartland, only the biblical truth of Samaria as the ancestral heritage of the Jewish People.

Oral Torah from Sinai

The author, looking closely at what is understood to be one of the holes for the original stakes by which the roof of *Mishkan Shilo* was tethered down.
(Courtesy of James D. Long 2009, used with permission)

2,899 years after the destruction of the Mishkan, the holes still remain in tact in broken lines along the rectangular stone perimeter, which once surrounded the sanctuary. (Ibid.)

Hard Science Reveals the Antiquity of the Oral Tradition

Seeing how trustworthy the Sages were in preserving such minute details about rituals which had been totally irrelevant and impractical for many centuries by their time, *consider how much more they can be trusted to have preserved the teachings that were relevant to them, and would remain relevant to Jews throughout the ages* – namely the details of the Oral Law of Moses: What really constitutes idolatry? Who is a Jew, who is not, and how can one convert? What are the actual Noahide Laws? What is the true interpretation of God's Commandments in the Torah regarding everything from the *kashruth* dietary laws to proper observance of Shabboth – the Sabbath day? And so on and so forth.

Moreover, this deep memory carried by the Sages of the Mishnah —extending back to Israel's hegemony of the land of Canaan over 3200 years ago— joins Point 14 above in establishing the Land of Israel as the aboriginal heartland of the People of Israel, her native sons.

I conclude this point with the immortal words of the Hasmonean hero Simeon the Maccabee, in his answer to enemies who would deny Israel's connection to her native land 2,150 years ago:

> We did not seize a foreign land, nor did we take control of foreign property; but rather the heritage of our forefathers that was conquered illegally at one point in time by our enemies. So when we had the chance, we took back the heritage of our forefathers.   (Book of Maccabees I, 15:33-34)[20]

18.
האם חז״ל היו צוללנים בעמוקי ים תהום רבה?
WERE THE TALMUDIC SAGES DEEP-SEA BIOLOGISTS?

The Talmudic Sages were experts in many things besides law and government: They had advanced knowledge in warfare, health, medicine, anatomy, psychology, astronomy, agriculture, and more. However, with all due respect, it can be assumed with some degree of confidence that they were not deep-sea divers. Neither they, nor any other people on earth at the time, had the technology to send deep-sea submersibles miles down to the bottom of the ocean's deep trenches, to learn what life existed.

Yet, while the Torah only teaches *this:*

> These you may eat of all that are in the water: *Whatsoever has fins and scales in the waters, in the seas, and in the rivers, them you may eat.* And all that have no fins and scales in the seas, and in the rivers, of all that swarm in the waters, and of all the living creatures that are in the waters – they are disgusting to you, and they shall be a disgust to you; you shall not eat of their flesh, and their carcasses you shall hold in disgust. Whatsoever has neither fins nor scales in the water – that is a disgusting thing to you. (Lev. 11:9-12)

…the ancient Sages of the Mishnah taught the following accompanying tradition about marine biology:

> Mishnah: Whatsoever has scales has fins, but there are some that have fins and no scales.
> (Tr. *Niddah* 6:9)

This rule is mentioned in RaMBaM's restatement of the law:

> With fish there are two signs [of ritual fitness], fins and scales. The fin is that with which it swims, and the scale forms the covering over its whole body. *Every fish [dagh] that has scales necessarily has fins.* If it possesses none at the moment, but is known to possess them when it matures, or if it has scales while it is in the sea but sheds them when it leaves the water – it is permitted. That whose scales do not cover its entire body, is permitted. Even if it has only one scale and one fin – it is permitted.
> (M.T. Laws of Forbidden Foods 1:24)

Note that although the Hebrew term *dagh* is loosely translated above as fish, the term includes all classes of swimming underwater creatures besides crustaceans and amphibians, ranging from squids and jellyfish to whales and dolphins. In other words, as the language of the Mishnah suggests ("Whatsoever has..."), the Sages taught a rule believed to apply to nearly all sea creatures.

Three things set this tradition of the Sages apart from the few, isolated beliefs about the physical world in Talmud (according to the science of the times) that have since been disproven[2] – (1) *its antiquity*, being from the Mishnah, (2) *in its not being taught as the opinion of a particular Sage*, and (3) its being hailed as a hallmark of the Torah's glory. According to Talmud, the Torah's mention of *both* scales *and* fins, which hints of this tradition, gave greatness and glory to the Law:

> Then why did not the All Merciful write scales and there would be no need for the mention of fins? Rabi Abahu replied and so it was also taught

at the school of Rabi Yishma'el: "To make the
teaching great and glorious."
   (Talmud, Tr. *Niddah* 51b, cf. Isaiah 42:21)

It stands to reason that Torah scholars of the stature of the Sages of the Mishnah would not teach a rule about the unknown in such emphatic terms, unless it was considered an undeniable, core Torah fact. They surely had enough foresight to know that, over the course of time, mankind would reach the deepest depths, and learn the truth. They might have best followed the ancient Mishnaic dictum, "Sages, beware of your words!" (Mishnah Tr. *Avoth* 1:11[13])

The true test of the "greatness and glory" afforded by this teaching, is if it stands up to the rigors of modern science. It should hold true according to the knowledge of the ocean's biodiversity amassed by our time. While much remains undiscovered, this is no small feat: We live in a time when man has sent three successful *manned* missions in deep-sea submersibles to the deepest known point of the ocean floor, the Mariana Trench. There, at 36,201 meters deep, the pressure is over 8 tons per square inch. If Mount Everest, the tallest point on earth were set inside, 2,183 meters (7,166 feet) of water would still remain above it.[21] This is besides the untold number of hours of filming, and physical samples of deep-sea life taken in unmanned scientific ventures over the years.

Indeed, according to what is known to modern marine biology, the ancient tradition recorded by Israel's sages 2,000 years ago has stood the test of time: *the "fins and scales rule" holds true to across all underwater creatures with no known exception.* For example, many sea creatures included in the term *dagh* —such as the Common Cuttlefish for example— indeed have fins, but only fish and reptiles (namely turtles and sea snakes) have scales.[22] However, we need only speak of fish, since they are the only sea creatures to have *both* fins *and* scales.

Not only do *all* fish have fins, it is their defining feature:

> *The fins are the most distinctive features of a fish,* composed of bony spines protruding from the body with skin covering them and joining them together, either in a webbed fashion, as seen in most bony fish, or more similar to a flipper, as seen in sharks. These usually serve as a means for the fish to swim. Fins can also be used for gliding or crawling, as seen in the flying fish and frogfish. Fins located in different places on the fish serve different purposes, such as moving forward, turning, and keeping an upright position.[23]

Such is not the case with scales, which is the feature of many but not all fish:

> The outer body of *many fish* is covered with scales. Some species are covered instead by scutes [a bony external plate or scale, as on the shell of a turtle, the skin of crocodilians, or the feet of some birds.[24] *Others have no outer covering on the skin;* these are called naked fish. Most fish are covered in a protective layer of slime (mucus). (Ibid.)

In summary, as the Sages taught: whatsoever has scales has fins, while some have fins but no scales.

Indeed, the Torah's mention of both scales and fins hints of this amazing fact, which was known to Israel solely by Oral Tradition for thousands of years, making the Torah "great and glorious." It conveys knowledge of the earth's biodiversity down to the ocean floor *from a time when such knowledge was unattainable.* It is evidence of the Divine origin of the Torah – the Oral and Written.

19.

האם חז"ל קבעו מראות על הירח?
DID THE SAGES MAKE USE OF MIRRORS ON THE MOON?

The Great Wisdom of the Ancients and Its Limitations

The way ancient civilizations and their technology have been traditionally treated in Western education is symptomatic of the widespread ignorance of the incredible wisdom of ancient civilizations. That is beginning to change. There is a growing awareness of ancient, colossal construction projects around the world that employed highly-advanced stone-masonry techniques, and growing dissatisfaction with the answers of the Scientific Orthodoxy. Evidence of ancient human flight and weapons of mass destruction, and even a 2,100-year old analog computer (or complex scientific calculator) from Greece,[25] can no longer be hidden from an increasingly open-minded public growing weary of the prejudices of the old guard of Darwinian-minded academia. The latter are finding it increasingly difficult to substantiate their dogma that civilization developed gradually from primitive stone-tool users.

While it is well beyond the scope of this book to treat this subject in any amount of detail, let the following assertion suffice: The weight of evidence supports the view of the ancients —from the Hebrews to the Chinese— that civilization began in a highly-advanced state, only to deteriorate over time on account of corruption, war, and natural disaster. That is, of course, before its recent climb in Europe. It took only 460 years since the beginnings of the Scientific Revolution for the West to evolve from a primitive technological state even lower than that of the Roman Empire, to our modern breathtaking abilities. No matter how sophisticated, our current level would have no doubt stunned the ancients of any previous age.

One technology that can be stated with a degree of confidence to be a brand new achievement for the human race is *space* flight. Even if valid evidence of "ancient astronaut" theory were found (much of it has been debunked), these theories center on aliens visiting the Earth (See Appendix III). *I have yet to learn of any serious theory promoting the notion that human beings ever conducted science in space before the modern age.*

Nasa's Science on the Moon, Israel's Tradition About the Moon

I venture there is not a single shred of any people's tradition —much less any other evidence— that could be twisted or spun to suggest that human beings ever did science on the moon, thereby learning the precise length of the synodic month: the exact length of time it takes for a complete monthly revolution of the moon around the earth. It would not happen until NASA's Apollo program, when retroreflectors were planted by men on the moon. By use of lasers on Earth aimed at the lunar retroreflectors, the precise distance between the Earth and moon could be determined, and the length of the synodic month could be discovered *to the sixth decimal place*. The Encyclopedia Brittanica writes:

> The synodic month, or complete cycle of phases of the Moon as seen from Earth, averages *29.530588 mean solar days* in length (i.e., 29 days 12 hours 44 minutes 3 seconds); because of perturbations in the Moon's orbit, the lengths of all astronomical months vary slightly.[26]

This information is general knowledge to be found in any online or printed source on the subject. What is glaringly absent from the public record, however, is that the elders of Israel had this information, accurate to the fifth decimal place, as an Oral Tradition for 3,300 years.

According to Oral Torah Tradition (M.T. Laws of Sanctification of Months 6:2-3), preserved and passed down by Israel's ancient Sages for millennia, the precise length of time between one new moon and the next is 29 days 12 hours and 793 parts of an hour (the hour is divided into 1080 parts). Note the following equation:

$$\frac{793}{1080} = \underset{\text{Hours}}{(0.734529)} = \underset{\text{Days}}{(0.03059)}$$

If 29.5 days (29 days + 12 hours) is added, we get a total of **29.53059 days**.[17]

Until the Babylonians learned this figure later (as will be explained below), such exactitude was unmatched in the ancient world. Other ancient peoples such as the Hindus came close, but their calendars are based on less-accurate approximations.[27]

According to the Sages, this knowledge of the precise length of the synodic month was an awesome secret taught to the Jewish People at Mt. Sinai by the Almighty, for Israel to fulfill one of the Commandments of His Torah.

It is a positive Torah Commandment to determine the first day of the month according to the sight of the New Moon. To briefly summarize one of the most complex laws of the Torah: Between two days —the 29th and 30th days of the Hebrew month— Israel's ordained Sages must declare the sighting of the new moon. They are to do so by following a formal procedure by which even lay witnesses come to the

Temple to testify to their sighting of the first sliver of the lunar crescent. Jews outside of Jerusalem could only know on what days their holidays would fall by the work of messengers on horseback, who would inform every Jewish community within a day's reach that the new month had indeed been inaugurated. Clearly the sages needed to be careful to ascertain whether or not a witness had merely seen a mirage, or was even sent as a spiteful ploy to mislead the public, God forbid.

They needed to employ astronomical calculations by which they could know the courses of the heavenly bodies in order to see whether or not it was possible for the new moon to appear at the time and place related by a witness. Knowledge of the precise length of the synodic month was a key tool Given to them by *HaShem* for this holy work.

It was known and referred to as such by Ezekiel, who wrote:

> And My hand shall be against the prophets who predict vanity, and who divine lies; *they shall not share in the secret of My people*, neither shall they be written in the register of the house of Israel, neither shall they enter the land of Israel; and you shall know that I am the Lord *HaShem*.
>
> (Ez. 13:9)

"The secret of My people" referred to in this verse refers to the council for the intercalculation of the months (Talmud Tr. *Kethuboth* 112a).

Why We Believe Israel Knew It First

Some may insist on believing the Babylonians arrived at this figure first – despite the evidence to the contrary. The Book of Daniel records the overwhelmingly superior wisdom of captive Hebrew scholars over their Babylonian counterparts, and their elevation by the king over all other scholars in the realm:

> Now as for these four [Hebrew] youths, God gave them knowledge and skill in all learning and wisdom; and Daniel had understanding in all visions and dreams. And at the end of the days which the king had appointed for bringing them in, the chief of the officers brought them in before Nebuchadnezzar. And the king spoke with them; and among them all was found none like Daniel, Hananiah, Mishael, and Azariah; therefore stood they before the king. *And in all matters of wisdom and understanding, that the king inquired of them, he found them ten times better than all the magicians and enchanters that were in all his realm.* (Dan. 1:17-10)

Chapter Two is an example of Divine secrets the Babylonians managed to learn from captive Hebrew scholars. In fact, after Daniel reveals secrets in Nebuchadnezzar's dream, the emperor proceeded *to worship Daniel as a god*, elevated him as his vizier over all Babylon, and placed him in charge over all the scholars of Babylon:

> Then the king Nebuchadnezzar fell upon his face, and worshipped Daniel, and commanded that they should offer an offering and sweet odours unto him. The king spoke unto Daniel, and said: 'Of a truth it is, that your God is the God of gods, and the Lord of kings, and a revealer of secrets, seeing thou hast been able to reveal this secret.' Then the king made Daniel great, and gave him many great gifts, *and made him to rule over the whole*

> *province of Babylon, and to be chief prefect over all the wise men of Babylon.* (Ibid. 2:46-48)

According to Oral Tradition (see footnote 1 of Part I) Daniel interpreted Nebuchadnezzar's dream in 3340 A.C., or 421 B.C.E. This follows the meteoric rise of Hebrew scholarship in Babylonia in the years before that, as the passages quoted above relate. Consider now the calendar system that was just set into motion three years prior:

> With the actual observation of the crescent by the Babylonians, eventually a pattern emerged, and this began to suggest a *cycle*. This was the *19 Year Cycle*, discussed below. The cycle settled down into its classic form in the 19 year period beginning in 424 BC
> [R.A. Parker & W.H. Dubberstein, *Babylonian Chronology*, Providence, R.I., 1956][28]

Is it pure coincidence that the 19-year cycle of the Babylonian calendar began in 424 B.C.E. – just three years before Nebuchadnezzar's dream? This is the exact time period, following the discovery of the genius of the captive scholars of Israel (bearers of the secrets of the 19-year-cycle of the Sinaitic calendar), when Hebrew wisdom was first integrated into Babylonian scholarship. *In other words, just as captive Israeli elders become dominant among Babylonia's elite scholarship, the 19-year-cycle Babylonian calendar (mirroring Israel's) begins.*

Besides the historical logic for Israel having been the original bearer of the secrets of the lunar cycle, one must remember that Israel's Oral Tradition —like the Bible— is no denier of non-Jewish wisdom, and no horn blower for inherent Hebrew "superiority." According to its brutal honesty, the Bible lays bare the memory of even the worst sins of the Hebrew nation. It exposes the faults of even its most righteous heroes, and gives equal treatment to the virtuous and wise men of foreign nations. Even the wisdom of the descendants of Cain (as the progenitors of cattle-raising, musical instruments, and metallurgy (Gen. 4:20-22) and the prophecy of Balaam (Num. ch. 22-24) are given eternal recognition.

The Oral Tradition follows suit. There is no shortage of respect for foreign science among the bearers of that Tradition, the Talmudic Sages. They taught candidly:

> If any man will say to you that there is wisdom among the gentiles, believe him.
> *(Ekhah Rabbah* 2)

In fact, RaMBaM considered the intellectual level of Aristotle close to that of prophecy *(Guide for the Perplexed)*. Considering this traditional view on foreign wisdom, besides it being out of character for the rabbis to lie in regards to origin of the wisdom of the lunar cycle, what benefit would it bring? *Yet these same Talmudic sages who established the belief in non-Jewish wisdom as a principle, insisted that this particular science —the secrets of the moon's cycle— was a divine secret from God to Israel at Sinai.*

In conclusion, we can put our well-deserved trust in Israel's humble, ordained scholarship of old, as to the source of this phenomenal knowledge known to them. It is rational to assume, in keeping with the Oral Tradition, that Israel's conquerors managed to learn to this secret from Israel, and not Israel from them. Israel's tradition of the precise length of the synodic month stands as further evidence of the antiquity of Israel's Oral Torah tradition, and hints to its Divine origin.

20.
האם חז"ל ראו שינויים מיקרוסקופיים בתוך גוף עובר אנושי?
WERE THE ANCIENT SAGES EMBRYOLOGISTS?

We can safely assume the scholars of old, who lived long before the microscope was invented and cells were first discovered, had only a rough, general understanding of human embryology (the study of the embryo from conception until the fetal stage, which begins at 9 weeks after fertilization). This understanding was, no doubt, the result of visual evidence: Over the centuries, scholars and healers would observe fetuses that, by chance, were aborted at different stages in their development, and would add their own observations to the wisdom they had inherited from earlier generations. This is how different ancient religious traditions had a good general idea as to when gender determination (when an embryo begins to develop distinctly as male or female) takes place.

However, at a time before cell theory —much less the awareness of the inner contents of cells— the ability to detect chemical reactions at the chromosomal level within cells was far beyond them. *It should therefore go without saying that they had no means of determining the precise time that gender determination in the embryo initially occurs, even before it becomes observable to the naked eye.* Unless we are to entertain the entertaining notion that certain ancient scholars had unfair access to *space aliens* who leaked such secrets, such knowledge in the hands of Israel's ordained Sages 2,000 years ago is clearly *prophetic*.

The following is a *beraitha* (an ancient ordained Rabbinical tradition that precedes the Mishnah, but is not included in it) taught by Rav:

> Within the first three days a man should pray that the seed should not putrefy [become impotent, that conception should occur],
>
> from the third to the fortieth day he should pray that the child should be a male;
>
> from the fortieth day to three months he should pray that it should not be a sandal; [a kind of abortion resembling a flat-shaped fish called sandal],
>
> from three months to six months he should pray that it should not be still-born; from six months to nine months he should pray for a safe delivery.

This is related to the ancient Mishnaic ruling that if a woman miscarries prior to forty days, it is not deemed a true pregnancy (Talmud Tr. *Niddah* 30a). Prior to 40 days, an embryo is considered "like water" (Tr. *Yevamoth* 69b).

Incredibly, the 40th day mark precisely matches the figure discovered by modern embryology under laboratory conditions. The crucial gender-determining event is a microbiological occurrence known as the "SRY event." "SRY" stands for the place where this microscopic event occurs: the "**S**ex-determining **R**egion of the **Y** chromosome. This minute place on this single chromosome is within the nucleus of the cell, which is about one tenth the size of the point of a pin! It occurs in "the second half of week six," which means between 39 and 42 days:

NOTE: *all males have both one X and one Y chromosome, while females have two Xs.*

> A crucial event that determines whether the embryo will develop into a male or female occurs

in the second half of week six. If the Y chromosome [the genetic component for maleness] is present in the embryo's cells, a gene within the short arm of the chromosome called SRY will turn, on initiating a chemical chain reaction that will turn on other genes and stimulate the production of male hormones. If the X chromosome is present, or if the SRY gene is missing from the Y chromosome, the embryo will develop into a female via mechanisms that are not fully understood.[29]

No ancient sage or text can match such exactitude. Compare, for example, the figure given in the Qur'an. Contemporary Moslem scholars —educated both in modern medicine as well as their religious texts— exult over the following Qur'anic teaching:

> When 42 nights have passed over the conception, Allah sends an angel to it, who shapes it (into human form) and makes its ears, eyes, skin, muscles and bones. Then he says; 'O Lord, is it male or female?', and your Lord decides what He wishes and the angel records it.[30]

While it is indeed close to the time frame revealed by embryologists in the laboratory, it is slightly late: The passing of 42 complete days marks the beginning of the seventh week, while 40 days rests neatly "within the latter half of the sixth" (the wording of the scientists). While we can conjecture that there may well be cases in which gender determination takes place only after 6 complete weeks; *in the majority of cases, the SRY event has already occurred by the time Allah is believed to have made the decision.*

As incredible as this proof of the Oral Tradition is by itself, the knowledge of the Sages was even more sophisticated.

Rabbi Yishma`el expressed his understanding that, while maleness is determined in 40 days, it actually takes *80 days* for a non-male embryo to become fully formed as a female. To debate his detractors who cited a story about handmaidens of Cleopatra, Rabbi Yishma`el related a similar account (note the blow this deals the above Qur`anic source):

> Then said R. Ishmael to them: A story is told of Cleopatra the Grecian queen that when her handmaids were sentenced to death under a government order they were subjected to a test and it was found that a male embryo was fully fashioned on the forty-first day and a female embryo on the eighty-first day.
> (Talmud Tr. *Niddah* 30a)

Leah Poltorak, an MS in biophysics and PhD in molecular biology, explains the marvel of the Rabbis' awareness of the binary nature of gender determination.[31] "If forty days pass and the fetus does not develop as a male, isn't it automatically deemed a female?" she asks. On a basic level, yes: Poltorak proceeds to explain the complex series of genetically-programmed events in the embryo that translate to the popular adage: "we all start out as girls" in the womb. In biological terminology, this means:

> By default, every embryo would develop as a female, and it only becomes male upon the successful expression of the SRY gene located on the short arm of the Y chromosome [the SRY event, as explained above] (Ibid.).

Before we continue, note how this alone reveals another marvel of the Sages' wisdom: The *beraitha* quoted earlier teaches "from the third to the fortieth day he should pray that the child should be *a male*." There is no prayer that the fetus should *not* become female. Why? *The ancient Sages seem to have been aware that, while the embryo develops by default into a female, something special must occur for the embryo to become a male* – warranting a special prayer if a son is desired.[32]

However, as the Sages apparently understood, even when the juncture to the path of maleness has been passed, there is no guarantee the process will continue uninterrupted, until 80 days have passed, and the fetus becomes fully female. A number of problems can occur. Poltorak explains:

> ... in the case of SRY slippage during the pairing of the parental chromosomes, if the resulting embryo had the XX composition [ordinarily female], it would produce a male, though infertile. If the embryo had the XY chromosomal composition [ordinarily male], without the SRY gene on the Y chromosome, the male development would not take place. Though such a child would look female, it would not have the ability to perform the essential female function of bearing offspring.
>
> Even if the parental chromosomes are intact, some chromosomal mistakes could interfere with the normal gender development of the embryo. ...
>
> Some authors' claim that up to 2 percent of live births may show deviation from the ideal male or female...
>
> In a normally developing embryo, the indifferent gonad begins to develop into recognizable female structures by the twelfth week [78 days]. Only at that period is it possible to judge the success of

female development. This coincides with Rabbi Ishmael's eighty days."

We can only marvel at the foresight of the Talmud Sages, who, almost a millennium and a half before the Age of Science, not only understood that both parents contribute to the biological development of their child, but were able to accurately determine the time line of embryonic gender development." (Ibid.)

Indeed: It is further evidence that the Oral Tradition has roots in Divine wisdom given to Israel at Sinai.

21.
מסורות בעל פה מימות שעיבוד ישראל במצריים
ORAL TRADITION PRESERVED SINCE OUR SLAVERY IN EGYPT

It is the firm belief of this author that *Riddle of the Exodus: Startling Parallels Between Ancient Jewish Sources and the Egyptian Archaeological Record,* by James D. Long,[33] should be required reading for high school and college students the world over. With his explicit permission, I will quote and borrow heavily from his book here, mainly in my own words, including my own insights.

Despite the naysayers as to the origins of *Sefer haYashar* (the *midrash* [piece of ancient rabbinical legendary literature] analyzed in *Riddle*), and the fact that new layers were certainly added to the original text over the millennia; the text in our possession is a primary source for the classical Torah commentaries of Rash"i and *Me`am Lo`ez*, who relied on it heavily. Its original translation into English in 1840 "contains endorsements from Hebrew linguists and biblical scholars attesting to the authenticity of the work." (Ibid. p.64-65) However, nothing more can be said for the accuracy or authenticity of the traditions recorded in *Sefer haYashar*, unless and until one finds precise correlations between details in the *midrash* and those discovered by archaeologists and historians. Precise and profound correlations are to be found.

According to *Sefer haYashar*, the pharaoh who imposed harsh servitude on the Hebrews, referred to by biblical historians as "the pharaoh of the oppression," lived a remarkable *94 years*. It is his death that *HaShem* referred to when telling Moses, "all who seek your life have died." The name of this sadistic tyrant was *Melol*. At the end of his long, accursed rule, *his firstborn son should have inherited his throne, but was found to be mentally incompetent.* His brother, Adikam, at the age of 20, became the next pharaoh, reigning four years – which explains how he escaped the destruction of the firstborn.

Consider the "Kings List, a record of seventy-five kings from the First to the 19th Dynasty" carved on the wall of the ancient temple at Abydos in Southern Egypt. Lo and behold, among the very last pharaohs of Old Kingdom — before it utterly crashed due to "unexplained causes" according to the Egyptologists— was Pepi II, also called *Merire*. (There was no hieroglyph for the "L" sound, so "L" was pronounced as "L," like in Japanese. M-R-R = M-L-L). He enjoyed the longest reign in Egyptian history: a stunning *94 years*. His reign is also recorded in the Turin Royal Canon (the official name for an ancient papyrus housed in Turin, Italy, with information about the pharaohs of the past) as being *succeeded by a son who reigned only a year,* preceding the last reign of the dynasty.

Although this may seem to contradict *Sefer haYashar*, it doesn't. The events of the death of pharaoh Melol (*Melol/Merire*), Moses' return to Egypt, and the beginning of the Ten Strikes (Ten Plagues) to Egypt *all took the span of a year*. According to midrashic tradition, pharaoh Melol suffered from an incurable skin disease for years. By the time he died, his body was already in an advanced state of decay. During his father's last years and even the short-lived rule of his handicapped brother, Adikam, may have fulfilled the functions of leadership, thus being remembered in *Sefer haYashar* as the direct successor to Melol. It is he who would have pursued the Hebrews into the sea with the finest soldiers of Egypt, only to be drowned in the Red Sea.

Who replaces "Neferkare the Younger" (Adikam) when he disappears from history after such a short reign? No surprise here: there being no male heir to the throne, *a woman becomes pharaoh* – a most rare event in the Old Kingdom. The empire was clearly plagued with a crisis that not only removed Neferare/Adikam's firstborn from the picture, but other senior male relatives who could have assumed the throne. This fact is extremely important, for the Torah tells us that the firstborn son and crown prince of Pharaoh (the newer pharaoh who pursued the Hebrews in the sea) died in the Tenth Plague that struck down the flower of Egypt – her firstborn sons (Ex. 12:29-30).

What is incredible is that this amazing parallel, besides agreeing with our Oral history, proves that these kings of Egypt (before *HaShem* brought them to their knees) were the last pharaohs of the 6th dynasty, which we know to be the fall of the Old Kingdom. There is consensus from mainstream academia that the Old Kingdom did, for unknown reasons, collapse seemingly overnight. When the discredited conventional dating is corrected (according the wave of modern scholarship mention above in Point #16), the fall of the Old Kingdom coincides with the Biblical timing of the Exodus.

Housed in the Museum of Leiden (Netherlands) is a damaged, ancient Egyptian papyrus, known to us as the

"Admonitions of Ipuwer." It is a list of dreadful, cataclysmic events that shook the Egyptian nation to its very foundations at the time. *It is dated to the end of the Old Kingdom, the same final days of Pepi II and his son, Neferkare the Younger (Melol and Adikam. It reads like a newscast straight from the scene of the Ten Plagues.* I quote from *Riddle of the Exodus* (In all quotes, the use of italics is my own addition):

* Blood...

> Papyrus 2:6 Plague is throughout the land. Blood is everywhere.

> Papyrus 2:10 Forsooth, the river is blood.

> Papyrus 7:4 Behold Egypt is poured out like water. He who poured water on the ground, he has captured the strong man in misery. *[According to Exodus 4:9 and 4:30, one sign Moses performed publicly was pouring water out on the ground, becoming blood. "The strong man" here might be a euphemism, even a degrading reference, to the pharaoh]*

* Fiery hail...

> Papyrus 2:10 Forsooth, gates, columns and walls are consumed by fire; while the [.......] of the king's palace stands firm and endures.

> Papyrus 4:14 Trees are destroyed...

* Plague...

> Papyrus 4:1 Forsooth, hair has fallen out for everyone.

Papyrus 5:4 Forsooth, all animals, their hearts weep. Cattle moan because of the state of the land.

* Darkness...

Papyrus 9:8-10 Destruction...the land is in darkness.

* Ex-slaves Spoil Egypt...

Papyrus 2:4 Forsooth, poor men have become the owners of good things. He who could not make his own sandals is now the possessor of riches.

Papyrus 3:3 Gold, blue stone, silver, carnelian, bronze and Yebet sone and ....are fastened to the necks of female slaves.

* The `erev rav... (mixed multitude of Egyptians who left with the *Banei Yisrael)*

Papyrus 3:14 Those who were Egyptians have become foreigners.

* The Pillar of Fire...

Papyrus 7:1 Behold the fire mounted up on high. Its burning goes forth before the enemies of the land.

* Hatred for the *B'nei Yisrael*...

...Would that he [pharaoh] perceived their nature in the first generation (of men); then he would have repressed their evils, he would have stretched forth (his) arm against it, he would have destroyed their seed and their inheritance...."

Long also discusses an unknown artifact of huge importance. The Egyptians apparently enshrined the memory of the Exodus in the hieroglyphs covering an ancient, black granite *naos* on display at Ismailia, in Egypt. It was a mystery until 1890, when it was translated, but it should not be today. It reads:

> Evil fell on the earth…the earth was in great affliction…great disturbance in the residence."
>
> …neither man nor the gods could see the faces of those next to them…

The granite artifact tells how the king and his men fight "the evil ones at the Place of the Whirlpool," whose location is described as *Pi-Kharoti* (= *Pi ha-hhiroth,* see Exodus 14:2,9, Leviticus 33:7). It relates how the pharaoh commands his men to follow him, and then disappears from their midst: "There at *Pi-Kharoti* the Pharaoh is thrown by a whirlwind high into the air and seen no more." (Consider the wind that blew the whole night, drying the seabed.) He is referred to as Pharaoh *T'hom*. Incredibly, *T'hom* is the Hebrew word for the depths of the sea. The memorial stone seems to refer to this pharaoh as *"Pharaoh of the Depths!"*

James D. Long, the esteemed author, makes a fascinating linguistic connection that directly links Pharaoh *T'hom* to Neferkare the Younger, who was lost in the sea. In the Egyptian records, he is also referred to as *Nem-t'm-saf* II." Could the consonants "t" and "m" be a shortened form of *T'hom*? An even more direct correlation can be made between the name of the pharaoh *T'hom* and one of the treasure cities we built in Egypt: *Pit'om* (Ex. 1:11). Long writes, "The prefix 'Pi' can be roughly translated 'city of' or 'dwelling of.' The above verse from the book of Exodus could be referring in retrospect to the "City of T'houm": city of the pharaoh who would be lost in the raging sea.

There are more amazing parallels and correlations, but they are beyond the scope of this book. One must ultimately read *Riddle of the Exodus*. In the context of this book, what is most incredible is that they not only prove the truth and accuracy of the Written Bible, but the truth and accuracy of the Oral Tradition by which the our national memory was preserved. We can say here as we did above in light of the finds at the *Tel Shilo* (Point #17). Seeing how trustworthy the Sages were in preserving minute historical details in Israel's legends, in regards matters that were not of practical use (names and lengths of rule of the pharaohs), *consider how much more they can be trusted to have preserved the teachings that were relevant to them, and would remain relevant to Jews throughout the ages* – namely the details of the Oral Law of Moses.

22.
הזכר בידי כומרי חבש לקבלה וזריקת
דם זבחים על פי תורת הכוהנים במשנה
HOW DID PRIESTLY RITES IN MISHNAH ENTER ABASSYNIAN TRADITION?

Imagine what a support for the antiquity of the Oral Law it would be, if we found a memory of the *same, unique* Torah traditions as preserved in the most ancient source of the Oral Law (the Mishnah), being preserved to this day by isolated elders of a people known to be descended from ancient Israelites – a people whose ancestors became separated from the Jewish people *much earlier than 2,000 years ago...* It would need to be an ancient people...

- who were known to have originated from the nation of Israel in ancient times.

- who separated from the Jewish People well before 2,000 years ago, well before the Sages of the Mishnah were born.

- whose traditions could not have been easily derived from the Bible by pure logic.

- and whose Oral traditions, a well-engrained part of their own traditions from time immemorial, were recorded *before* their elders had any access to rabbinical literature.

The Abyssinian Christians of Ethiopia happen to be all of the above.

KEY CLARIFICATIONS:

1) It must be made clear that there is no intention or desire in this section to infer our approval of the Abyssinian Christian religion or practices, Heaven forbid. According to Torah Tradition, which the Jewish People preserved in its entirety, worshipping a man, or any created thing for that matter, is pure idolatry (M.T. Laws of Idolatry 2:1, 3:1-6). Even if its devotees had somehow preserved the way Moses himself worshipped *HaShem*, and worship their idol accordingly – it adds no legitimacy: It is idolatry, through and through. Moreover, since the Holy Temple in Jerusalem was built, even burnt-offerings to *HaShem* outside of the Temple are a severe Torah crime for Jews (Deut. 12:13-14).

On the contrary, we are examining details of Abyssinian oral tradition that hark back to their pre-Christian past, when they worshipped *HaShem* only – the common past they share with today's Ethiopian Jews. It reveals a totally distinct, isolated, ancient memory of Hebrew altar service with matching details to the Oral Torah instruction preserved only in rabbinical literature. Despite widespread misconceptions, it matches the oral tradition of another isolated people descended from Jews: the Lemba-Igbo tribe. It is a profound yet unknown proof of the authenticity of the Oral Law as it was preserved by the Sages of the Mishnah.

2) *There is no intention here to promulgate the belief that the Ark of the Covenant is in Ethiopia.* This would contradict the majority opinion of the ordained sages who discussed this matter in the Sanhedrin (Jerusalem Talmud, Tr. *Sheqalim* 6:1). It is my opinion that the Tabernacle cult brought to Ethiopia by Israelite priests was centered on a replica of the Ark. There is much evidence for this. The point of this section is purely to discuss traditions from that ancient Tabernacle cult, regardless of the origin or nature of the relic at its center.

Background: The Ancient Israelite Origin of Ethiopian Religion

The Abyssinian Christians of Ethiopia are a non-Jewish people with an Israelite past in remote antiquity. They share a common ancient past with today's Ethiopian Jewry, the *Beta Yisrael* (the commonly-used term *Falasha* is a derogatory term), a tiny remnant of a once-mighty Hebrew kingdom that flourished for centuries in antiquity. Despite their genetic dissimilarity to other ethnic communities of the Israelite Diaspora (whose genetic markers indicate their common origin in the Land of Israel), in light of the customs they have maintained and written testimonies about them from travelers, their Israelite heritage is undeniable.[34]

The ancient Hebrew ancestors of Ethiopia's Jews and Christians separated and were isolated from the rest of the Jewish People so far back in time, that until the *Beta*

Hard Science Reveals the Antiquity of the Oral Tradition

Yisrael's recent repatriation to the land of Israel by the modern state, *they had no tradition of the public fasts ordained after the destruction of the First Temple – only their own fast day 'Sigd', which expresses their longing to return to Zion.* Yemenite Jewish elders maintained a little-known tradition regarding the earliest origins of the community: During Israel's bitter sojourn in Egypt, Ethiopia was a safe haven to which many Hebrew slaves escaped. When their Israelite brethren were eventually led out of Egypt by Moses and received the Torah at Sinai, the community learned of the covenant, and voluntarily accepted it upon themselves (from private conversation with Rabbi Yosef Qafihh of blessed memory).

According to the common tradition of Ethiopian Jews and Christians of the region, accepted as historical fact by mainstream academia, Christianity only entered Ethiopia in 331 C.E., by a Syrian monk. According to a rare Ethiopic manuscript from the Tigrayan fortress of Magdala:

> Christianity was introduced into Abyssinia 331 years after the birth of [the Christian deity] by Abuna Salam, whose former name was Frumentos or Frumentius. At that time the Ethiopian kings reigned over Axum. *Before the Christian religion was known in Ethiopia half the inhabitants were Jews,* who observed the Law; the other half were worshippers of Sando, the dragon (p.141).[35]

Another common tradition of local Jews and Christians is that the Ark of the Covenant was brought into Ethiopia during the First Temple era.

NOTE: See Appendix IV for 1) a background on the cult of the Ark of the Covenant, 2) how it arrived in Ethiopia, 3) the strong archaeological and historical evidence that supports this, 4) how this in no way contradicts rabbinical tradition, and 5) how it corroborates the ancient traditions of the Lemba-Igbo tribe of

Nigeria [a tribe whose members possess the Kohen gene and Semitic practices from the pre-colonial era in Africa].

The Ancient Memory of an Oral Tradition that Still Remains

Theorizing over the true fate of the Ark and what the Abyssinian church truly possesses at this time is a popular subject of conjecture that is beyond the scope of this work. In Appendix IV, I substantiate the tradition of the Ark's movement through Ethiopia so that the reader can fully appreciate the significance of the traditions of the Abyssinian priests at Tana Qirqos – a remote island in Lake Tana that provided a totally isolated haven for its monks for millennia. Significantly, the site is revered by both local Christians and Jews alike as having been a past resting-place for the Ark, and its monks maintained a vivid memory of the unique traditions from that bygone era. Of particular interest to us is their living memory as to how the Israelite priests in Ethiopia collected and sprinkled the blood of animals prepared for sacrifice *as it is written in a book they never possessed: the Mishnah.*

In his rigorous pursuit of the lost Ark, British researcher Graham Hancock combed Ethiopia in search of the truth behind the myths and legends. Despite the criticism from the jealous academia, and notwithstanding his subtle anti-Orthodox bias, Hancock's research contained in his bestseller *The Sign and the Seal*[35] yields the most significant finds on the subject this author has as come across in his own research. They match what I have learned from traditional, Torah-observant Ethiopian Jews in Beit Shemesh, Israel.

Taking a tip from the locals, Hancock journeyed to the isolated Lake Tana and its island, Tana Qirqos. When he, by means of translator, asked the senior priest by the name of Memhir Fisseha for details as to how they would offer their burnt-offerings; the monk proceeded to describe a process so similar to Israel's ancient priestly tradition, that it included details found only in the Mishnah Tr. *Yomah*. Fisseha explained:

> We were Jews. We performed sacrifice. The blood from the lamb was collected in a bowl...a gomer [not belonging to any Ethiopian language, this is a plainly Hebrew word meaning "finish, complete" – i.e. the vessel that "completes" the sacrifice, when the animal's life is "finished"]. Then it was scattered over some stones, some small stones. They are here still here. ... After the sacrifice, some was scattered over the stones and some on to the tent that contained the Ark. The remainder was poured into these hollows.' (Ibid. pp. 214-215)

When the researcher asked if he could be shown how this was done, Memhir Fisseha did the following:

> He then positioned himself next to the stones with the bowl in his left hand, dipped into it with his right forefinger, *swept his right hand above the level of his head and commenced an up-and-down motion.* 'The blood was scattered in this way,' he said, 'over the stones and over the tent of the Ark. Afterwards, as I told you, what was left was poured thus.' He then tipped the bowl sideways above the cup-shaped hollows in the tops of the pillars. (Ibid. p. 216)

In the exhaustive book on his findings, Hancock makes the following observation:

> *It was not until I turned to the Mishnah, however, the compilation in written form of the early oral Jewish law, that I realized just how authentic Memhir Fisseha's account in fact had been.* In the

tractate known as Yomah, in the second division of the Mishnah, I found detailed descriptions of the sacrificial rituals carried out by the High Priest within Solomon's Temple in front of the curtain that shielded the Ark of the Convenant from the gaze of the laity. ...

I read that the blood of the victim —whether lamb, goat, or bullock— was collected and given 'to one that should stir it up ... so that it should not congeal'. *Then the priest, having emerged from the sanctuary, 'took the blood from him that was stirring it and entered and stood again on the place whereon he had stood, and sprinkled the blood once upwards and seven times downwards.*

Where, exactly, did the priest sprinkle this blood? According to the Mishnah he sprinkled it 'on the curtain outside, opposite the Ark, once upwards and seven times downwards, *not as though he intended to sprinkle upwards or downwards, but as though he were wielding a whip* ... He then sprinkled the cleansed surface of the altar seven times and poured out the residue of the blood.

It seemed highly improbable that Memhir Fisseha had ever read the Mishnah. As a Christian he would have no reason to do so; nor would he have had access to such a book on his remote island; nor could he have understood any of the languages into which it had been translated. *Yet his hand movements, when he had shown how the scattering of the blood was done, had been precisely those of a man wielding a whip.* And he had spoken confidently of the blood being poured not only upon the altar stones but also 'on the tent of the Ark.'   (Ibid. pp. 217-218)

Hard Science Reveals the Antiquity of the Oral Tradition

Remember, Tana Qirqos is so remote that it provided a haven of near total isolation for priests for millennia. Add to that the fact that the Abyssinians —both Christians and Jews— had no awareness of the Mishnah, no access to it, and certainly no ability to read or have it translated. Yes, even the Ethiopians who remained Jewish, ignorant of the events of Purim and Rededication of the Temple (Hannukah) until the last century, are known to have lost contact with mainstream Jewry *centuries* before the Mishnah was written – in fact, considering their own Torah scroll was traditionally written in the language Ge'ez (Ethiopic), the Jewish elders had most likely lost their knowledge of Hebrew by then as well.

Only now one can appreciate what significant proof this is of the deep antiquity of the Oral Law and how faithfully it was recorded by the Sages of Israel.

Ironically, the Abyssinian Christians, historical enemies and decimators of the Ethiopian Jewish community, would be among the last people on earth with a desire to lend such credibility to the Jewish faith. Ironically, *HaShem* would have it that the traditions taught from their own mouth give testimony to the authenticity of the Oral Tradition from Sinai: the hallmark of the precious faith they tried to destroy.

(For a full analysis of the authenticity of the traditions at Tana Qirqos and my understanding as to the nature of the relic at its center, see Appendix IV.)

NOTES

(1) Known in Hebrew as *Yam Kinnereth* (Jerusalem Talmud, Tr. *Meghillah* 2a [bottom]), *Yam Tiveriyah* (M.T. Laws of Monetary Damages 5:8[6]) and *Yam shel Ginosar* (Talmud Tr. *Bava Bathra* 122a).

(2) Rabbi Avraham son of RaMBaM, *Ma'amar `Al Derashoth Hhaza"l* ("Discourses on the Sayings of the Rabbis"). Published online at the website of Mikhleleth Hertzog - Gush Etzion: *Da`ath Limude Yahaduth we-Ruahh*, managed by Prof. Yehudah Eisenberg. *www.daat.ac.il/daat/mahshevt/agadot/hagada1-2.htm*

(3) For sources of dates, see footnote 1 to Part II. All post-475 C.E. dates are based on commonly accepted historical dates from online encyclopedias.

(4) An elucidation of RaMBaN's identification of the two Temples as the historical manifestation of the "heavenly lights" by Rabbi Benjamin Blech *shlit"a*. It is based on the Second Temple having lacked five things which had been in Solomon's Temple: the Ark, the sacred fire from Heaven, the *Shekinah* (Holy Spirit), and the *Urim* and *Thummim* (Talmud Tr. *Yomah* 22b), and the "lion" and "dog" symbolism in the commentary of the Maharsha (Rabbi Shemuel Eidels, 1555-1631) on Tr. *Yomah* 21b.

(5) As explained in Point 8 of Part I, the prophet Jeremiah wept over his vision of the future demise of the Sanhedrin (ordained Torah judgment), crying *"ein Torah"* – there is no ordained Torah judgment! (Lamentations 2:9) He foresaw the many centuries during which his nation would stumble without any single, nationally recognized, compulsory legal authority. The planting of the Torah in Babylonia marked the beginning of the end for the light of *Torath EreS Yisra'el* – the Torah of the Land of Israel, save that which was preserved in the exile. Its uniqueness is briefly discussed in the latter two sections of Point 7 of Part I.

(6) Kelly, Jack, *Gunpowder: Alchemy, Bombards, & Pyrotechnics: The History of the Explosive that Changed the World.* Basic Books (2004). ISBN 0465037186 . Cited in entry for "Gunpowder" in Wikipedia, The Free Encyclopedia. *en.wikipedia.org/wiki/Gunpowder*

(7) "It happened that Rabbi Hhiyya Rabbah [Hhiyya the Great] and Rabbi Shim`on ben Hhalafta were walking in the Arbel Valley at the break of dawn [lit. 'the wink' of dawn]. They beheld the early dawn as its light broke out. Rabbi Hhiyya Rabbah said to Rabbi Shim`on ben Hhalafta: "Verily, my master, thus is the Redemption of Israel - at the beginning it comes slowly, slowly, and as it progresses it increases more and more." (Jerusalem Talmud Tr. *Berakhoth* 4b)

(8) Artscroll Commentary of RaMBaN on Genesis.

(9) Rabbi Hillel Rivlin of Shaklov (1758-1838, devoted student of the Vilna Gaon), *Qol Ha-Tor* (Voice of the Turtledove, translated and annotated by Rabbi Yechiel Bar Lev). Published online by: The *Yedid Nefesh* Institute. *www.yedidnefesh.com/kaballah/kol-hator/2.htm*

The reader should be aware that this is the seminal mystical work of the rabbi who –besides one of the greatest Torah geniuses ever– is may well have been the single greatest halakhic mind in the history of the exile, besides the RaMBaM. Notwithstanding his mystical beliefs, which he kept separate from the *halakhah*, the legal approach of the Vilna Gaon (or "Gra" [Gaon Rabbenu Eliyahu]) was purely rational, taking into consideration the entire sum of Oral Torah literature – including that of the Land of Israel, like the RaMBaM. It is said in the name of late Yemenite sage, Yoseph Kafihh of blessed memory, that the only real halakhic differences the Gra had with the RaMBaM are due to the corrupt, censored manuscripts of *Mishneh Torah* available to the Gra in his day.

(10) Rebbetzin Devorah Fastag, "Zionism." Published online at: Messiah Truth Project. *www.messiahtruth.com/zionism.html*

(11) Entry for "Israeli Declaration of Independence" in Wikipedia, The Free Encyclopedia:
en.wikipedia.org/wiki/Declaration_of_the_Establishment_of_the_St ate_of_Israel#Context_and_content

(12) *Discoveries in the Judaean Desert*, I, p.7. Oxford, 1955. Cited in "The Qumran Community: Artifacts from the Qumran Site."

Published online at: Scrolls from the Dead Sea: The Ancient Library of Qumran and Modern Scholarship. *www.loc.gov/exhibits/scrolls*

(13) Golb, Norman, *The Origins of the Dead Sea Scrolls* (See "The Phylacteries"). Published online at: Fathom Archive, The University of Chicago Library Digital Collections. *fathom.lib.uchicago.edu/1/777777190227/*

Online citation:

Professor Norman Golb has achieved worldwide renown through his manuscript discoveries and historical writings. A prolific author and twice a Guggenheim Fellow, he is the first holder of the Rosenberger Chair in Jewish History and Civilization at the University of Chicago and a voting member of its celebrated Oriental Institute.

COPYRIGHT | Adapted from pages XV, 95-104, and 382-385 of "Who Wrote the Dead Sea Scrolls?: The Search for the Secret of Qumran" by Norman Golb. Copyright 1995 by Norman Golb. Reprinted by arrangement with Scribner, an imprint of Simon & Schuster, Inc., New York.

(14) Hakham [sic] Meir Yosef Rekhavi, "Phylacteries: 'A Sign Upon Your Hand and as [sic] Frontlets Between Your Eyes.'" Published online at: Teachings of Hakham Rekhavi, The Karaite Community of The Diaspora. *www.karaites.org.uk/index.shtml*

(15) The original source of this photograph is unknown and assumed to be part of the public record. It was found at a racist website with photos from the tomb of King Tutankhamon, called "Egypt: The Nordic Desert Empire" *www.vivamalta.org/forum/showthread.php?t=2299*. There is no reason to doubt the authenticity of the images: The author has personally seen the throne below at the Egyptian Museum in Cairo.

(16) It appears that, underneath Jesus' tirade of insults against the character of Israel's Torah scholars –publicly condemning them as hypocrites and snakes (Mat. 23:29, 33)– is that they could not

accept his messiahship. After all, he had failed to fulfill any of the requirements that would prove him to be the prophesied Messiah, namely: bringing all of Israel to follow the Written and Oral Torah, fighting the wars of *HaShem* and beating all of Israel's surrounding foes, rebuilding the Holy Temple and ingathering Israel's exiles (M.T. Laws of Kings and Wars 11:8[4]).

In the name of fairness, an analysis of Jesus' character (if the NT is to be believed), for comparison, can be found in Rabbi Aryeh Kaplan's work, "Behold the Man: The Real Jesus" in *A Jewish Response to Missionaries*. Published by National Conference of Synagogue Youth/Orthodox Union. New York, NY (1997). 106 pp.

(17) Rabbi Tovia Singer, *In-depth Study Guide to the "Let's Get Biblical" Tape Series*. Published by Rabbi Tovia Singer, Outreach Judaism. Monsey, NY (1998). 178 pp. p.111 for Point 19.

(18) Michael Avi-Yonah, entry for "Shilo" in *Encyclopaedia Judaica*. Published by Thomas Gale (2006)

(19) Rabbi Yitzkhak Etshalom, 1Samuel: First lecture of the Book of Samuel (audio lecture). Etshalom.com.
www.etshalom.com/audio_rating/audio_31.htm

(20) Original translation from the Hebrew translation of *Book of the Maccabees* in *Ha-sefarim Ha-hhiSoniyim* (*The Apocrypha*, translated by Avraham Kahana), Vol. II. Published by Lichtenshtein and Son Bookstore. Ra`anana, Israel (2006). Copyright by Ben Zion Kahana.

(21) *The Mariana Trench, Oceanography*. (© 2003). April 04, 2003 (last modified). Published online at
www.marianatrench.com/mariana_trench-oceanography.htm

(22) Hall, Brook Ellen, *Scales, Feathers, and Hair*. An Animal Sciences (2002) reference article published online at: www.encyclopedia.com. December 29, 2010 (web).
www.encyclopedia.com/doc/1G2–3400500293.html

(23) Entry for "Fish Anatomy" in Wikipedia, The Free Encyclopedia. *en.wikipedia.org/wiki/Fish_anatomy*

(24) Entry for "Scute" in Wikipedia, The Free Encyclopedia. *en.wikipedia.org/wiki/Scute*

(25) Entry for "Antikythera Mechanism" in Wikipedia, The Free Encyclopedia. *en.wikipedia.org/wiki/Antikythera_mechanism*

(26) Entry for "Synodic Month" in Encyclopædia Britannica. Published online at: Encyclopædia Britannica Online (2010). December 30, 2010 (web). *www.britannica.com/EBchecked/topic/578490/synodic-month*

(27) Goldstein, Bernard R., Ancient and Medieval Values For the Mean Synodic Month. JVA, xxxiv (2003), Science History Publications Ltd. Published online at: *www.pitt.edu/~brg/pdfs/ brg_i_2.pdf*

(28) Ross, Kelley L., Ph.D., The Babylonian Calendar after R.A. Parker & W.H. Dubberstein, *Babylonian Chronology* (Providence, Rhode Island, 1956). Copyright (1999, 2010) by Kelley L. Ross, Ph.D. Published online at: *www.friesian.com/calendar.htm*

(29) Groleau, Rick, "How is Sex Determined? Week 6 (later)—Male." November 2001 (last updated). A flash video published online at: *www.pbs.org/wgbh/nova/ miracle/dete_nf06.html*

(30) Al Ghazal, Sharif Kaf, Ph.D., "Embryology and Human Creation between Quran and Science." Published online at: Quran & Science: Where Religion Meets Science. *quranandscience.com/human/129-embryology-and-human-creation-between-quran-a-science-47-.html*

(31) Poltorak, Leah, MS, "On the Embryological Foresight of the Talmud." Published in *B'or Ha'Torah,* Vol. 19, 2009. (Papers from the 2007 Miami International Conference on Torah and Science.) pp.19-24.

(32) Note that there is no preference of male children over female children in the Torah Commandment "to be fruitful and multiply" (Gen. 1:28, 9:1, 9:7). The Law, in true egalitarian spirit, requires that an Israelite produce at least one son and one daughter, who will themselves marry and produce at least one son and one daughter (M.T. Laws of Marriage 15:4-5). Jewish fathers whose wives bear son after son or daughter after daughter cannot fulfill their Torah obligation until an individual of the other gender is born.

(33) Long, James D., *Riddle of the Exodus: Startling Parallels Between Ancient Jewish Sources and the Egyptian Archaeological Record.* Published by Lightcatcher Books. Springdale, AR (2006). 227 pp.

(34) One possible reason for the genetic distinctiveness of Abyssinian Jews and Christians would be if they were originally descended of early converts to Judaism. Aside from converts who have a Jewish father, converts do not normally share Jewish DNA markers.

(35) Hancock, Graham, *The Sign and the Seal: The Quest for the Lost Ark of the Covenant.* A Touchstone Book published by Simon & Schuster, Inc. New York, NY (1992). 600 pp.

Oral Torah from Sinai

CONCLUSION

כֹּה אָמַר יְהֹוָה עִמְדוּ עַל־דְּרָכִים
וּרְאוּ וְשַׁאֲלוּ לִנְתִבוֹת עוֹלָם,
אֵי־זֶה דֶרֶךְ הַטּוֹב וּלְכוּ בָהּ,
וּמִצְאוּ מַרְגּוֹעַ, לְנַפְשְׁכֶם;
וַיֹּאמְרוּ, לֹא נֵלֵךְ. (ירמיהו ו:טז)

Thus says *HaShem*: stand on the highways
and see and ask for the ancient paths,
which is the good way for you to walk therein,
and find rest for your souls.
But they said: 'We will not go.' (Jeremiah 6:16)

Oral Torah from Sinai

As we read in the title verse, the old ways, the ancient paths – these are the Will of *HaShem*. I hope that through the candid, researched answers and twenty-two points of evidence in this book, the reader has gained clarity as to which way, between that of the teachers of the Oral Law and that of its detractors, represents "the ancient paths" that God desires: the way of the Oral Law —a tradition far older than 2,000 years— or the way of the rebels and revolutionaries who effectively declare "We will not go!"

The main root of this old conflict, however, is revealed in a single verse from Isaiah that summarizes an epic, continuing tragedy in Israel's history:

> Your children make haste; your destroyers and those who cut you down shall issue *forth from you*.   (Isaiah 49:17)

Israel's greatest enemies have always come from within. Fittingly, it is none other than the Sadducees (*Sadduqim*), a Jewish sect, who were the first group in history —Jewish or gentile— to launch an ideological attack aimed at the Oral Tradition of Israel's elders. I will conclude with a voice from a vantage point of 2,000 years ago, close to the time when this group began its treacherous campaign. I believe we can gain from it one last ancient proof, one final ray of light that can illuminate for us which group —Sadducee or Pharisee— represented the voice of antiquity, and which represented a revolution, coming to supplant the old.

Josephus Flavius was the turncoat *kohen*-priest who defected to the Roman enemy of Israel. I regard Josephus as a neutral voice in the controversy between the Jewish movements, for two reasons:

Josephus describes how he undertook in his youth (between the ages of 16 and 19) to test all three sects —Pharisees (*Perushim*), Sadducees and Essenes— even enduring suffering and hardship to give asceticism a fair chance (*Life of Flavius Josephus* 1.2 [10-12]).

Josephus' even-handed treatment of the "three sects" is clear in the contempt he shows for the Pharisees he loathed. It is most clearly apparent in his account of how they angered the Hasmonean High Priest, John Hyrcanus, causing him to defect to the Sadducees. Josephus greatly admired this figure, even claiming that God had given him prophecy! The reader cannot come away with the impression that Josephus had any special loyalty to the Pharisees, when he wrote his books.

This same Josephus describes the Pharisee-Sadducee conflict as follows:

> What I would now explain is this, that the Pharisees have delivered to the people a great many observances by succession of their fathers, which are not written in the law of Moses; and for that reason it is that the Sadducees reject them and say that we are to esteem those observances to be obligatory which are in the written word, *but are not to observe what are derived from the tradition of our forefathers*; and concerning these things it is that great disputes and differences have arisen among them, *while the Sadducees are able to persuade none but the rich,* and have not the populace obsequious [subservient] to them, but the Pharisees have the multitude on their side.
>   (Antiquities of the Jews 13.10.6[297]*)

Josephus reveals what was clearly a well-known fact in his day: *The legal foundations of the Perushim (the Oral Law) were, in fact, the traditions of their forefathers.* This was so well-known, that the Sadducees were only able to convince the rich of their doctrine. After all, the rich had the most to gain by being aligned with the pet political party of the pro-Roman Hasmonean government. The multitudes, on the other hand, not blinded by the trappings of wealth or power, knew which path faithfully carried forward the teachings of their forefathers – and which did not.

Not surprisingly, the young, yet uncorrupted Josephus — following his three years of religious investigation— chose to live according to the teachings of the *Pharisees* (*Life of Josephus Flavius* 1.2[12]*).

For there is a teaching in the Written Torah of Moses that all parties were aware of, whether or not they practiced the Torah accordingly:

> Remember the days of old, comprehend the years of past generations; ask your father and he will declare it to you, *your elders, and they will tell it to you.* (Deut. 32:7)

HaShem Himself enjoins Israel to trust the traditions of her forefathers as they are preserved in the communal memory: the way they were passed down within the institutions of family, and the nation's elders – the Sages. This verse in itself presents a challenge to Bible-believing naysayers to Israel's Oral Tradition. If God knew the normative, Orthodox tradition of Israel's elders would contain lies and gross distortions, why would He enjoin Israel to cling to it?

Considering all the blessings promised in the Torah to the individual, the nation, and the world that obeys the Torah's precepts, for the sake of all mankind, we would all —Jew and non-Jew alike— be wise to comply.

* Whiston, William (1667-1752). *The Works of Josephus: New Updated Edition.* Hendrickson Publishers, Inc. Peabody, MA (1987). 756 pp.

APPENDIX I

Why Were Jews of Israel Pressured to Abandon Their Tradition?

Without mentioning names, there are private scholars in Israel who advocate going even further than RaMBaM did to purge Jewish practice of what they consider to be mistakes by the Babylonian Jewish Sages. In places where there appears to be a contradiction between a Babylonian Talmudic ruling and the ancient practice of Jews in Israel (as evinced by the Israeli Talmudic literature), they practice according to the latter.

However, they do so not only against RaMBaM's teachings, but against his great predecessors all the way back to Babylonia: centuries of equally-brilliant rabbis – critical scholars who revered authentic Israelite tradition no less than our non-standard scholarly friends. Moreover, the rabbis of centuries past wrote from a vantage point much closer in time to their ordained legal source (the Great Sanhedria of old), giving them access to traditions and cleaner (uncensored) manuscripts that no longer exist, not to mention a far better understanding of the language of the ancient sources than we have today.

One "example" these scholars give of how supposedly-crooked Babylonian tradition came to "unfairly" replace supposedly virgin, Israelite tradition of many centuries, is found in the critical commentary of the *Ba`al ha-Ma'or* (Zechariah ben Isaac Ha-Levi Gerondi, 1125-c.1186) on the Talmudic commentary of the *Rif* (Rav YiShhaq Alfasi, 1013-1103). The *Ba`al ha-Ma'or*, along with his contemporary Rabbi Ephraim, noted that the remaining Jewish inhabitants of the land of Israel continued to keep one day of Rosh HaShanah. They considered this to be an unbroken custom in Israel since the advent of the Jewish calendar when all doubt was removed as to which day the holidays should be kept. That is, until Jews from Provence, France came and pressured the community to accept the Babylonian teaching that —unlike other holidays— Rosh HaShanah is two days in Israel, as in the Diaspora.

While we are tempted to view the beleaguered 11th century Jewish community in Israel as unfortunate victims of rabbinical power politics, we must not forget that authentic Torah was no less a value for the sages who ruled according to the Babylonian view. It turns out —and the *Ba`al ha-Ma'or* admits this— that a question about this very situation had been asked centuries earlier to Rav Haye Gaon, the leading Torah giant of the generation, by his student Rav Nissim. Rav Haye responded according to what RaMBaM would later rule in *Mishneh Torah*: like Jewish communities in the exile, the inhabitants of Israel are obligated to the custom of their forefathers, which is to keep two days of Rosh HaShanah. In fact, the Rav Alfasi, RaMBaM, and later RaMBaN (Nachmanides) in his book *Milhhamoth HaShem**, all teach what had been passed down as historical fact:

> There had been a 'taqanah' —an actual Sanhedrin decision— that despite the new calendar system (which removed any doubt as to what day Rosh HaShanah was on), every community must follow its original custom from the days when the months were determined by the sight of the new moon. Since the first day of the month of Tishre is the sacred holiday of Rosh HaShanah; unlike on other holidays, witnesses of the new moon would not leave on that day to give testimony. *The result is that it was so common an event in Jerusalem — even when the Holy Temple stood— for there to be*

> *two days of Rosh HaShanah, it became viewed as the original custom to which the inhabitants of Israel became obligated by rabbinical decree.*
> (M.T. Laws of Sanctification of Months 5:8)

The few Jews who remained in Israel at the time apparently accepted this ordinance, giving the ruling the force of law. After all, RaMBaN relates that the recent practice of Jews in Israel was due to ignorance, not defiance. Due to the tumultuous exile, nearly all the Jews who once remained in Israel had left. Unlike previous generations, the few remaining Jews who innocently understood there to be only one day of Rosh HaShanah in Israel like the other holidays, were simply not sufficiently learned. Even Rav David Bar Hayim, an advocate for returning to the halakhic perspective of the Jerusalem Talmud, attests to this impoverished state of Torah knowledge in Israel at the time (from private conversation).

Another understanding of Rav Haye Gaon's teaching is that there never was a rabbinical decree to uproot the second day of holidays from Jewish practice – even in the parts of Israel where it was regularly kept. While it was originally instituted because of doubt as to what day of the month it was (a reason which ceased to exist with the advent of the calendar), there is an uncontested, foundational law that *even if the reasoning for a rabbinical decree is no longer present, the decree remains in force* (M.T. Laws of Rebels 2:3). It remains in force until it is changed or removed by a Sanhedrin having both greater wisdom and a larger number of scholars adhering to its decisions than the one that made the ordinance. No lesser legal authority has the authority to uproot rabbinical legislation. When one considers the wisdom and power of the Great Court that instituted the second day of holidays back in the Temple era, vis a vis that of the Sanhedrin in its final era before it was dissolved, there is no comparison. *To remove the second day from practice was not legally possible however desirable it was.*

From a simplistic point of view, for the beleaguered post-Sanhedrin Israeli scholars, who no longer enjoyed access to the Sanhedrin archives, one day of Rosh HaShanah today made sense. However, as noted above, those archives had been moved to Babylonia around the time the last Great Court in Israel dissolved. (See above section: "Needed: The Most-Updated Court Record") *Between the view of the Babylonian court —a thriving community of scholars with the precious Sanhedrin archives at their disposal— and the view of the few, impoverished, less-learned Jews who managed to remain in Israel – in this case, the author relies on the former.*

One individual, private scholar who I know and respect has a unique solution to this controversy worthy of mention. Due to sound arguments on both sides, this pious rabbi (who prefers to remain anonymous) chooses to fully observe only one day of Rosh HaShanah *out of doubt*. On the second day, in order not to separate from his community, he still refrains from labor forbidden on holidays and goes to synagogue. This despite the fact that abstaining from forbidden labor and hearing the shofar blasts *on the second day* are, at the most, rabbinical obligations – and he is in doubt.

However, he prays the *weekday* prayers, and refrains from reciting the special blessings of the holiday *qidush* (marking the sanctity of the day), or upon hearing the shofar blasts. After all, considering the possibility that a Sanhedrin never decreed a second day for Rosh HaShanah in Israel after the advent of the calendar, one runs a risk of invoking God's sacred Name in vain —a severe Torah prohibition— by reciting the blessings on the holiday *qidush*, hearing the shofar blasts, and those in the special

Appendix I

holiday prayers of the day. On the contrary, according to the authoritative Yemenite manuscripts of M.T., RaMBaM rules that one who mistakenly prays a regular weekday prayer on the Sabbath has fulfilled his obligation (M.T. Laws of Prayer 10:7).

In light of this reasoning, that scholar's choice to fully observe only one day of Rosh HaShanah is actually in faithful keeping with the rules mentioned above in Part I, Point 3. Significantly, this exacting scholar is one who generally regards the traditions of RaMBaM as the most authoritative. Indeed, it is possible —within the framework of the Oral Law as codified in *Mishneh Torah*— for qualified individuals to question Babylonian Jewish tradition in light of the ancient sources from the land of Israel. However, as we can see, this is no simple or advisable undertaking.

I, for one, am among a growing number of scholars who believe we have no greater legal guide than RaMBaM's *Mishneh Torah*, according to the authentic Yemenite manuscripts. Until the Sanhedrin is restored, we can do no better than faithfully follow this ultimate code of the Oral Law, unparalleled in its scope and accuracy.

* Rav Moshe ben Nahhman (RaMBaN/Nachmanides). *Milhhamoth HaShem* in Tractate *BeSah* of the *Talmud Bavli* (Babylonian Talmud), Friedman Edition. Oz ve-Hadar Publishing, Jerusalem 5766/2006. (See *"Ba`al ha-Ma'or, ha-Ra'avad, we-ha-RaMBaN `al Masekheth BeSah"* p.6. It is RaMBaN's defense of Rav YiShhaq Alfasi's commentary to the Talmud, against the criticism of the *'Ba`al ha-Mor'*, found here as well.)

Oral Torah from Sinai

APPENDIX II

The Sixth Day Continues to Unfold

(Original Torah Commentary by the Author)

As explained in Part III Point 15, we currently find ourselves in mid-afternoon of the 6th "Day" of world history, the 6th millennium of world history.[1] While it continues according to *HaShem*'s primordial plan, it is continually shaped by our actions, for better or for worse. While all roads lead to Israel's prophesied Redemption and the Messianic Era, it is we who choose which route – be it through blessing or hardship. The following is my own original Torah commentary of how it all began – the first three chapters of Genesis. Being that these insights are the product of years of study, it may not be easy to follow for those who are not yet fluent in these profoundly cryptic chapters and rabbinical tradition.

According to the tradition mentioned above, Adam repented of his sin —his eating of "the fruit of the Tree of Knowledge of Good and Evil" (Gen. 3:6)— near the close of the 6th Day of Creation. If the "fruit of knowledge of Good and Evil" were identifiable with the grape, Adam and Eve may have been intoxicated with wine.[2] Allowing their imagination (the seat of our evil inclination) to overcome their sense, they gave into the tempting notion of "becoming like God" (3:5). This means that they started to redefine Good and Evil, Right and Wrong, *for themselves*, according to their fancy (3:6). (This is also in harmony with a deeper, sexual meaning that is implied in the whole episode.) By making morality subjective, they had abandoned *HaShem*'s definitions of Right and Wrong as an external, objective discipline to which they must subjugate —and thereby improve— themselves.

By placing the Tree of Life in the center of the Garden (2:9), *HaShem* intended to guide mankind away from that choice. The Tree of Life symbolizes Torah (Proverbs 3:18), God's objective instruction and wisdom. It was given center stage to encourage mankind to subsist on it and thereby merit experiencing the eternal life of the soul *in our physical lifetimes*. However, once Adam and Eve ate of the wrong fruit, their free access to the Tree of Life had to be removed (Gen. 3:22). Why?

No matter how he may think about himself or dress up externally, *a human being ultimately has room for only one master: either his own ego, or HaShem*. The moment that mankind chose to redefine Right and Wrong according to what was "delightful to their eyes" (Gen. 3:6), we created our own false, subjective reality. By making that initial choice to try out living according to faulty human logic instead of God's, we cut ourselves off from the possibility of eternal, blissful life in the physical realm (3:22). From then onwards, "heaven" was no longer "a place on earth": the eternal bliss of the Garden could only be achieved by a departed soul after a lifetime of Torah and good deeds, together with hard labor.

To safeguard the possibility for our soul's return to the Garden, mankind was "punished" measure for measure (in ways that exactly fit the crime) for "playing God." (See 3:16-19) Far from acts of Divine cruelty, they were purely for the sake of reminding them of what they had denied: their humanness and the fact that only *HaShem* is God. In other words, *these punishments were actually blessings in disguise.*

Appendix II

To save Man from being led astray by his godly ability to bring food from the ground with little effort, the earth was cursed, so he could only sustain himself through hard labor.

Note another way the punishment fits the crime: Just as Adam sinned through eating, his punishment, too, was through food. Instead of the idyllic life of Eden, they would now suffer hunger, and could only fill their stomachs as well as their souls through hard labor.[3]

To save Woman from being led astray by her godly ability to bring forth life painlessly, she would now suffer in childbirth (3:16-19).

I believe it is here, at *this* point, that Adam –while still in the Garden of Eden– accepted *HaShem*'s Six-Law Edenic Covenant.[4] According to the rabbinical tradition, the Edenic code was the original form of the Seven Noahide Laws. (Only after the Great Deluge did God add the 7th Law, the prohibition of consuming flesh from a living creature (M.T. Laws of Kings and Wars 9:2[1]).

To my reading, God's next action at the end of Chapter Three is actually a fuller description of what was briefly related much earlier in verse 1:28; *the two actually describe the same event.* In 1:28 we read:

> And God blessed them; and God said unto them: 'Be fruitful and multiply [note connection with Eve's new condition in 3:16], and replenish the earth, and subdue [or "conquer"] it; and have dominion over the fish of the sea, and over the fowl of the air, and over every living thing that creepeth upon the earth.'

Clearly, mankind being sent out to settle the wide earth, to subdue and dominate the natural world, connotes a different picture than the Edenic existence referred to in Chapter Two. It makes sense in the context of the *post-*Edenic world. It brings us to verse 3:23, where *HaShem sends forth* Adam and Eve from the Garden (the word *wa-yishlahh* – "sent out" connotes a positive mission) to conquer the earth (1:28). It begins in a most special place, the land from which Adam was originally taken (see below).

It might still be difficult to connect the end of Chapter One, where *HaShem*'s blesses mankind, with the end of Chapter Three. Isn't the end of Chapter One where God blesses man (1:22), while verse 3:23 is clearly in the context of punishment and curse?

Besides those punishments being blessings in disguise as explained above, the verses that follow relate how *HaShem* proceeded to bequeath mankind with two "lifelines," so to speak – two means by which the path to the Tree of Life would be safeguarded for him. By these lifelines, access to Torah law and wisdom would be secured for Adam's future generations. *By a life of commitment to Torah and good deeds, they [we] could still merit the eternal life of the soul (albeit only after our physical lives).* They are symbolized by the *keruvim* (angels) and the *hherev ha-mith'happekheth* ("the overturning sword") (3:24).

What are these, and what does all this mean for us?

The Torah is hinting that the path to the Tree of Life —the ability to live a full Torah life, according to God's Will, privately and communally, thereby ensuring our eventual return to Eden— can be safeguarded by two forces. The first is the *spiritual* means of character refinement through the study and fulfillment of Torah, prayer, the Temple Service, and deeds of kindness (represented by the *keruvim*, which became manifested on the Ark of the Covenant[5].)

Appendix II

The second is the *physical* means to bring the sword of the wicked upon their own head (represented by the "overturning sword").

In other words: through a lifetime of developing oneself both spiritually and physically (namely training in holy warfare so as to preserve one's life physically and execute justice), man merits to live a life of Torah, thereby enabling his return to the "Garden": the unspeakably blissful, eternal life of the soul. *Considering how Adam and Eve had initially distanced themselves from HaShem, what greater blessing could there be?*

As noted above, the Torah relates that Adam was not simply banished from Eden, but *sent out* on a *positive* mission to a specific place – the very place from which he was formed (see verse 3:23). According to sacred Oral Torah Tradition, this is none other than Mt. Moriah, the sacred site of the altars of Adam himself, Cain and Abel, and the future Holy Temple (M.T. Laws of the Chosen House 1:1[2]). These verses are a profound message to the nation of Israel: *Through the spiritual (establishing HaShem's Temple) and the physical (willingness to fight in God's Name to defend our lives and land, and establish His kingdom), we can merit the eventual return of our world to the paradisiacal state of Eden.*

Accordingly, the Jewish People are destined not only to continue returning to the Holy Land, but ultimately to return in full repentance to the Covenant. When King David, ancestor of the future Messiah-king, brought the Ark (with the *keruvim*) and the sword of Goliath ("the overturning sword") to Mt. Moriah —*the very spot where mankind was created and to where our mission from Eden began*— it was the beginning of the fulfillment of Creation: He set the foundation for the return of that intense connection to the Creator in this world. It would be the site of a Holy Temple – the heart of a kingdom established so that the nation that had chosen the Torah could pursue the 'Tree of Life' in peace and strength.

When the process will be complete, with the Holy Temple rebuilt in the place of man's origin, we truly come full circle: Once again, Jerusalem will become the center of connection to the Creator for mankind. Ultimately, even death will be a thing of the past: the dead will be revived and Eden will again be a place on Earth.

Appendix II

NOTES

(1) Talmud Tr. *Sanhedrin* 97b

(2) This is why, in Torah tradition, a Jew who takes a Nazirite vow — by which he is forbidden to cut or even comb the hair of the crown of his head for the length of the period of his vow— must abstain from any grape product (grapes, raisins, wine, etc.). Resembling the first human beings with his long locks, he aspires to the level of Adam in the Garden of Eden before his sin. For this, Torah tradition regards him as equivalent in stature to a prophet (Num. ch.6 cf. M.T. Laws of the Nazirite 10:21[14]).

This is keeping with the general Torah value of sobriety (i.e. Lev. 10:9, Deut. 29:5, etc.).

(3) I thank Noahide author, teacher and archaeologist James D. Long for this phenomenal, original insight.

(4) The original Edenic Covenant was based on the following Commandments: The prohibitions of idolatry, cursing a Name of God, murder, forbidden sexual relations, theft, and the obligation to pursue justice by enforcing these laws.

(5) See the section "Lose the Spaceship, Become a *Merkavah*" in Appendix III below.

Oral Torah from Sinai

APPENDIX III

A Brief Guide for Those Perplexed by "Alien Astronaut" Theory

INTRODUCTION

The degree of attention I've given this subject here may surprise some. After all, it is a non-issue for the great majority of Torah observant Jews, as it should be. Rabbis traditionally stay away not only from this subject, but refrain from discussing the metaphysical world in plain terms. Beyond their just fear that unlearned be led astray, it is not our focus as faithful Jews: *Whether there are aliens or not, we leave the heavens to HaShem, focusing on **our** responsibility: doing **our part** in making the world a better place.* This fills us with joy, purpose, and strength. After all, metaphysics cannot heal a broken heart or a mend a broken world. The study of Torah law, on the other hand, educates us in proper action, by which we fulfill our purpose on earth: to build a just and Godly world.

RaMbaM taught that Torah scholars —healers of the soul— often prescribe for the sick (including the spiritually ill) a diet or mode of behavior that deviates from those recommended for a healthy person (Ibid,. Laws of Personal Dispositions 2:1-4[1-2], 4:31[21]). In the sick state of our world, powerful media are not only intent on moving the belief in "aliens in flying saucers" into the realm of accepted fact,[1] they vigorously promote alien astronaut theory.[2] Beyond a general weakening in Torah faith (I personally know of three individuals whose faith has been badly damaged by it), it has spawned large, growing cults that prey on the souls and psyche of the public worldwide.

Recognizing the sick state of our world, I will therefore pour out a non-standard teaching for whoever feels it will be of benefit.

* * *

"Alien astronaut" theories are based on the speculative interpretation of various ancient artifacts, dubbed "Ooparts" (Out-of-place-artifacts). Interpreted as being far beyond the creative abilities of ancient peoples, these artifacts supposedly point to extra-terrestrial involvement with mankind in our early history. Much of this is a product of a proponent's agenda and *a priori* assumptions. I have found most other-worldly explanations for "Ooparts" to have been debunked, or to have more plausible, mundane explanations.[3]

Nevertheless, it may well be confirmed in the future what some of the world's eminent scientists believe: that extra terrestrials not only exist, but once visited the earth. RaMBaM, may peace be upon him, taught that there can be no contradiction between the Torah truths which *HaShem* has revealed, and the findings of science.[4] Any apparent contradiction between them is by definition the result of a misunderstanding of one or the other. It is critical to know what beliefs on this subject, however erroneous, can be tolerated within the borders of authentic Torah faith.

Even to imagine that the angels of the Bible (*mal'akhim* – heavenly agents) are powerful, organic, extra-terrestrials from Planet Xenon, employed in the service of the Creator of All, is not, in itself, apostasy. If a human being can act as a *mal'akh* (an agent of God's Will, as we see in the Bible as well[5], why cannot a heavenly, extra-terrestrial being? So long as one fully accepts the 13 tenets of faith, his faith — despite the errors it may contain— is kosher.

Appendix III

If, for sake of argument, such a belief were one day proven to be scientific fact, this would only imply an error in RaMBaM's Aristotelian understanding of the cosmos – *not in his understanding of the Written or Oral Torah.* Similarly, errors are discovered in the understanding of science and metaphysics of history's wisest men, as will our own one day, no doubt. *Whatever their nature, such 'mal'akhim' would be no less a part of the Creation than anything else in heaven or on earth. HaShem would still remain the invisible, eternal, non-corporeal Creator of all space, time, and matter.* (See Part I Point 1)

Even if, for the sake of argument, it were conclusively determined that such extra terrestrials indeed visited the earth and interbred with humans, producing the giant *Nefillim* referred to in Genesis, again, while it would suggest a more blunt interpretation of Gen. 6:2, 6:4, Job 1:6 and 38:7, it would do nothing to undermine the 13 tenets of Torah faith. In fact, it would suggest what "alien astronaut" theorists believe about UFO's – that their alien pilots are humanoid. *Such a discovery would show the human form to be the design of a Universal Creator whose creations exist far beyond our planet.* We would rejoice in what Torah-observant Jewish scholars have known for 3,300 years: that *HaShem*'s realm extends to all other worlds that exist, have existed in the past, or will ever exist in the future.[6] *It would serve to support the same Torah that declares the existence, Creatorship, and Kingship of HaShem according to His Abstract, Incomparable Oneness.* (See Part II Point 1)

However, such rational thinking escapes much of the world. Eager to find another strategy to debunk the Torah and absolve themselves of Divine Commands, secular astronomy (personified by the late Carl Sagan) has found an unlikely bed partner in alien astronaut pseudo-science – all without realizing the true implications of a universe brimming with intelligent life. *Such an awesome universal order —with governing laws for wildly diverse environments from the scale of sub-atomic particles all the way to the inter-galactic scale— declares a Law-maker.*

- How could conscious intelligence spontaneously arise from dead material *anywhere* in the universe?

- How could order have spontaneously generated from disorder?

- How could very primordial building blocks of matter in the early universe invent themselves from absolute nothing?

- In fact, how could *space itself* exist without a primary being to conceive of and prepare it?

- Finally, how could the necessary inventor of space, the building blocks of matter, and order, and life be a physical being itself?

The universe in all its wonder, which continues to slowly yield its secrets to us, declares the existence of a non-physical Law-Giver, a Creator, and governing King outside of space and time.

LOSE THE SPACESHIP, BECOME A *MERKAVAH*

My intent in what is written above is to show how flexible the Torah can be for those who cannot shake alien astronaut beliefs. However, it would be a disservice to the Torah for me to leave the open-minded truth-seeker without a taste of the awesome depths of authentic Oral Torah on a subject he may be eager to chalk up to aliens and spaceships: Ezekiel Chapter 10.

Appendix III

Ezekiel is the prophet whom alien astronaut enthusiasts swear experienced an "alien abduction" into God's "spacecraft" (*HaShem*-forbid). In truth, Ezekiel's description of the Divine Chariot —*merkavah*— is textbook material for the highest, most sublime, abstract, and guarded realm of Torah learning there is. It is so guarded, in fact, that it is literally a legal prohibition for a Torah teacher to reveal more than mere "chapter headings" and a hint of its secrets – and that to one student only (M.T. Laws of Foundations of Torah 2:17-18[12]). I have no intention of breaking this rule, which we hold sacred. However, I will allow myself to teach enough Talmudic knowledge to help the truth seeker to look at the Bible as our tradition teaches: a prism for looking inwards, as much as outwards.

The root of *meRKaVah* in Hebrew is the verb "R-K-V," meaning "ride," as in a person riding an animal. Note that, according to the preconceived notions of a generation raised on Star Trek and Star Wars, space travelers do not "ride" in spacecraft as one "rides" on the back of an animal. It is a vehicle. The verb for travel, either in or accompanied by vehicles, is "N-S-`A." The verb for flight is "T-W-S." If the *merkavah* were a sort of spaceship, we might expect one of these to be the root of the Hebrew term for the Divine Chariot. Neither one is. On the contrary, the sublime subject of *merkavah* has nothing to do with such nonsense.

One can begin to scratch the surface from the profound Oral Torah teaching from *Sifre*, one of the oldest written sources of the Oral Law: "The idolaters ride [*RoKh'Vim*] on their gods, but the Holy One Blessed Be He rides [*RoKheV*] upon his servants." It is a baffling, perhaps nonsensical teaching to outsiders; those who were desperately hoping for such a verse to end "but the Holy One Blessed Be He rides in a spaceship!"

Indeed, the verse's true meaning is so awesome, yet so profoundly simple, it puts such "alien" thinking to shame.

The Hebrew-literate reader who is familiar with the Bible may suddenly remember the role of the *KeRuV,* angel (same three letters as in the word root of *meRKaVah,* albeit in a different order) in Ezekiel 10 ("cherub" in English). He may then recall the angelic *KeRuV* figures atop the most sacred man-made vessel on this earth: the Ark of the Covenant. The golden-winged *KeRuVim*-angels atop the Ark-cover (according to tradition, one with the face of a boy and the other with the face of a girl) model the attributes of the ideal relationship: *modesty* (they don't stare at one another) and *focus on Torah.* This represents holy love, forever young, between individuals who merit that the *Shekhinah* (*HaShem's* holy Presence) *rest between them.* Being overlaid with gold from without and inlaid with gold from within, with a layer of wood in between, is a lesson as to the ideal character of a human vessel of Torah and Godliness. *We must strive to be 'golden'* (true, humble, in awe of and in love with *HaShem*) *inwardly as well as outwardly. Our* heart must not be of stone, but organic, requiring the 'water' of Torah as a tree. (To see how Torah is likened to water, see M.T. Laws of Talmud Torah 3:8[9]).)

If it is not clear by now, *merkavah* science —based on the teachings of Ezekiel— is about becoming just that – *a perfect vessel, a chariot, for HaShem's Presence.* The four animal faces and exotic creatures —all biologically impossible— revealed to Ezekiel while in a state of deep prophecy, are keys to sublime, hidden insight. Once understood, it can help the deserving servant of *HaShem* to become such a vessel.

This is why the Sages' figurative teaching about *HaShem* "riding" upon His servants is in the context of the Torah's wording about two of the greatest *merkavoth* in history – Abraham and Jacob. When Abraham's prophecy would end, the Torah writes:

> And He [*HaShem*] finished talking with him, and God *went up* ["rose up"] *from* [literally, "from on"] Abraham. (Gen. 17:22)

When Jacob's prophecy would end, the Torah writes:

> And God *went up* ["rose up"] *from* ["from on"] him in the place where He spoke with him. (Gen: 35:13)

RaMBaM hints of this when he teaches that *merkavah* science, which is part of the wider field of sublime study called *Pardes*, is one of the keys to achieving true prophecy (M.T. Laws of Foundations of Torah 7:2).

It is my hope and prayer that this book should inspire many to consider the flimsiness of newer, man-made religious doctrines who claim legitimacy based on a shallow reading of the Bible, next to the awesome integrity and accuracy of Torah tradition over 3,300 years old. Perhaps they might even consider throwing off the lies and vanity in this world to begin the road towards becoming a real *merkavah:* a pure vessel —a "chariot"— for the universal Law-Giver in His glorious universe. *The first step is by accepting His body of laws for **our** world: the Written and authentic Oral Torah.*

NOTES

(1) In example, The Disclosure Project © Copyright 2010 www.disclosureproject.org/

(2) In example, the popular film series *Ancient Aliens* from The History Channel © Copyright 2011 (a registered trademark of A&E Television Networks.) *shop.history.com/detail. php?p=263610&icid=mybuys&green=17565440661*

(3) For a page-by-page refutation of Von Däniken, look for *The Space-Gods Revealed*, by Ronald Story.

Other good books refuting ancient-astronaut claims are *Frauds, Myths, and Mysteries: Science and Pseudoscience in Archaeology* by Dr. Kenneth L. Feder, and *The Cult of Alien Gods* by Jason Colavito. The second one details how HP Lovecraft's *fiction* influenced writers like Däniken.

(4) Entry for "Maimonides" found in Wikipedia Fact Index: *www.fact-index.com/m/ma/maimonides.html*

(5) Note the human *mal'akhim* sent by Moses (Num. 20:14, 21:21, etc.) and Joshua 6:17, 6:25, etc.

(6) See Psalms 145:13 in light of Talmud Tr. *Avodah Zarahhh* 3b [God's presence is among 18,000 worlds]. See Judges 5:23, and the opinion in Tr. *Mo`ed Qatan* 16a that *Meroz*, whose inhabitants were cursed, is a heavenly body.)

APPENDIX IV

The Shared Tradition of the Ancient Ark-Cults of Africa, and Its Significance until Today

INTRODUCTION

The length of this Appendix may surprise some. However, the notion that the original Ark of the Covenant today lies safely and securely in a church (a place of idolatry according to authentic rabbinical tradition) in the hands of the Abyssinian Christians —a view promoted in secular pop scholarship today— is one that challenges the faith of some. Even if it were true, God forbid, considering Jeremiah's words of consolation (Jer. 3:16), it should not faze those who cling to authentic Torah belief:

> And it shall come to pass, when you will multiply and be fruitful in the land in those days, says *HaShem*, they shall say no more: The ark of the covenant of *HaShem*; neither shall it come to mind; neither shall they make mention of it; neither shall they miss it; *neither shall it be made any more.*

However, those last words "neither shall it be made any more" may hint to a solution to the mystery: the Ark had been *replicated* in the past. In the spirit of this book, strengthening the rational base for belief in Torah tradition, I believe the insight *HaShem* gave me into this mystery may buoy the faith of those confused by popular claims.

Finally, while Ethiopian Jewry has been embraced by the Israeli rabbinate, their Ark traditions are ignored by the

Orthodox Jewish world, who do not know what to make of them. Worse, the worthy Lemba-Igbo tribe of Africa with its traditions has been largely ignored as a whole. This has contributed to the feeling of estrangement among Africans of Israelite descent, leaving many to fall prey to deviant religious streams. In hopes that my respectful reconstruction of their past may draw them close to authentic Torah, I will give this topic the full treatment it deserves.

PART I
ESTABLISHING THE AUTHENTICITY OF THE ETHIOPIAN TRADITION OF ARK-SERVICE AT TANA QIRQOS

1. The Ancient Ark-Cult in Ethiopia: A Jewish Tradition

To repeat and expound on the ideas introduced in Part III Point 22, the Abyssinian Christians retain traditions from their ancient Israelite past. Although their practices have changed significantly over the millennia, remaining hints of their undeniably Israelite past permeate their religious observance. That religious heritage once included the offering of *qorbanoth* (burnt offerings) outside a Tabernacle-like tent they believe to have housed the Ark of the Covenant – *Aron ha-Berith*. According to both meticulous records of the Christians (oral and written) and the oral tradition of the native Jewish elders, this Tabernacle service continued on a remote island in the midst of Lake Tana called Tana Qirqos. It persisted for 800 years, from 400 BCE to about 400 CE, when King Ezana brought their sacred relic to a church in Axum. When senior priest on the island, Memhir Fisseha, was interviewed by Western researcher Graham Hancock, (*The Sign and the Seal*[1], henceforth *S.A.S.*), he said candidly:

> We were Jews. We performed sacrifice... the sacrificial lamb [the Passover offering]. And we continued to practice until the Ark was taken from us to Axum." (Ibid. p.214)

According to Ethiopian Jewish tradition as well, their own ancestors were the custodians of the Ark (or a good replica thereof) until their brethren —the new Christians— stole it from them. This Jewish tradition of the Ark's movement through Ethiopia (or a replica thereof) was learned from the mouth of none other than Raphael Hadane, the aged Chief *Kess* (traditional religious leader) of the *Beta Yisrael* (the Ethiopian Jewish community. He was father to Rav Yoseph Hadane, the first rabbi of the community to be ordained in Israel. According to the traditions learned by the elderly sage from the elders back in his own youth, *their own ancestors* had brought the Ark out of the Land of Israel into Egypt, where they built a Temple "at Aswan." Moreover, the *Kess* related that the island of Tana Qirqos was the most important, venerated site to his people in Ethiopia, and how a half of the people exiled from Egypt had settled there (Ibid. p.427,445).

*NOTE: Ethiopian Jewish priests are also called "Kahen" from the Hebrew "Kohen." "Kess" appears to be the exact equivalent of an ancient Hebrew family name that is quite common today: "Katz" (or "KaS" in the transliteration scheme of this work described at the beginning of the book). Both are differing pronunciations of the acronym for the term "**K**ohen **S**edeq" – "righteous priest."*

2. How and When First-Temple Service Came from Israel to Ethiopia

There is much evidence to support the *Kess* tradition.

The Hebrew temple at Aswan (a perfect model of the First Temple built by Solomon), which stood on Elephantine island, is well-known to archaeology. Scholars believe it stood between the 7th and 5th centuries BCE, and it is alluded to in prophecy in Isaiah 19:19-20. According to *secular* chronology, this fits neatly in between the reign of the wicked King Manasseh (7th century BCE) on the one hand, and the Ark's arrival at Tana Qirqos according to both Ethiopian traditions, Jewish and Christian (400 BCE) on the other.

> NOTE: Although secular chronology of Biblical dates is off, it is not as far off as the older dates – such as those of the Exodus and Hebrew conquest of Canaan. Between its inaccuracy and the inherent inaccuracy of scientific dating techniques, the coinciding dates may still indeed have merit.

The notion that the forebears of the Ethiopians left for Africa during the intensely wicked reign of King Manasseh is bolstered considering the strict reforms of his successor – the righteous King Josiah. He was the first king to enforce the Torah's prohibition of giving *korban*-offerings outside the Holy Temple (II Kings 23:8-9); even King Solomon who built the Holy Temple in Jerusalem had embraced the practice (I Kings 3:2-3). Being that sacrifice outside the Temple was an active part of the observance of the ancestors of the Ethiopian Jews when they left Israel, they must have left before King Josiah's crack down on the practice, eliminating it from Judea.

According to the Chief *Kess*, their Temple in Aswan was destroyed by the Egyptians after an invasion of Egypt by a foreign king:

> There was a great war in Egypt. A foreign king who had captured many countries came to Egypt and destroyed all the temples of the Egyptians. But he did not destroy our temple. So when the Egyptians saw that only the Jewish temple was not destroyed they suspected that we were on the side of the invader. Because of this they started to fight

Appendix IV

against us and they destroyed our temple and we
were forced to flee.   (S.A.S. pp.427,445)

This matches the results of archeological research on Elephantine, which has yielded no human bones or other evidence of a massacre of the community. The evidence clearly suggests that the community indeed fled. According to Ethiopian tradition they fled southward into Ethiopia, continuing the service of *HaShem* as they saw fit – a service alluded to by the prophet Zephaniah:

From beyond the rivers of Ethiopia shall they
bring My suppliants, even the daughter of My
dispersed, My offering.   (Zephaniah 3:10)[2]

3. Why Researchers Believe the Actual Ark was Stolen into Africa at That Time

Considering the accuracy of the ancient traditions preserved by both Christians and Jews regarding the Tabernacle cult in Ethiopia, there can be no doubt that an Ark-like relic was at the center of ancient Jewish worship in Ethiopia. Researcher Ibrahim M. Omer writes[3]:

The Jews of this community regarded their temple as no less holier [*sic*] than the temple of Solomon in Jerusalem, and their settlement as no less blessed than the land of Israel. For example, reference was made in one of the archives to *Yahweh* [an incorrect and offensive rendering of God's four-letter Name promulgated by mainstream academia] *the God who dwells in the fortress of Elephantine."*   -K 12:2. (S.A.S. p.440)

The wording from the papyrus that *HaShem* literally "dwelled" in their fortress, clearly alludes to a sacred Ark in their midst. As I explained above, when *HaShem* is

225

described as *yoshev* —"dwelling"— it is a figure of speech referring the Divine Presence upon the Ark.

All evidence points to the progenitors of the community leaving the Holy Land for Africa during the wicked reign of King Manasseh. Secular researchers claim it is no coincidence that that the Ark of Covenant itself was removed during the reign of King Manasseh.

Unlike any rebellious Jewish king before or after, Manasseh placed an idolatrous image in the Holy of Holies. Whoever entertains that Manasseh's wicked deed would have been possible even when the Ark was still in its place, should consider the fate of King Uzzah upon his unlawful attempt to approach the Ark (II Chronicles 26:19-20). Even if it somehow were possible, the *kohen*-priests would never have allowed it. It had to have already been removed. Now note how *just before Manasseh's reign,* King Hezekiah (Manasseh's righteous father) prayed to "*HaShem* God of Israel Who dwells upon the *keruvim* [the angelic figures adorning the cover of the Ark]." (II Kings 19:15) In the context of I Samuel 4:4, II Samuel 6:2, we find that to be a figure of speech referring to the Ark with men in its presence. *King Hezekiah was praying in the presence of the Ark.*

Now note what happens *soon after Manasseh's reign,* when the righteous King Josiah purifies and renovates the Temple after the damage his grandfather had caused. Among a list of orders to the priests, the young king commands the Levites:

> …Put the holy ark in the house that Solomon the son of David king of Israel built; that it should no more be a burden upon your shoulders….
> (II Chron. 35:3)

Graham Hancock believes it significant that, unlike the other commands of the king, there is no corresponding mention that this command was complied with, as if the order was met with silence. He strengthens this notion that the Ark itself seems to have disappeared, with the words of the prophet Jeremiah, King Josiah's contemporary. *(The fact they were contemporaries is proven by Jeremiah 35:25, in which the prophet bitterly eulogizes King Josiah's death.)* Jeremiah consoled his people with following words:

> And it shall come to pass, when you will have multiplied and increased in the land, in those days, says *HaShem*, they shall no longer say 'the Ark of the Covenant of *HaShem*'; neither shall it come to mind; neither shall they make mention of it; neither shall they miss it; neither shall it be made again. (Jer. 3:16)

In other words, *before* King Manasseh's reign of terror, there is a direct reference to the Ark's presence. Just *after* his reign, it had clearly disappeared. Based on this, Hancock attempts to prove that, at this precise time, the Ark was stolen into Africa. As I explain below, while I do not support this conclusion, I do believe it marks the beginning of the story of the *Ark-replica* taken in to Africa.

4. The Tradition of the Early Talmudic Sages
Versus an Isolated Opinion

However compelling the possibility for modern Ark-hunters that the Ark itself was secreted out of Jerusalem, the conservative Torah scholar is unfazed. Loyally restating the teaching from the Talmud, *RaMBaM teaches that King Josiah Commanded that the Ark be placed in its deeply hidden vault prepared by King Solomon (builder of the Temple) in the Temple Mount, in case the Temple would ever be overrun* (M.T. Laws of the Chosen House 4:1 cf.

Talmud Tr. *Yomah* 52b). It is not less than a Levite tradition recorded in the Mishnah, that the Ark was 'hidden in its place' – in a subterranean chamber beneath the Temple (Mishnah Tr. *Sheqalim* 6:1-2).

This is the reason, according to our tradition, that King Josiah ordered that the Ark be returned to "its place," and the Bible is silent about the details. It was purposefully hidden by the Israel's righteous leadership at the time, who heeded the warnings of the prophets concerning the upcoming destruction of Jerusalem. It is in *this* context that Jeremiah's words of consolation to the people over the Ark's disappearance should be understood.

Another traditional rabbinical opinion that excites Professor Tudor Parfitt, an Ark researcher whose theory we will discuss later, is that there were two sacred Arks in use simultaneously. If true, this would give the Ethiopian tradition that they possess the actual Ark of the Covenant much greater credence, since it would not contradict the tradition of the Sages. This view is taught by the classic Torah commentator, Rashi, in his notes on Deut. 10:1. Rashi cites an ancient opinion recorded in the Jerusalem Talmud that, while the Ark built by Bezalel housed the unbroken set of Tablets and resided in the Holy of Holies, there was another Ark of wood only, constructed by Moses, which was taken out to war (Jerusalem Talmud Tr. *Sheqalim* 6:1). However, what Parfitt does not mention (if he is even aware of it), is that *this is the lone opinion of a single sage, which the majority of Rabbis soundly refute.* The first proof they bring is from I Samuel 4:3:

> And when the people arrived at the camp, the elders of Israel said, "Why has *HaShem* smitten us today before the Philistines? Let us take for ourselves the Ark of the Covenant of *HaShem* out

of Shiloh, so He may come among us and save us from the hand of our enemies.

It is clear from this, and elsewhere, that there was no special "Ark of War"; rather, the Ark in the Holy of Holies itself was taken out to war. *The majority opinion of the ordained Sages, as recorded in the Jerusalem Talmud, is that the wooden Ark was never used simultaneously with the Ark of Bezalel.* This point is noted by RaMBaN (Nachmanides) in his Torah commentary. He explains how *both* sets of Tablets —the original set broken by Moses and the second set of whole tablets— were originally kept in a *temporary* wooden Ark built by Moses until the Tabernacle was completed. Once it was ready, all the sacred contents were transferred to the one permanent Ark, and the first Ark was hidden.[4]

This matches the Levite tradition recorded in the Mishnah, which mentions no second Ark, as well as the understanding of RaMBaM, whose accurate restatement of the Law has no parallel. Therefore, *if a holy Ark was indeed at the center of the faith of the forebears of Ethiopian Jewry, it could only have been a replica.* Indeed, the Ark traditions of the Lemba-Igbo people (which I will show in the next part to match the Ethiopian legends) indicate that the *kohen*-priests who carried the sacred Ark-relic through Africa had no taboo against replicating the object when it needed to be replaced.

5. Why Forebears of Aswan Jewry Would Have Built an Ark Replica

Again, considering the authentic traditions of sprinkling the blood discussed in Point 22 and the coinciding historical and archaeological facts, there can be little doubt: an Ark-like relic, revered as sacred, was brought to Egypt and from there to Ethiopia. To the careful Torah scholar, this could only have been a replica of the Ark created by *kohen*-priests (see below). The question is: Why would they invest the time and resources in creating a replica?

The key solution to that question is to be found in the answer to a much more basic one: *Why would they re-create Temple worship outside the Land to begin with?* Consider the severe Torah violations the Jews of Elephantine transgressed, far beyond the widespread, quasi-accepted Torah violation in those days of sacrificing outside:

- Returning to live in Egypt

- Building a perfect Holy Temple outside of its Divinely-ordained site in Jerusalem (the place *HaShem* chose forever) (see Deut. 17:16, 28:68)

Yet the Jews committing these violations were zealous *kohen*-priests. What could have justified such behavior in their own eyes? If we can understand that, we can easily understand how they would have felt justified to create a replica of the Ark, for which no halakhic prohibition exists.

Fulfillment of a Vow

The following insight may be a key to that mystery: Isaiah's prophecy of the altar in Egypt, clearly an allusion to the Temple in Aswan, is in the context of *freedom from oppression:*

> In that day shall there be an altar to *HaShem* in the midst of the land of Egypt, and a pillar at the border thereof to *HaShem*. *[Note: Aswan is close to the southern border of Egypt]* And it shall be for a sign and for a witness to *HaShem* of Hosts in the land of Egypt; for they shall cry to *HaShem*

because of oppressors, and He will send them a savior and a defender, who will deliver them.
(Isaiah 19:18-20)

The altar in Egypt was likely to have been built as the fulfillment of a vow, in gratitude to *HaShem* for having saved her builders from oppression. In his reign of terror, King Manasseh "filled Jerusalem with blood from one end to the other" (II Kings 21:16). This certainly included the innocent blood of righteous priests who opposed him, who were ready to give up their lives to prevent the desecration of the Holy of Holies (see above). For them the flight to Egypt would have been a salvation from persecution and death. *The building of a Temple in Egypt —no matter how wrong-headed— may well have been the stubborn fulfillment of a sacred vow* (Ibid. 19:21), in the spirit of Jephthah with his vow (Judges ch. 11).

Intentions of Breaking Torah Law in order to Save the Torah

It is most likely that the *kohen*-priests who lead the small exodus into Egypt would have viewed themselves as saving the Torah. Watching in horror at the demise of holy priests and precious Torah scholars at the hands of King Manasseh's wicked regime, they may well have perceived the Torah to be in danger of extinction. They would have naturally used a line of reasoning employed historically by Torah leaders in dire straights, justifying otherwise forbidden actions in the name of saving the Torah, often based on Psalms 119:126: "It is a time to act for *HaShem*, for they have broken Your Torah." According to this most-easily corruptible concept, the Torah can be broken, God-forbid, in order to save it.

A Maximal View of Israel's Borders

In fact, it could well be that they did not consider their flight into Western Egypt as leaving the borders of Greater Israel. There is a rabbinical opinion that the borders promised to Abraham, and described by Ezekiel —from the River of Egypt to the Euphrates— means from the Nile River. Those details in Ezekiel 47 and 48 have been understood to imply that the Land continues southwards to the source of the Nile in the Ethiopian highlands. It is no coincidence that was a common belief among the elders of the Beta Yisrael that they had been within the borders of the Promised Land all along! Similarly, an opinion existed among Habbani Jews in Yemen that their own native region (just across the strait from Ethiopia) was but an extended part of *ereS ha-Negev* (the land of the south) of the tribe of Judah (Joshua 15:19, Judges 1:15 cf. Ez. 47:19).

Appendix IV

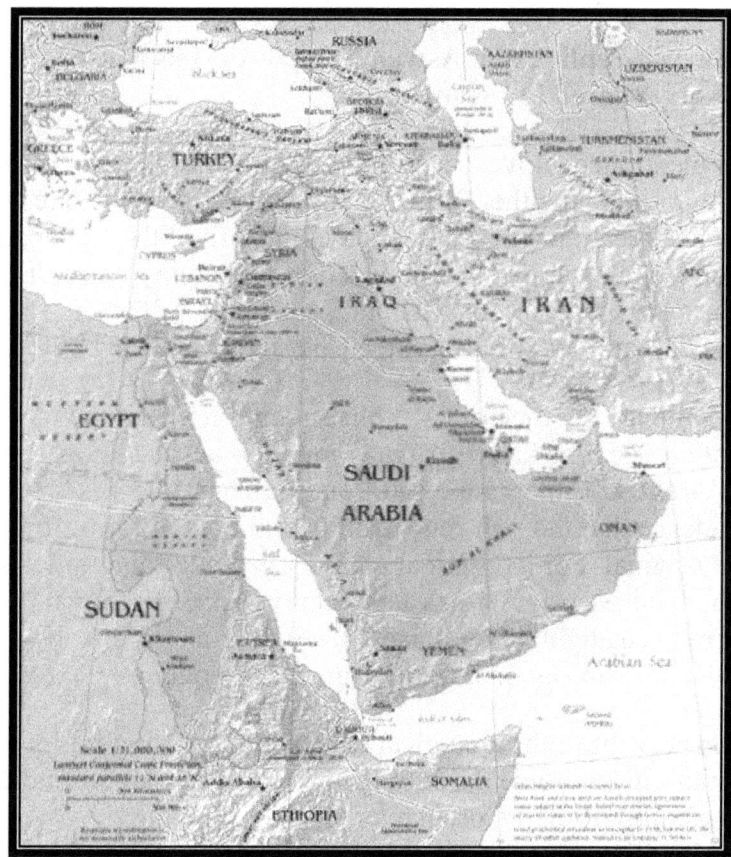

A minor, maximalist opinion of the borders of Israel revealed to Ezekiel (ch.47-48).[5]

While the founders of Aswan-bound *kohen*-priests had given up on Jerusalem, they likely intended to *rescue the Jewish religion by replanting it not on foreign ground, but in what they believed to be a far-flung part of the Israelite heritage.*

The Ark-replica and Aswan Temple Vessels Most Likely Altered in Form

As mentioned above, according to RaMBaM, there is no prohibition —neither from the Torah, nor from the Sages— against creating an exact replica of the Ark of the Covenant – only against creating a replica of the Temple edifice, its courtyards, the Golden Menorah, and Table of the Showbread. (M.T. Laws of the Chosen House 7:9[10])

Despite the absence of an explicit prohibition and the fact that no one who knows is ready to speak out as to how the Ark-relic in Ethiopia looks (or once looked), there is evidence that the Ark-relic itself *was* altered in form from the original. For its original creators, zealous *kohen*-priests who held the original Ark in great reverence, altering its form even slightly would have freed their plan from any possible taboo against creating an exact replica.

Consider the anthropological evidence supporting this notion. In an article describing his own research and finds, Ark hunter Robert Cornuke writes the following:

> Subsequent to this initial investigation, we located and interviewed two people who have claimed to have seen the object resting in St. Mary's of Zion. The first was a 105-year-old priest who once was the Administrator at St. Mary's of Zion. On two occasions, he said, when the Guardian of the Ark died and a new guardian was trained in the worship rituals, he was able to gaze upon the relic. He described it as a gold box with two winged angels on top.

In his detailed inventory of the treasury, he also described 24 smaller angelic-type figures forming a molding around the top, with two green stones (not described in the Bible) at either end. Is this the Ark of the Covenant described in the Bible? At this juncture, we cannot say with certainty that it is, but neither can we say for certain that it isn't. What we have concluded is that St. Mary's of Zion church in Axum, Ethiopia, is the resting place either of an incredible replica of the biblical Ark of the Covenant, or, of the actual Ark of the Covenant itself.[6]

I believe the Ark traditions of the Lemba-Igbo people to be a shared tradition with Ethiopian Jewry. Lemba-Igbo tradition not only indicates that their Israelite priestly forebears would replicate the sacred relic if it needed to be replaced, but *their Ark-like relic in its present state —with a circular drum-like bottom— is clearly an obvious change from the Ark of the Covenant as it was described in the Torah*. The unanimous belief that the original Ark had a rectangular base is not only based on the Torah's description (Ex. 25:10,12) and tradition; it is evident from the impression that marks the spot where the Ark once rested on the sacred stone under the Dome of the Rock. Based on the dimensions of its chamber, the Holy of Holies, this rectangular indentation (noted by archaeologist Kathleen Kenyon[7]) remains to this day in the precise spot where the Ark rested upon its much smaller, flat, moveable foundation stone – *Even Shettiyah* in Hebrew (Mishnah Tr. *Yomah* 5:1[2]).

Therefore, rather than a strike against the Lemba-Igbo relic being a replica based on the Ark of the Covenant, its altered shape is precisely what we would expect of pious Hebrew priests. Out of reverence to the original, they would have been careful to introduce some noticeable change in form.

The purported remains of the *ngoma lungundu*, the Ark-relic sacred to the Lemba-Igbo.

In summary, for the progenitors of the Beta Yisrael (and the Lemba-Igbo people, according to my theory), it was like pioneering a re-birth of the Israelite nation. To that end, they likely saw themselves in the position of Moses, leading the Israelites from oppression. They, too, would need to maintain the loyalty and faith of their flock over a long sojourn laden with difficulty and strife. *For that, they would need a replica of the Ark itself – and they would have felt perfectly justified in creating one.* What else would invoke the awe and faith of their flock over the long term? The *kohen*-priests would have planned this exodus well in advance. *Given their intimate knowledge of the relic, diligent kohen-priests would have had the ability and feeling of justification in creating such a replica over the long period of King Manasseh's oppression.*

Appendix IV

6. Understanding the Respect by the Kohen-Priests of Jerusalem

In his effort to prove the fugitive priests made off with the actual Ark of the Covenant, Graham Hancock notes the respect of the kohen-priests in Second Temple Jerusalem for their counterparts in the Temple in Aswan: Ostraca (pottery shards) on the island record the correspondence between the *kohen*-priests of Aswan and the kohen-priests in Jerusalem... The respect between them was so great, that when the temple in Egypt was destroyed, *her priests had the nerve to request help from Jerusalem to have their temple rebuilt!* Researcher Ibrahim M. Omer writes:

> The Jewish leaders of the community pleaded and begged before the authority of Jerusalem to interfere on their behalf by requesting from the Persians to rebuild their temple at Elephantine. When their letters went unanswered, they begged for a response.

Hancock wonders what they might have had at Aswan that was so sacred, that it warranted its own Temple service – a service that the *kohen*-priests in Jerusalem not only felt powerless to protest, but could only give their respect and support? It must have been the Ark itself, he claims. He reasons that even in Jerusalem they understood that the Aswan priests had something they believed to be equal in sanctity to the site of the Holy Temple in Jerusalem.

However, there is no necessary connection between the Aswan priests bearing a relic they revered as the Ark itself (nobody doubts this), and the respectful support of the *kohen*-priests in Jerusalem. *There are other possible reasons for the respectful communication from Jerusalem.* Struggling under the thumb of Persia and later Greece, what security or messianic hopes could the priests of the embattled Judeans offer their brother priests in Aswan, who had fled oppression? Perhaps the Judean priesthood saw the Aswan community as a key ally and even a potential safe haven if their dream of restoring Jewish hegemony in the Land failed, much as modern-day Israel looks up to empowered Jewish communities in the Diaspora.

How much more would Second Temple Jerusalem have offered its begrudging support and shown a level respect if the Temple in Aswan were the fulfillment of a vow, if her vessels —particularly the Ark— were slightly varied in form, and if they respected the noble intentions of those who led the established community, as explained above.

7. Conclusion

In conclusion, the tradition maintained at Tana Qirqos (the way blood was sprinkled at the tabernacle) is no contradiction whatsoever to the tradition of the Talmudic Sages that the Ark of the Covenant remains buried in Jerusalem. *When we understand the true context for their tradition, we are free to recognize it for what it is: a time capsule preserving a point of law according to the ancient Oral Tradition of Israel – as it was recorded by the Sages of the Mishnah.*

PART II
THE TRADITIONS OF THE LEMBA-IGBO AND THE ETHIOPIANS: A SINGLE STORY REMEMBERED BY A DIVIDED PEOPLE

1. Who the Lemba-Igbo Are, and Why Their Tradition Matters

It is narrow-minded to rest the reputed history of the ark in Africa on the shoulders of Ethiopian tradition and Egyptian archaeology alone: There is another, lesser-known Israelite-descended people whose oral history lends the story even greater strength. While the Ethiopian Jews have a fuller

Appendix IV

memory of the movement of their Ark-like relic through Africa, they do not have the famed "*kohen* gene,"[8] linking them to Israel's priestly clan. While the Lemba-Igbo tribe of Nigeria cannot be recognized as Jews at this time (so must the Ethiopian community undergo formal conversion rites to intermarry with other Jews), *they actually bear the "kohen gene" and ancient Semitic customs, and have maintained an Ark-tradition of their own that happens to fit the Ethiopian legend more than anyone may realize.*

In 1996, a genetic test proved that over 50% of the Y chromosomes of Lemba-Igbo males were Semitic in origin.[9] In 1999, Tudor Parfitt genetically-tested 136 males of the Lemba-Igbo tribe, and found that they possessed the "*kohen* gene." This gene is shared by an overwhelming majority of Jewish males worldwide who bear family traditions that they are *kohanim*.

One particular sub-clan within the Lemba, the Buba clan, is considered by the Lemba to be their priestly clan, while among Jews, the *Kohanim* are the priestly clan. The Buba clan carried most of the CMH [Cohen Modal Haplotype] found in the Lemba. Among Jews the marker is also most prevalent among Jewish *Kohanim*. As recounted in Lemba oral tradition, the Buba clan "had a leadership role in bringing the Lemba out of Israel" and into Southern Africa (Ibid.).

Since Jewish identity is passed down through the mother's line, (see Part II Point 10 in this book) their priestly gene does *not* establish today's Lemba-Igbo as Israelites according to *halakhah* (practical Torah law). Neither do their old, unique Semitic customs, and the growing Israelite identity of a growing number of Lemba-Igbo. I mention their genetic proof of priestly origin —literally sealed in their blood— since it gives us all the more reason to consider their ark tradition seriously. After all, who other than zealous *kohen*-priests would have escaped with the Ark in the wake of the pagan kings of Judah?

NOTE: Despite their non-halakhic Jewish status, to my humble understanding the Lemba-Igbo tradition of Israelite descent **has no less legitimacy** *than that of Ethiopian Jewry. Considering the moral obligation felt by the Jewish people to embrace Ethiopian Jewry and facilitate their formal return to the Covenant by conversion in order to remove all doubt, we owe no less to those Lemba-Igbo whose Torah beliefs are pure and desire to live according to 'halakhah' (Jewish law) as full Israelites.*

2. Discerning the Factual Elements from Wishful Thinking

In short, the Lemba-Igbo believe it is *their* ancestors who removed the Ark from Israel in antiquity *(or the replica thereof, as the author has proposed)*, and brought it into Africa.

Now, insofar as one can reconstruct genuine Lemba traditions, what they say essentially is that they came from the North, possibly from Judea. They subsequently went to a place called Sena, then they crossed from Sena to Africa via Pusela. We don't know what that is, and they don't know what that is, but they say, "We crossed Pusela and we came to Africa."

Then they say, "We rebuilt Sena, and then we went inland and had something to do with the construction of the Great Stone City [Great Zimbabwe]. At that point, we broke the law of God and we ate mice" – which were not ritually fit for Lemba consumption. And then they were scattered, as they put it, among the nations in Africa.[10]

The Lemba-Igbo revere the memory of their dwelling in Sena (pronounced "Senna") because they believe the Ark, removed from Jerusalem, resided there with them. They maintain the tradition that "their ancestors carried the Ark

Appendix IV

south, calling it the *ngoma lungundu* or "voice of God," eventually hiding it in a deep cave in the Dumghe mountains, their spiritual home."[11] They recall that, *"The drum could not be looked at. Once, when the people quarreled among themselves, Mwali, angry, spoke through the drum and many died."* This may well recall the tragedy at Beit Shemesh, when thousands were struck dead when non-priests looked into the Ark (I Samuel 6:19).[12]

Every researcher I have come across on the subject seems to accept, without critical analysis, the theory put forth by British researcher, Tudor Parfitt, that "Sena" is the ancient city "San`a" in Yemen. However, there are significant holes in this theory:

a) *There is no evidence or traditions among Yemenites of the Ark ever being in San`a, or any part of Yemen.* This is based on discussions with two respected elders: Rabbi Yosef Maghori-Kohen (born in San`a to a San`anite family) and Yehoshua` Sofer Ma`atuf-Dohh, an elder of the Habbani Yemenite community in Israel.[15] It should be noted that, to my own private research, the Jews of Habban have the oldest traditions of the communities in Yemen, hailing from the times of kings David and Solomon.[13] According to Yehoshua`, they first dwelled for a time in San`a before moving to Habban about 2,000 years ago. There they controlled the desert and trade routes. It is unlikely that such an event as the passage of the Ark of the Covenant would have escaped their communal memory. Those aware of the breadth and accuracy of Yemenite Jewish tradition know that such a history would not be forgotten among them.

b) The fact that Parfitt found Lemba Y-chromosomal DNA (inherited through the fathers) —which in many cases contained the distinct kohen gene— to be closely related to that of the inhabitants of the Hadramaut region (greater

Yemen), should come of no surprise: Considering the assimilation of untold numbers of Jews over the centuries to Islam, the majority of the modern population of the region would have Jewish genetic markers. In other words, if the Lemba-Igbo are indeed patrilineally-descended from Jews (which the Kohen-haplotype research establishes), they are bound to show a certain genetic similarity to most inhabitants of the Hadramaut region. *This does not prove the Lemba-Igbo came from Yemen.* However, there is a stronger reason for this unique genetic similarity that will soon become clear...

c) If "crossing Pusela into Africa" meant crossing a sea, we would expect there to be at least be one remaining place-name resembling the name "Pusela" along the sides of the Indian ocean, between Yemen and Africa. On the contrary. A search of all possible variants of "Pusela" in Africa and the Middle East, using the index of the exhaustive *Oxford Atlas of the World*[14], only yielded locations from southern Ethiopia and south-eastward across the heart of Africa: *Buslei* (Ethiopia), *Possel* (C.A.R.), *Bousso* (Chad), *Bouza* (Niger), *Boussé* (Burkina Fasso), *Basile* (Eq. Guinea), *Foso* (Ghana), etc. As Parfitt conjectures, Pusela appears to have been a desert. *Evidence points to this being a desert that led them from a "Sena" in the North, deep into the heart of Africa.*

d) Note the wording of the tradition: *"We rebuilt Sena, and then we went inland and had something to do with the construction of the Great Stone City."* To get to Zimbabwe from San`a, Yemen, you do not merely "go inland"; you cross a strait of open sea. Yet an exodus of thousands of men, women, and children crossing the Gulf of Aden is absent from the Lemba-Igbo tribal memory – only an exodus on dry land. *"Sena" seems not have been across the sea, but a place in the Africa nearer to the coast.* Egypt and Ethiopia fit this picture.

Appendix IV

The true identity of the Lemba-Igbo's fabled "Sena" becomes clear when one considers how closely related their tradition is to that of Ethiopian Jewry:

- Both recall the Ark being brought from the North into Africa by their ancestors.

- Both recall, with reverence, a blessed place where they dwelled in the Ark's presence, before they were exiled deeper into Africa.

- The elders of one community, who remained close to Egypt and are aware of its Arabic name, refer to the place-name as *"Aswan."* In ancient times it was known as *Swenet* (ancient Egyptian), *Sinim* (Hebrew) and *Syene* in ancient Greek. The other community recalls the name as as *"Sena."*

- (The Hebrew reference, in Isaiah 49:12, is from the mouth of the very prophet who foretold of the Temple in Aswan. He prophesizes of those from "the land of Sinim" will eventually return to Zion. According to ancient rabbinical tradition, "the land of Sinim" means "the Land of the South.")

In light of the above and considering how languages evolve, the land called 'Swenet', 'Syene', and 'Seeneem' and the fabled "Sena" appear to be one and the same place. *The Lemba's fabled 'Sena' appear to be none other than the Aswan of Ethiopian Jewish tradition.* The traditions of both isolated Hebrew communities of Africa suggest a common origin. I believe that both peoples come from a single root, and that the Arks they remember are one and the same. *The Lemba-Igbo represent a group of true kohen-priests who split off from their brother Jews of Ethiopia who had brought a replica of the Ark from Elephantine Island.*

One important point of evidence is a key point of the Lemba's oral history:

> After entering Africa, the tribe is said to have split off into two groups, with one staying in *Ethiopia*, and the other traveling farther south, along the east coast. The Lemba claim this second group settled in *Tanzania* and *Kenya*, and built what was referred to as "Sena II."[15]

In fact, this theory provides a compelling explanation from their genetic similarity to the inhabitants of Hadramaut [see above]. It may be for the same reason that Ethiopian Jews were found to be genetically similar to Yemenite Jews: it is well-known that there was a certain level of contact and even intermarriage between those two communities. In other words, being related to Ethiopian Jews would give the Lemba-Igbo, by extension, similarity to Yemenite Jewry. The Lemba-Igbo, however —by their own account— fell out of strict Torah observance and became scattered among the tribes of Africa. This was accompanied by their Hebrew ancestors' intermarriage with local women (a fact to which they admit), clearly giving the Lemba their robust, Bantu-type appearance, as opposed to the slighter features shared by Ethiopians and Semites.

Most telling is that the Lemba belief that the present *ngoma* drum, which was buried in the deep cave *(see above)*, was a *replica* of the previous one, which they believe was destroyed.[16] *In other words, the Lemba are heirs to a culture in which it was natural to replace a previous ark with a new replica.* Could this practice hail from forebears who brought a replica of the original Ark out of Israel? Moreover, as explained above, the form of the *ngoma lungundu* discovered by Tudor Parfitt, made without gold and round on the bottom like a drum, is clearly changed from that of the Ark. Considering Jewish law on the issue,

Torah-observant forebears would have *only* created an ark-replica in altered form – a point that considerably strengthens the theory presented here.

Conclusion

Based on all the above, it is most likely that the Jewish Ethiopian and Lemba-Igbo communities have a common origin, and their respective traditions of the Ark's descent into Africa derive from a single memory. It is further evidence that a replica of the Ark was indeed brought to Ethiopia in Israel's First Temple era.

In light of the traditional memory maintained by the priests at Tana Qirqos as to just how the blood was once sprinkled at their tabernacle, these finds are truly significant. *It is revealed to be a time capsule for a vivid memory of details of Israel's Oral Tradition, as they were recorded by the ordained Rabbis in the Mishnah, some four centuries before the Mishnah was ever written down.*

As written in Point 22 above, it can only be such, considering how isolated the Abbyssinian priests remained until very recently, and their lack of access, much less any ability to read the Mishnah, or have it translated. Even the Ethiopians who remained Jewish. Being ignorant of the events of Purim and Rededication of the Temple (Hannukah) until the last century, they clearly lost contact with mainstream Jewry centuries before the Mishnah was written. In fact, considering their own traditional Torah scroll written in Ge'ez, the elders had most probably lost their knowledge of Hebrew by then as well.

Ironically, *HaShem* would have it that the Abyssinian Christians –among the last people on earth who would wish to prove the foundation of the Jewish faith— became the unwitting bearers of testimony that establishes the authenticity of the Oral Tradition from Sinai. It is the foundation of the very faith they tried in vain to extinguish.

Appendix IV

NOTES

(1) Hancock, Graham, *The Sign and the Seal: The Quest for the Lost Ark of the Covenant*. A Touchstone Book Published by Simon & Schuster, Inc. New York, NY (1992). 600 pp.

(2) My understanding of this verse in its surrounding context in Zephaniah Chapter 3 is as follows:

After the prophet laments the spiritual pollution of Jerusalem, he levels a veiled rebuke at the exiles "beyond the rivers of Ethiopia." One day in the future, he prophesizes, after *HaShem* will have gathered the nations together and poured out his wrath upon them and Israel will no longer be ashamed of her past misdeeds, a great *tiqqun* (rectification) will occur: the returned Ethiopian exiles will bring *HaShem*'s offerings – *this time in Jerusalem*. The rest of Israel's remnant will be inspired by the humility and noble faith of this poor, afflicted people who took refuge among them in the Name of *HaShem*. For in that time, *HaShem* will remove all the haughtiness and arrogance from Israel's exulting leadership – both secular and religious.

(3) Omer, Ibrahim M., *Investigating the Origin of the Ancient Jewish Community at Elephantine: A Review.* Published online at: www.ancientsudan.org by Ibrahim Omer (Copyright 2008). *www.ancientsudan.org/articles_jewish_elephantine.html*

(4) According to *halakhah* (applied Torah Law) this hiding away (*Genizah*), usually by burial, is the traditional retirement of holy objects that that are no longer used.

(5) From the *Ahavat Yisrael* website:
www.ahavat-israel.com/eretz/future.php

(6) Cornuke, Robert. *Search For the Ark of the Covenant: Israel, Egypt, Ethiopia*. Copyright 2009 by Robert Cornuke BASE Institute. Published online at: Robert Cornuke – Research, Discovery, Dialogue. *www.robertcornuke.com/search- ark-covenant-israel-egypt-ethiopia*

(7) Ritmeyer, Leen and Kathleen. *From Sinai to Jeruslaem: The Wanderings of the Holy Ark.* Published by Carta Ltd. Jerusalem, Israel (2000). 72 pp. See page 70.

(8) Keiman, Yaakov. *DNA & The Bible: The Genetic Link – Special Edition.* Published by Lightcatcher Books. Springdale, Arkansas (2010). 224 pp.

(9) Entry for "Lemba people" in Wikipedia, The Free Encyclopedia: *en.wikipedia.org/wiki/Lemba_people*

(10) Tudor Parfitt's Remarkable Journey (updated November 2000): *www.pbs.org/wgbh/nova/israel/parfitt.html*

(11) Entry for "Ark of the Covenant" in Wikipedia, The Free Encyclopedia: *en.wikipedia.org/wiki/Ark_of_the_Covenant*

(12) Entry for Ngoma-lungundu, A Drum That Is the Voice of God (from Oxford Dictionary of African Mythology) Copyright 2011 by Answers Corporation. Published online at in Answers.com – Reference Answers: *www.answers.com/topic/ngoma-lungundu-a-drum-that-is-the-voice- of-god#copyrights_d*

(13) See interview with Habbani elder Mori Awadh ben Seleiman Ma`atuf Dohh of blessed memory. In the interview he speaks about the early roots of Habbani Jewry in Yemen: *Abir Qesheth Interview 1 (ראיון אביר קשת).* A video posted to Habbani's Channel. Published online at Youtube.com: *www.youtube.com/user/habbani?blend=2&ob=1#p/u/9/1p4LjmpmYY0*

(14) *Oxford Atlas of the World – Ninth Edition.* Published in North America by Oxford University Press, Inc. New York, NY (2001). All Rights Reserved to George Philip Limited. 304 pp.

(15) *THE LEMBA: The Story of the Lemba as told by Dr. Rudo Mathivha.* Copyright 1999/2000 by Rudo Mathivha MD. Published online by Haruth Communications: *haruth.com/jw/JewishLemba.html*

Appendix IV

IMPORTANT NOTE:

The letter by Dr. Mathivha may reveal an actual oral tradition of the Lemba-Igbo that their ancestors came from Yemen. While neither the Habbani nor the San`ani Yemenite Jews elders I spoke to have any tradition of a Tabernacle or Temple being in their midst while in exile, a friend hailing from the Yemenite Jews of Najran related to me the following:

"Najrani Jews maintain that their ancestors were once bitterly divided over two competing interpretations of the design of the original Tabernacle in the desert, as described in the Torah. Their stubbornness led them to actually construct two competing Tabernacles. They reasoned that the Tabernacle that would elicit God's fire from Heaven would prove its correct design. In the end, so the legend goes, God's fire did indeed come down, but devoured both the correctly-designed structure as well as those who participated in the competition."

While I believe that the bulk of evidence points to an Aswan origin of Africa's Israelite-derived peoples, the above Najrani tradition just might —together with a genuine Lemba Oral tradition— suggest a Yemenite origin after all.

(16) Anderson, Troy. *"Professor claims to have discovered Arc of the Covenant."* Media News, March 1, 2008. Copyright 2007 by and published online at Ethiomedia.com - An African-American news and views website: *www.ethiomedia.com/abai/arc_of_covenant.html*

Oral Torah from Sinai

ABOUT THE AUTHOR

Mori Michael-Shelomo Bar-Ron is an ordained rabbi and publishing Torah scholar. His first work, *Guide For the Noahide* (Lightcatcher Books ©2009,2010) has been hailed by rabbis and students as a groundbreaking primer in Noahide Law and outlook. He also has a BA in Anthropology from the University of California San Diego. His broad Torah journey ultimately brought him to formal rabbinical training at Shehebar Sephardic Center in Jerusalem, and under the tutelage of master halakhic decisors according to RaMBaM.

However far he has journeyed from his own beginnings as a young, truth-seeking college student, Mori Michael-Shelomo never lost his respect and sensitivity for serious, academically-trained truth-seekers, their valiant struggles, and their valid, critical questions. After years as an understudy of rabbis and scholars with opposing outlooks, all the while maintaining a critical, balanced mind, he has found compelling answers that have helped others not only to return to Torah observance, but to the practice of *mitzvot* according to authentic Talmudic tradition. *The many he has helped were the inspiration for this book.*

He is currently based out of his Torah center in Beit Shemesh, *Beth Midrash Ohel Moshe* (www.torathmoshe.com), where he continues to study, teach and write. A father of six children, Mori Michael-Shelomo makes a living as an English instructor.

---

* Mori Michael-Shelomo (pronounced *"Mee-kha-el She-lo-mo"*) prefers the title *m'ori* (מאורי), the humble title of the teachers of children in Yemen, over the title "rabbi."

www.ingramcontent.com/pod-product-compliance
Lightning Source LLC
Chambersburg PA
CBHW050134170426
43197CB00011B/1832